(continued)

Inviting Families into the Classroom

LEARNING FROM A LIFE
IN TEACHING

Lynne Yermanock Strieb

Foreword by Joseph Featherstone

Teachers College, Columbia University
New York and London

National Writing Project
Berkeley, CA

Published simultaneously by Teachers College Press, 1234 Amsterdam Avenue, New York, NY 10027, and National Writing Project, 2105 Bancroft Way, Berkeley, CA 94720-1042

The National Writing Project (NWP) is a professional development network of more than 200 university-based sites, serving teachers across disciplines and at all levels, early childhood through university. The NWP focuses the knowledge, expertise, and leadership of our nation's educators on sustained efforts to improve writing and learning for all learners.

Work on portions of this book was funded by the Spencer Foundation Practitioner Research Communication and Mentoring Program for an Intensive Research on Practice Grant.

Library of Congress Cataloging-in-Publication Data

Strieb, Lynne Yermanock.
  Inviting families into the classroom : learning from a life in teaching / Lynne Yermanock Strieb ; foreword by Joseph Featherstone.
      p.   cm. — (Practitioner inquiry series)
  Includes bibliographical references and index.
  ISBN 978-0-8077-5082-7 (pbk : alk. paper) — ISBN 978-0-8077-5083-4 (cloth : alk. paper)
  1. Parent-teacher relationships.   2. Teacher-student relationships.   3. education—Parent participation.   I. Title.

  LC226.S87 2010
  371.19'2—dc22

                                                                        2010003680

ISBN: 978-0-8077-5082-7 (paper)
ISBN: 978-0-8077-5083-4 (cloth)

Printed on acid-free paper
Manufactured in the United States of America

17   16   15   14   13   12   11   10   8   7   6   5   4   3   2   1

To Bert

with love and appreciation for your patience

and to our grandchildren

Jenna, Jacob, Zachary, and Ariana

so that you'll know a little about what your Bubi did

Contents

Foreword

LYNNE YERMANOCK STRIEB'S *Inviting Families into the Classroom* is an important book about the neglected topic of families and schools. It is also unique. There are a handful of good books in this area—Sara Lawrence-Lightfoot's wise books on parents and parent-teacher conferences; Annette Lareau's studies of social class, families, and schools; Deborah Meier's account of her work with parents as principal of Mission Hill School in Boston; and the collections of letters to parents by Ted and Nancy Sizer and by Meier. But I know nothing that approaches the depth and complexity of Strieb's account. This is the story of the development of a systematic practice of communication with parents on the part of a classroom teacher of young children over a long span of time. The documentation here is amazing: Strieb seems to have saved scraps of paper for 30 years, sorted them, analyzed them, and picked out essential pieces. The participatory picture she draws is more remarkable because the school in question is a city school in Philadelphia, subject (especially in recent decades) to the tightening screws of what is called "reform"—the standardization, heightened managerial control, and obsessive testing that now make it hard for urban classrooms to become communities of any sort, and much harder for teachers like Strieb to reach out to parents.

Strieb demonstrates the nuts and bolts—the practice—that allows one teacher to create a classroom community in which parents play an important role and in which the constant dialogue that is such an essential part of her approach to teaching children is also a part of how the teacher connects to their parents. Strieb's teaching practice is deeply, profoundly participatory—it assumes that children have ideas, and can construct and share meaning—but so is the practice of this classroom community in relation to parents. This is a modest book—Strieb draws herself as an astringent character, albeit a sensitive and vulnerable person—a worrier, in fact; she has few illusions about herself or parents. Though she believes that the teacher will (barring racism or other forms of malpractice) necessarily be the authority of last resort within the small classroom community, she often points to her own mistakes and misunderstandings—at times those of a middle-class White woman attempting to work past the blinkers of race and social class. She is scrupulous in showing examples and evidence to back up her claims, as well as instances where she slips badly. Her candor is welcome, and rare. The notes from parents to Strieb (and her reactions and thoughts) are worth the price of admission. An anthology of these exchanges with parents would do a lot to help novice teachers begin to see and value children's families and find ways to listen to them more carefully. Novices could also find in these exchanges ways that a thoughtful teacher learns to correct the mistakes that are the inevitable result of all attempts to teach.

The level of communication with parents that *Inviting Families into the Classroom* shows is rare in city schools, which can feel like colonial outposts or prisons; true communication can, however, be equally rare in the swankier environs of empowered parents in suburbs and private schools. Most parents anywhere in the United States who read this account will feel envy that they have not been able to communicate so well with a teacher of a young child or play a significant role in classroom life. Teachers who read this book may want to open up their approach to parents. (Teachers in schools where parental bullies get their way will yearn for its more positive picture of possibility.) Yet this is also an intensely practical work, not a hymn of longing for utopia. Despite its big implications, the book is full of many examples of small first steps that beginning teachers and veteran teachers alike could try out reasonably safely. It's unusual to see a book so philosophically consistent and of a whole piece that also manages to be practical and low-key. Parents, do you want your young kids to learn how to cut an apple safely with a knife? Strieb tells you how. Teachers, what's a good format for a classroom newsletter to parents? Here are several. Everybody: what happens when a White teacher in a city school messes up as she treads into such loaded topics as discipline or homework or the hair of the African American kids? Read on, and become wiser with Strieb.

The story of Strieb's practice with parents starts with her own involvement as a parent activist in Philadelphia during the 1960s, a time when participation in many forms in the United States had what the Chinese call "the mandate of heaven." Parent and community involvement took many forms, from local action groups and community school boards to the parent boards of Head Start and other local governance mechanisms created as part of President Lyndon Johnson's War on Poverty. In the United States of Amnesia we need reminding of the wealth of creative school and institutional experiment and variety that lies in the past, awaiting exploration. Particularly in the current time of economic depression and diminished possibility, we are too easily convinced that nothing much ever works. Hope is at risk. Our current era of reform from the top down in the name of standards and testing may therefore be an especially apt moment to rediscover the rich creativity and inventiveness available at the grass roots. Strieb's reshaping of the lofty and often unexamined 1960s participatory ideals into a hard-headed and intelligent approach that continued to work well in the more constrained atmosphere of an urban school in the 1980s and 1990s is a part of her wider story: how democratic visions translate into our own time's version of sober and productive reality.

This is a revolutionary story. Lacking the perestroika we need for our stricken and suffering America and its many failing institutions, we also lack organizers to help ordinary teachers and parents find a voice and strike a blow for democratic education in the place where it matters most, the local classroom itself. Strieb emerges as a canny organizer who has written a manual of how to organize parents at the classroom level. She has, as I say, the big advantage of having started out as a parent activist, too, and that may be an important ingredient in her success. Like most good organizers she has learned many ways to draw on the formidable power and talents of those she is attempting to organize. This book amounts to a catalogue of the contributions adults can make to one classroom. They range from tutoring to helping with paperwork to such skills as gardening and demonstrating how to cut hair—and to telling Strieb about the complexities of their own children and each family's circumstances and troubles, on which, not surprisingly, a lot of parents turn out to be experts. Those who are too stressed and overworked to contribute in obvious ways can sometimes make their own kinds of contributions, if a teacher is listening. This last point may seem implausible to teachers in schools not set up to communicate with families well. It is not necessarily, as Deborah Meier has put it, that a particular school lacks respect for children or parents—although the matter of respect is always a relevant question to raise in schools dealing across the lines of race and class. It's more often that those in the school have not found concrete ways to make respect manifest, and so it curdles. Strieb shows many different ways to make respect manifest: Her vignettes feel like the real thing. She is tactful but tart about the way that school administrations have over the years raised barriers to genuine parent participation. Whether our schools will continue in their current top-down, one-size-fits-all mode, or whether they will open to more democratic and pluralistic visions of education is one of the questions this wonderful book raises but of course cannot answer.

Strieb advances a democratic approach to teaching that may in the long run (I believe) survive our current era of top-down reform. Though its message is scarcely mainstream discourse, this book comes at a good time; skepticism about continuing to create standardized learning, what David Tyack has called The One Best System, is mounting in the general public, and among teachers. Many classroom teachers and parents are already sympathetic to Strieb's values and her approach; in their own way, many are working to topple The One Best System and make classrooms and the curriculum more open, democratic, and participatory.

Strieb makes her argument in clear, literate prose, not by abstractions and theory, but case by case, kid by kid, parent by parent, each story and each bit of evidence contributing to a cumulative, powerful (and deceptively modest) claim: Participation and sharing knowledge are good ways to build a learning comunity. It's a good idea to draw on the strengths of everyone involved. A classroom that works in this fashion—in which routines and habits and practices make participation a daily possibility—emerges as a very powerful learning environment, for teacher, parents, and children. Such an environment helps produce a synergy. A civilized and fun and intellectual place to be emerges, a place where people of all ages generate enthusiasm and ideas. When was the last time you read the word "fun" in relation to a discussion of a U.S. classroom? Among their other sins, the testers and the gradgrind reformers have so narrowed the school curriculum for young children that it is now harder for parents to contribute academically or socially in the many ways that Strieb demonstrates. Her parents' use of the babies and younger children they bring in to show the older kids develops into a fascinating and powerful elementary curriculum. The baby and toddler sessions bring together many threads of the book's argument, demonstrating the way that Strieb's approach encompasses all the complex elements of classroom life—not least its intellectual life. The idea that poor and working-class as well as middle-class parents might play a role in contributing to a classroom's intellectual culture is so quietly revolutionary that some readers will miss it on the first reading. The fact that a classroom teacher, not a principal or outside reformer, would orchestrate such bold reforms, is also startling in an era when the classroom teachers have been marginalized in discussions of educational reform.

Family participation in young children's classrooms should naturally be the ordinary, expected thing, as well as an end in itself: All of education and civilized life start with community, conversation, dialogue, and common action. But the participation documented so carefully here also serves other important purposes. The young children in Strieb's classroom are involved in a highly intellectual and very interesting classroom world where their parents and people in their families count. These kids are becoming intellectuals in a world that includes people they know; their teacher has helped parents from many walks of life add to the intellectual mix. By demonstrating how to make the classroom an open space in which grown-ups can demonstrate their ideas and skills, Strieb makes a fresh contribution to theory and practice: This is one method by which a teacher can help young children from families without money to acquire the crucial habits of having and expressing powerful ideas. Strieb's big news goes way beyond the bake sale. Her book explores a democratic philosophy in action, persuades as it charms, and enlists the reader as it goes. The text itself is participatory, a call to small first steps of action as well as deeper thought about the ultimate purposes of education, reaching out in Strieb's modest, teacherly way to what Lincoln called the "unfinished work" of American democracy. I believe it will make an impact and find many diverse readers, especially among the rising generation of young teachers and parents.

—Joseph Featherstone

Acknowledgments

THOUGH I AM completely responsible for the final words and ideas, a large number of people have helped me complete this book. I can't possibly mention all of them by name because in an attempt to be comprehensive and to list every name, I fear I might inadvertently leave someone out.

Those whom I do not mention by name have been members of five groups that have helped me analyze my data: the Philadelphia Teachers' Learning Cooperative (PTLC), two Prospect Summer Institutes (the Summer Institute on Descriptive Practice and the Summer Institute on Descriptive Inquiry), the Philadelphia Writing Project Literature Circle, and Research for Action.

Much of the data analysis for this book was done by groups using the Descriptive Processes, developed at The Prospect Center for Education and Research. These are Format for Close Reading of Documents, Texts, Etc.; Descriptive Review of Children's Work; Descriptive Review of the Child; and Reflections on a Word.

The PTLC, which I have attended since 1978 as a founding member, gave me valuable insights into the chapters on homework and behavior, and into the 1996–1998 notes and letters from parents that I have used throughout this book. Without the support of the many educators who have attended our weekly meetings over the years, and who always asked me how the book was coming along, I'm not sure I could have completed it.

At Prospect Summer Institutes on Descriptive Practice and on Descriptive Inquiry from 2001 to 2005, groups of participants read and analyzed my newsletters to parents, the story of Tonya, notes and letters from parents to me, portions of Chapter 6, and drafts of my Prospectus.

I especially want to mention Cecelia Traugh (Chair), Gina Ritscher, and Jean Stevenson, who worked with me to describe and analyze early versions of Chapters 1, 2, and 4. We also did a Reflection on the words *bring/bringing*, summarized in Chapter 6. The book began to take shape after our sessions. I am grateful for their help.

The Philadelphia Writing Project Literature Circle discussed a draft of the entire book. I am grateful to Diane Waff, convener, for suggesting that the draft be its selection for January 2009. Those who attended that

January meeting were Rhoda Kanevsky (Chair), Michelle Bell, Marilyn Boston, Esther Cristol, Randi Calbazana, Jackie Jackson, Lisa Kelly, Tamar Magdovitz, Paula Paul, Robert Rivera-Amazola, Mary Silverstein, Bert Strieb, Judith Sussholtz, Diane Waff, and Milton Watkins. Susan Threatt and Connie Sekaros also read and commented on portions of the book.

I thank the Spencer Foundation Practitioner Research Communication and Mentoring Program for providing me with an Intensive Research on Practice Grant for the years 2001–2003. During the period of that grant, Eva Gold, founder and Principal at Research for Action, was my research mentor. She helped me to think about data analysis and to refine my thinking about the book. Research for Action is a Philadelphia-based, non-profit organization engaged in education research and evaluation. It works to bridge the gap between research and practice, and assures research that is attuned to local conditions. The staff at Research for Action described and made suggestions for Chapter 1, which proved to be extremely helpful as I began to write.

In addition to the important work that these groups did, there are also many individuals whom I want to thank. In June 1998, Patricia Carini led the PTLC description and analysis of all the notes and letters that parents wrote to me during the years 1996–1998. This session opened our eyes to how much we can learn from describing collections of seemingly mundane documents. In addition, Pat's thinking about educating, learning, and the importance of closely observing and describing people, objects, and events has been a shaping influence in my work and life. For 45 years I have appreciated Rhoda Kanevsky's sensitivity to tone, her friendship, and her support. I learned a great deal when Margaret Himley and I had a discussion about race and culture, and also from her close reading of one of my stories.

Early in the summer of 1981 I sorted my journal entries into themes by cutting and pasting copies with scissors and tape. I am indebted to Steve Longo, Professor of Mathematics and Computer Science at LaSalle University, who, in 2003, developed a simple but elegant program that did exactly what I needed—sorted my coded chronological data into themes and printed them in their entirety.

Thea Abu El Haj, Katherine Schultz, and my daughter-in-law, Shari Golan, read and made helpful comments about my Spencer proposal. Shari pointed me to bibliography on parental involvement for both my Spencer proposal and this book. I had fruitful discussions with another daughter-in-law, Karla Strieb, about data integration for qualitative research. And I appreciated that my daughter-in-law, Marci Bortman, was always willing to answer technical questions.

Certain friends and colleagues gave my drafts an enormous amount of attention—possibly much more than I should have requested. I am truly indebted to them, and I hope I didn't try their patience. They are Mary Daniels, Kathryn Keeler, Edith Klausner, Susan Lytle, Tamar Magdovitz, Katherine Schultz, and Anne Burns Thomas. Each took time from her already busy life to fill the margins of the drafts with extensive and thoughtful comments and suggestions. I give special thanks to Betsy Wice, who, because of her love of literature, has an ear for words like few people I know. Up to the last moments of my writing this book, she was exceptionally generous with her help.

Long ago, after reading many of my journal entries, Carol Chambers Collins, then an editor at Teachers College Press, recommended that I write about working with families. It was an excellent suggestion. Brian Ellerbeck, Senior Acquisitions Editor at Teachers College Press, has been a sensitive editor, and I've enjoyed our sometimes humorous discussions about the book. Marilyn Cochran-Smith and Susan Lytle, editors of the Practitioner Research Series, have shown their unwavering commitment to publishing teachers' research and writing. They know how valuable it can be to students, teachers, and administrators, and I am honored that they have been so strong in their support of this book.

I thank Nancy Shawcross (mother of a former student) and Paul Farber of the Library of the University of Pennsylvania for the help they gave me.

Peggy Perlmutter Stone was my teacher and my children's first teacher. Friends and colleagues will recognize much of Peggy in my practice and words.

I am honored that Louise Fishman, my friend of 60 years, has allowed the use of her painting on the cover.

My children, Lee, Saul, Max, and my grandchildren, Jenna, Jacob, Zachary, and Ariana have not only shown great interest in this book, but have also been patient with me through my many years of working on it. Our three sons, Lee, Saul, and Max have been central to my education. I appreciate their enthusiastic interest and support since its inception. Marci, Max, Shari, and Lee shared personal experiences about working in their children's schools. Some of their experiences have made their way into this book.

Throughout the many, many years I have worked on this book, my husband, Bert Strieb, has shown more patience than I ever thought humanly possible. I can't imagine the number of drafts of each chapter he has read. His comments, on both big ideas and small points of grammar and vocabulary, have been helpful and supportive. I have always admired his interest in teaching and in learners of all ages. It has been my greatest pleasure to have shared 50 years of marriage, friendship, children, hard work, music, many movies, good fun, and this completed book with him.

And now, Ariana, the quilt is on the way. Thanks for waiting patiently.

Inviting Families into the Classroom

Introduction

THIS BOOK is the story of my teaching life, told through the lens of my relationships with parents and families. I taught first and second grade for many years and loved doing so. I could have told many other stories about teaching—stories about building community in the classroom; about the provision for choice; about helping children become readers, writers, mathematicians, scientists. But as I read through the many documents I wrote both before and while teaching, I noticed that even as a quite young parent, I had realized that if the doors were open to them, parents could and would make enormous contributions to classrooms. As I taught, I often thought of the classroom as a kind of home, and I wanted to make it as homelike as possible for the children, in spite of constraints placed on us from outside the classroom. I believed that in doing so, schools could encompass much more than what the curriculum, with all its testing, demanded. I knew from the beginning that, though schools could never really be like home, parents could help to blur the sharp edges and could contribute some of what I could not provide. I am grateful that at every point in my teaching life I had opportunities to learn from other educators, other parents, and the children I taught.

In the book I describe concerns that I had as a parent, concerns held by the parents of children I taught, ways in which I invited parents into classrooms and schools, what parents did when they entered the classroom, and other ways in which parents and I connected with one another. I have been considering parent–teacher relationships since even before I was a full-time, certified teacher, when I was an activist parent of three children. I brought my experience as an activist parent to my work with the parents of the children I taught. It is because of my experiences, and because I so valued my many relationships with parents and learned so much from working with them over the course of those years, that I have chosen to address some of the complexities of parent–teacher interactions in a book.

Children, most precious to parents, are in the care and under the supervision of teachers for only about 5 hours a day—a time when parents usually are not present. Every day parents and teachers come into contact with one another—if not face-to-face, then indirectly, through their connection with their children. For teachers, the issues connected to parent–teacher relationships and parental involvement are complex. These relationships involve much more than showing parents how to help their children at home to prepare them for school or to do homework. They may involve more than meeting with parents at twice-yearly report card conferences,[1] more than using them as chaperones on trips. They may include day-to-day conversations in the schoolyard about homework, behavior, and myriad small matters. They may also involve inviting parents into the classroom, where parents then have opportunities not only to observe but also to interact with (and sometimes informally evaluate) the teacher.

For parents, too, the issues connected to parent–teacher relationships and parent involvement are complex. Sara Lawrence-Lightfoot (1978) notes that parents are most concerned about their own children, while a teacher's concern must be for an entire class.[2] It may sometimes be difficult for parents to understand a teacher's reasons for handling matters as she does. Whether because of experiences with schools in their own childhood or experiences with schools as adults, parents sometimes see schools and people who work in them as creators of barriers, rather than as potential connectors between the home and school. Parents sometimes have good reasons for not wanting to become involved in classrooms: too many children at home, inability to take time off from work, belief that the classroom is no place for parents—it's the teacher's job. At other times, parents may be grateful for contact with the teacher and for invitations to join with her in educating the children.

The overall purpose of this book, with its story of one teacher's work with families, is to help elementary school teachers and parents think broadly and deeply about the opportunities and challenges of parent involvement in schools, to help teachers and prospective teachers examine and reexamine the daily encounters they have had or will have with parents, and to prompt new discussions and initiatives. Though written primarily for an elementary school audience, particularly for teachers, it may also stimulate thinking about parental involvement in secondary schools. Readers may not agree with some of the practices described in this book, but if, in disagreeing, questions are raised about one's own practice, it will have served a useful purpose. If it becomes a starting place for discussions between teachers and teachers, teachers and parents, it will have been successful.

The following are only a few of the questions that might arise: Where school-age children are concerned, who's really in charge? What are the realms of authority of parent and teacher? What are the areas of overlap? Are there areas of conflict? What are they? What happens when parents' and teachers' expectations and goals are different? How does a teacher's own experience shape attitudes about parent involvement? What are the interactions that work? What does it mean to genuinely invite parents into the classroom? What happens when parents enter into classroom work and life? What do children, parents, and teachers learn when parents are involved? How can parents and teachers come together in ways that support their children and one another? What is the administrator's role? How can teachers, parents, and administrators together critique established policies and think about them in new ways?

This book makes a case for having education policy grow from the experiences of actual teachers in the classroom, policy grounded in practice. Policy issues are embedded in every one of the classroom stories that appear in this book. More often than not, policy is created at the managerial level of a bureaucratic entity such as federal, state, or local government. It travels from there to the administrators and then to the advisors or coaches, to be carried out by teachers. This is usually called "top-down delivery" because people who carry out policy are considered to be at the bottom. When teachers are involved in writing policy, they often are asked by the authorities who created it to find ways to implement what has already been decided. This book enters the policy conversation from a perspective outside the usual one; here, policy is looked at through a teacher's practice or "from the bottom up" (Lytle, 2008).

It is now a critical time to think about connecting schools and families and about involving parents in schools. For years, research from a variety of different approaches has documented the finding that students are more likely to succeed in school when their parents are involved. Other lines of research have consistently shown that among the features of the most effective schools are strategic approaches to including parents in constructive relationships (Booth & Dunn, 1996; Jeynes, 2005). Government policies now mandate parent involvement. For example, from its inception No Child Left Behind legislation specified a central role for parents in their children's education (NCLB, 2003). This book offers possibilities for parental involvement that are meaningfully related to student learning.

MY CLASSROOM AND SCHEDULE

In this book, I use the word *parents* to designate all of those who care for the children who attend school, including mothers, fathers, grandparents, aunts, uncles, foster parents, and guardians. I have changed the names of all children and parents. Finally, I have not changed the grammar and spelling in parents' and children's letters to me.

My views about parent–teacher relationships are closely tied to the ways and settings in which I taught. My practice was influenced by what I'd learned as a substitute kindergarten teacher before earning certification, as a parent in the Parent Cooperative Nursery, from reading about education, and from attending workshops during the 1960s and 1970s with advisors who were knowledgeable about English infant schools. From the start of my full-time employment, I was an "open classroom" elementary school teacher, which meant that I taught in a "progressive," nontraditional way. Whether in an "open-space" school in which many classrooms shared a large space or in a self-contained classroom, nontraditional or "open" meant to me that my first- and second-grade classrooms resembled kindergartens and nursery schools, both in the way the room was arranged (Figure Int. 1) and in the ways I taught. Though I occasionally taught "formal" or whole-class lessons, more often the children had many choices and could move around, rather than being seated at desks for most of the

Figure Int.1. Map, Room 214, John B. Kelly School, 1981–82

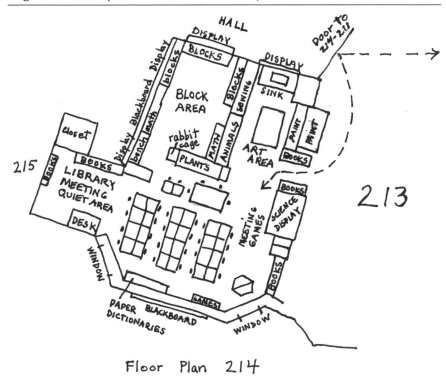

Floor Plan 214

day. Among those choices were most of the books they read, the materials they worked with at Project Time, and the projects they carried out. Materials not usually found in first- or second-grade public school classrooms (and which have even become scarce in kindergartens) were found in mine: blocks; home corner; puppets; many kinds of art materials (clay, paint, chalk, papier mâché, cloth for sewing, yarn for weaving); and science materials such as magnets, mirror cards, attribute games, playing cards, puzzles, live insects and other live animals. During Project Time it might have looked like the children were "playing." They were. But I believed (and still do) that children learn not only from being taught by an adult from the front of the classroom while sitting still, but also (and sometimes even more) from playing—by themselves, with one another, and with adults. Play gives them time to practice things they've been taught in ways that have meaning to them. Play for young children (and here I mean children even as old as eighth grade) and "playfulness" are not wastes of time but are central to learning. Furthermore, it is through social interaction that language is enhanced and community is built.

Though it was unusual in most schools, from 1974 to 2000 I taught the same children for 2 years, a system that is now often called "looping." The entire class came to me in first grade and I kept it through second grade.

Teaching as I did, in schools where most classrooms were traditional, often meant compromises. I had time in the school day for only about three-quarters of an hour of Project Time (Figure Int. 2). I would have liked to have allowed more time for choice, and I did earlier in my teaching, but I came to believe that I needed to set aside designated times for reading and math during the day. I did this so that the principal and parents would see that I gave enough time to teaching these subjects. I allowed the children much choice of what to read and with whom. Fortunately, throughout my teaching life, principals supported the way I taught, probably because parents seemed satisfied that their children were learning.

Schools have changed since I retired from teaching in 2000. The focus on testing and improving test scores now shapes what is taught. Many teachers must follow scripts and tightly controlled curricula. If I were still teaching, it's possible that I would not be permitted to set aside a time for children to choose activities according to their interests, to have blocks, games, and art materials in my classroom.

Nevertheless, parents still send their children to schools and still trust their teachers to provide educational experiences. Teachers must still think about their relationships with parents. Administrators must still consider how to make schools welcoming to parents, and parents must be invited to use their strengths and abilities to enhance the education of both their own children and other parents' children.

Figure Int.2. Approximate Schedule of a Typical Day

8:30–9:00. Discuss homework, read reading homework
   together, sing songs, point to words as we read and sing.
9:00–9:45. Writing workshop and regularly scheduled
   conference with teacher or volunteer.
9:45–10:30. Reading instruction for individual children or
   small groups, either from books I assigned or books of
   their own choice, according to their ability. The rest of the
   children do quiet reading, either on their own, with an
   adult, or with other children, usually books of their choice.
10:30–11:15. Project time (some teachers call it "choice time").
11:15–11:30. Clean-up, discuss work.
11:30–12:15. Lunch.
12:20–1:00. Story, discussion, social studies.
1:00–1:45. Math (whole-class lessons or groups) using manipula-
   tives, school-provided workbooks, and/or games, or teacher-
   directed instruction from the chalkboard or overhead projector.
1:45–2:30. Teacher's planning time (art, music, science, gym,
   library; children usually left the room for these classes).
2:30–3:00. Prepare for dismissal, homework in books, discuss
   homework and how to do it.

HOW I WORKED ON THIS BOOK

Raymond Williams, in *The Long Revolution* (1961) states, "We learn to see
a thing by learning to describe it" (p. 39). I have learned a great deal about
my students, their work, and my own work by observing and describing.
Both were central to my teaching. The written material that I saved, which
I call my documentation, became data for this study of parent–teacher
relationships. Among my data sources were my journal; letters I wrote as
a parent and to parents, and those that parents wrote to me; and my newsletters to parents (see Appendix A).

Data Sources[3]

My major data source has been my journal. In it, I described what happened in the class during a particular day; events I wanted to further reflect on; things that seemed important about children (individuals, small
groups, the whole class); incidents that I might not want to share with a

parent about a child but that were important to remember; details that represented the daily life of the classroom through the eyes of a teacher. The journal was also the place where I made plans for teaching, based on my daily records on children and on previous journal entries. The notes in the journal were reminders so that if I wanted to write more fully, I would have something to jog my memory.[4]

A second data source for my research is notes and letters: letters I wrote when I was a young parent in 1968, and notes and letters that parents wrote to me and that I wrote to them. These were the primary sources for Chapters 2, 3, and 4.

A third important source of data was my newsletter to parents. I started writing a biweekly newsletter in 1971 to inform parents and the principal about what was going on in my classroom and to serve as a record for me. I describe this newsletter further in Chapters 2 and 5.

Finally, I also observed and then wrote brief descriptions of each child on a daily record sheet. Every 3 weeks, I wrote a narrative based on these daily records. I used these narratives for report card conferences and curriculum planning. I also collected student work for parents and me to view together. Though these were very important to my teaching, I only occasionally refer to them in this book.

As I chose the journal entries, letters, excerpts, and stories to include in this book, I had to leave behind hundreds of other wonderful examples. I know from past experience that 1 year's journal entries or a 2-year collection of parents' letters can provide the basis for discussions about teaching. In the future, I hope to make much of my data available on a website.

Data Analysis

I worked both by myself and with other educators in inquiry groups to analyze my data and drafts of portions of this book. I typed all the entries on families in my journal in chronological order so that I could describe and learn about the continuities and changes in my work over my many years of teaching. I coded the entries according to themes that emerged as I read each of them. Sometimes an entry fit into more than one theme. Then, using a computer program developed by Steve Longo, Professor of Math and Computer Science at LaSalle University in Philadelphia, I sorted each theme's entries into a file and then printed them. For example, as I searched for stories about parents who worked in the classroom, I was able to see all the entries on parents working in the classroom in one file. I read all those entries, noted the kinds of work parents did, chose examples that stood out and that also represented many parents who could not be mentioned for lack of space, and wrote about these examples in detail. I worked in a similar way with the notes and letters from parents to discover parents' major concerns, interests, and issues.

I didn't do this work by myself only; I had a great deal of help working through my data with educators in the inquiry groups in which I participated. In 1974 I began to attend Summer Institutes at the Prospect School. Formerly part of the Prospect Archives and Center for Education and Research in North Bennington, Vermont, it was there (and at workshops in Philadelphia) that I learned about phenomenology (Himley, 1991) and the group descriptive processes that Patricia Carini and the staff of the Prospect School were then developing. The first of these was Prospect's Descriptive Review of the Child in which

> The teacher organized the portrayal under five headings, each designed to call out a facet of the child's presence. Beginning with physical presence and gesture, the successive headings for the portrayal are disposition and temperament; connections with other people; strong interests and preferences; modes of thinking and learning. With the teacher's portrayal before us, everyone participating in the review added observations, and through questions and dialogue invited the presenting teacher to amplify the emerging portrait.
>
> The primary aim of the Descriptive Review of the Child was to recognize and specify a particular child's strengths as a person, learner, and thinker, so that as a school we could respond to and build upon those capacities. As we came to the close of a review, our attention turned to suggestions for how that might happen, with all of us contributing ideas. (Carini, 2001, pp. 3–4)[5]

I also participated in the Philadelphia Teachers' Learning Cooperative (PTLC) and continue to do so.[6] Since 1978 we have met weekly to discuss educational issues, with a focus on children and classrooms. The Literature Circle of the Philadelphia Writing Project, where I am a teacher-consultant, is the third group in which I participate. Like the Prospect Summer Institutes and PTLC, we use the Prospect Descriptive Processes.

During Summer Institutes, at the Literature Circle, and at the PTLC meetings where my book was discussed, we used the Format for Close Reading Documents, Texts, Etc. to describe and analyze my data.

> Close reading is the polar opposite of debating a text or offering opinions about it. The aim is to stay as close as possible to the text itself. The yield is an unlayering of meanings, with attention to ambiguities as interesting and important in their own right. Understandings of the text are usually both heightened and deepened. In these ways it is precisely parallel with a description of any work—visual art works, constructions, writings, drawings, etc.

> Close reading a text is a variation on the process used for describing children's works. The process can be applied to any text (poetry, essays, etc.) or a set of notes. . . . Close reading is slow, intensive work.
>
> [After the chairperson collects first impressions from participants] if the document or notes to be described are lengthy, the next step is to have participants identify and read aloud passages that are particularly meaningful to them, commenting as they do so about what makes the passage important to them. The chair may then elect to pull this reading of passages together or move on to a selection of a "starting point" passage. The passage is often obvious for the reason that several persons chose it. Sometimes more deliberation is needed. (Carini, 1996, p. 49)

At the Prospect Summer Institutes in 2001–2005 we described and analyzed newsletters to parents, the letters I wrote to administrators when I was a parent, and drafts of two chapters. PTLC noted themes and important issues that emerged from describing many documents: the notes and letters from parents, the many examples from my journal, and several of the book chapters. And the Literature Circle described my entire book. These descriptive sessions ended with suggestions. The Prospect group descriptive processes were especially helpful to me in analyzing data. I noticed that when I was part of a group of individuals contributing their own perspectives but discussing the same text, I often learned more than when I worked alone.

ORGANIZATION OF THE BOOK

Chapter 1 provides an autobiographical background. Parent involvement has, for me, been closely linked to issues of equality of educational opportunity. The results of my activism as a parent, both as an individual and as part of a group, anticipated what would eventually become state and federal policy. It influenced my teaching and my desire to invite parents into my classroom.

Chapters 2, 3, and 4 describe concerns that parents of children I taught had for their own children in school. In Chapter 2 I describe and analyze many of the things about which parents informed me, such as their families and lives at home; about difference; about their concerns with school policies; and about the well-being and happiness of their children. I introduce my newsletter to parents, which was one location of my invitation to them to communicate with me. At the end of the chapter, I compare my concern as an activist parent (and those of the group with which I was associated) to those of the parents of children I taught.

Chapter 3 discusses homework as a site where home and school most often meet. It was one of the parents' major concerns. I describe why I gave homework, how I informed parents about homework, some examples of assignments, and parents' responses. I then describe my current thinking about homework.

In Chapter 4 I address the ways in which children's behavior (specifically inappropriate behavior) influences, affects, and interacts with parent–teacher relationships. Behavior was a major concern to parents and to me, though our expectations were sometimes different. This chapter addresses many of the complexities involved with children's behavior, such as school district policy; my classroom policies; the effect of disruptive behavior on the creation of classroom community; and matters of power, control, authority, and democracy in the classroom. I describe why and how I informed parents about children, the range of their responses to my informing them, times when parents informed me about the behavior of children other than their own, and what I learned from thinking about this issue.

Chapters 5 and 6 bring parents into the school and classroom. Chapter 5 describes why I wanted parents to work alongside me. I address differences between my assumptions in involving parents and assumptions found in some government policies requiring parent involvement. For the second time in the book, I discuss my newsletter to parents, this time as my primary vehicle for inviting parents into the classroom. Chapter 5 also provides examples of how I prepared parents and myself for working together. Finally, I describe times when it was difficult to have parents in the classroom, and include some thoughts about parents who don't enter the classroom.

Chapter 6 tells stories of parents working in the classroom in a variety of ways. These examples show the range of what parents are capable of doing if a teacher encourages such involvement. It includes parents who simply did anything that needed to be done for the day-to-day fine-tuning of the classroom and parents who participated by bringing and sending special objects and sharing aspects of themselves and their skills.

Chapter 7 provides a summary of the book. It addresses issues of authority and trust—and perhaps progress in involving parents since the late 1960s. I discuss what I've learned from examining my teaching and what I might have done differently, as well as some of my further concerns. I describe ways in which administrators can support welcoming settings for parents. I end with responses to questions I have raised in this Introduction about parent involvement as well as questions about practitioner research.

Through my examples, analysis, and reflections, I illustrate school context and classroom situations that both facilitate and hinder parent–teacher interactions. I explore major aspects of parental involvement and how each of these plays out in the classroom. I try to capture the day-to-day challenges of making parent participation an integral part of children's school experience. I suggest ways for parents to be involved in their children's education. I offer some new ways to think about parent–teacher relationships and parent participation that integrate the daily lives of schools and communities and that challenge traditional roles for parents as mere consumers of school services.

❧ 1 ❧

I'm a Parent and a Teacher:
How My Own Experiences Have Informed
My Stance Toward Parent Involvement

My LIFE as a teacher, and particularly the attitudes toward parents that I held throughout my teaching life, were deeply influenced not only by my first-time experience in teaching, but even more by experiences that I had as a child and a parent, before I officially became a full-time teacher.[1]

MY FAMILY

I am the great-granddaughter and granddaughter of immigrants to the United States from a shtetl[2] in Ukraine. Neither my great-grandparents nor grandmother, whom I called Bubi, had attended school. They could not read English, though they were able to read Yiddish. I am the daughter of a woman who did not graduate from high school because she failed a course in her senior year and didn't think it was important to make it up. At the age of 7, Bubi began to sew velvet collars on men's coats at her father's home tailoring "factory." Such home workplaces were common in Philadelphia when she arrived in the United States in 1898. Bubi's parents were rarely involved in their children's education. Whatever the teacher said was law, and even when a first-grade teacher changed my two great-aunts' first names from Goldie and Sophie (too foreign) to Lillian and Josephine (more American), they said nothing. My bubi and mother had active intellectual lives. Bubi read the Yiddish newspaper every day and occasionally read Jewish literature or English literature translated into Yiddish. As a young adult, even though she sewed all day, she and her friends often attended Yiddish theater. I remember talking with her about the Yiddish versions of *King Lear* (with a happy ending, unlike Shakespeare's original) and Ibsen's *Memories, Dreams, and Reflections*, both of which she'd seen. My mother constantly read novels long into the night.

My bubi and then my mother were both widowed early in their marriages, and they worked all of their adult lives in the grocery store that they owned. We lived behind and above the grocery store until my mother remarried when I was 9. My mother and bubi did have one connection to public schools. Occasionally, teachers from the elementary school across the street came into our grocery store to buy sandwiches for lunch, and my family got to know them in a less formal way. At Passover, they invited any teacher who wished to come, to eat a home-cooked Passover lunch. In addition, in the years before I went to kindergarten, if we had a family emergency and all the adults had to be away from home, the kindergarten teacher cared for me by allowing me to spend time in her classroom. These things made me feel quite comfortable when I finally went to the school when I was 5.

My grandmother raised my mother and her sister, children from her first marriage, and three stepchildren from her second marriage, which ended with her husband's death after 6 months. Like many immigrants, she was too busy supporting my mother, aunts, and uncles to help with their schoolwork. Even if she had had the time, because she could not read English, she would have been of no help whatsoever. My mother, when also widowed a second time, had to work to support my sister and me. Her lack of time to help me with schoolwork (and perhaps her lack of confidence, since she hadn't graduated from high school) was not a hardship when I was young. Parents were not really expected to help their children with homework or to work in the schools. They were invited to join parent–teacher organizations, perhaps to volunteer in the school library or on trips. An especially helpful mother might have been invited by the teacher to be a room mother, someone who acted as a liaison between the teacher and the rest of the parents.

I remember asking my mother for help only with practicing spelling words or memorizing history facts. In spite of this, she expected me to keep attuned to current events by reading the newspaper daily, to receive good grades and a good education, and to attend college. My mother experienced great pride in whatever academic achievements I attained.

EARLY TEACHING EXPERIENCE

In September of 1962 I became a long-term substitute teacher for 1 year (see Appendix B). This was long before policymakers began to mandate parent involvement in schools. I was inspired by President John F. Kennedy's call to serve the country. I was unable at the time to join the Peace Corps because I was newly married, in graduate school, and didn't want to leave my husband, who was also in graduate school. On a visit to a friend's kindergarten classroom, I fell in love with young children and became intrigued with all I might accomplish by teaching them. I was immediately curious about how those exuberant, expressive children learned. And so, with the help of my own kindergarten teacher and her contacts, I was fortunate to get a job as a long-term substitute at the Paul Lawrence Dunbar Elementary School.[3] Just short of a master's degree in the history of art, with no special training except a 2-week workshop for kindergarten teachers, I began to teach. I loved working with children from the moment I started until the moment I retired in June 2000. I still miss being in a classroom with children, and I also miss the interactions with their parents.

In 1962 it was rare for parents to be invited into classrooms to work alongside teachers. As members of the officially sanctioned parent–teacher organization—in Philadelphia called the Home and School Association—parents worked in the halls to help maintain order and safety; in the library to organize, shelve, and repair books; at recess to supervise pretzel sales; and to chaperone children on class trips. The Home and School Association also raised funds and made suggestions for and then "rubber stamped" local or school district decisions, but parents rarely worked alongside teachers in classrooms.[4] During that year at Dunbar, I realized as soon as I had met some of the parents that they were valuable, though untapped, resources in that school neighborhood of generally very poor people. I wondered about all the time so many mothers spent on pretzel sales, and I came to believe that parents should be welcomed to contribute their knowledge and experience to classrooms if they wanted to be there. Like many new teachers, I was overwhelmed teaching 35 kindergarten children in the morning and a different 35 in the afternoon. (Until my supervisor demonstrated it, I didn't even know how to hold a book so that everyone could see the pictures.) I think I was too inexperienced and unsure of myself to ask for extensive help. One parent must have sensed my need, and I was grateful that she volunteered in the classroom once a week.

PARENT ACTIVISM IN GERMANTOWN

But what if, as is often the case, the teacher is also a parent—a parent/teacher who believes that it is the job of citizens and educators to make public schools so good that parents would not want either to send their children to independent schools or to educate them at home, who believes that parents like her (even though they are not necessarily teachers) have important contributions to make in schools? I believed both, and where I resided helped to shape me as a teacher. In 1967 we bought a house in Germantown on Schoolhouse Lane, a good street in a good neighborhood for someone who was concerned about schools.

Germantown, in the northwest area of Philadelphia, was integrated racially and economically.[5] While in the late 1960s most children in Philadelphia attended neighborhood public schools, in Germantown this was not always the case. The neighborhoods in Germantown were integrated, but the schools, for the most part, were not.[6] Our Westside and the nearby Southwest Germantown communities had two public elementary schools, Fitler and Keyser, under the leadership of the same principal. Though the schools were within walking distance of each other, they were effectively segregated. In 1967 Fitler was a school with almost all White students, reflecting the surrounding working-class, largely White, Catholic population. Keyser, three blocks from our house, had almost all Black students, even though the surrounding area was integrated. Many White children in the Keyser neighborhood went to either Quaker or archdiocesan schools if their parents could afford them. If they wanted to send their children to public school, they were encouraged or permitted (I never found out which) to send their children to Fitler. From personal experience, I know that real estate agents, who were anxious to maintain or increase Germantown's White population, played a role in this. One agent, whom we did not use, promised us that our children could gain admittance to one of the local Quaker schools if we bought a house there. Finally, some Black families from Westside sent their children to the Catholic Saint Catherine's School for "Indian and Colored Children," founded by Mother (and Saint) Catherine Drexel.

Like ours, many of the White families who bought homes in Germantown during the 1960s intended to send their children to public schools, but my husband and I did not want to engage in undercover antics. I was angry about special treatment for White families. I was angry that so many people sent their children to private schools or Catholic schools. I was angry because I believed that public schools would never live up to their promise unless those who had a choice (both Black and White) sent their children to them. Within a year of moving into our home in Germantown, my beliefs and convictions led me to become active in the education committees of two local civic groups—the Westside Neighborhood Council and the Germantown Community Council. These groups advocated for public schools.[7] The small group of White parents, who had recently moved into Germantown and had begun to send their children to Keyser, along with active African American families, hoped that we could find some ways to interest other neighborhood White parents in sending their children there.

We saw the Westside Parent Cooperative Nursery, established by our neighborhood group in 1958, as one way to do this. When our oldest child turned 4 (1967–1968), he began to attend the nursery's half-day program.[8] The Philadelphia Board of Education provided the teacher's salary and

some basic supplies, while we parents were expected to work in the classroom once a week or, if that was not possible, to contribute in other ways.
We were also expected to attend a monthly meeting at which a variety of
issues pertaining to educating and parenting were addressed. If possible,
the population of the nursery school was to be 50% White, 50% people
of color, and of different economic classes. The first teacher was Peggy
Perlmutter (now Stone), and many of us who were parents consider her
to have been our teacher, too. Some parents who had not completed high
school before their children attended the nursery were inspired by her to
earn high school diplomas. They then became classroom assistants, attended college, and became teachers.[9] Peggy was a wonderful model for
working with children, and throughout my teaching life I heard myself
repeating words and phrases she had uttered. Peggy was also a model for
working with parents, showing us how we could all contribute to our
children's learning alongside the teacher, how all of us, regardless of race,
class, and educational background, could enrich the classroom.

The school district and neighborhood activists also thought integration could be encouraged through the construction of two new schools.
The John B. Kelly Elementary School would merge the populations of,
and replace, Fitler (the "White") School and the rapidly physically dete-
riorating Keyser (the "Black") School. The second, the Pickett Middle School,
would make room for the increasing number of children in Germantown.
During the 1960s, there was a national climate of interest in schools and
a desire for community control of or, at the very least, intensive community involvement in schools. This interest had grown out of the civil rights
movement and the federal government's War on Poverty. Many of us in
Germantown wanted to push for community involvement in our new local
schools. Pickett Middle School was one of the first schools chosen by the
school district to have a community advisory board, and my husband served
on that board as an advisor on science curriculum. For me, community involvement in schools was a perfect coming together of my interest in national political action, my concerns about education and teaching, and my
parent cooperative nursery experience.

In addition to national interest in community involvement and control, there was also interest in the progressive education practices of the
primary schools in England. American adaptations of this way of teaching—
where children had choice—took on the name "open" or "informal" classrooms (see the Introduction). Both my husband and I supported this way
of educating young children. We purchased reprints of Joseph Featherstone's article "The Primary School Revolution in Britain" and distributed
them to anyone who might share our interest. We believed that the progressive practices illustrated there could be adopted in public schools in

Philadelphia. We also believed—arrogantly, I now think—that open classrooms would be good for all children.

Addressing Inequities

In the fall of 1967 I had heard Mr. Gideon, principal of both Fitler and Keyser Schools, speak at a meeting of the Germantown Community Council. The stated topic of the meeting was the results of the Iowa Achievement Tests, but it was also a chance for the community to meet the new superintendent of schools, Mark Shedd. During the meeting, Mr. Gideon said that he was not surprised that the children at Keyser School had done so badly in the standardized tests. I asked him if children who do badly on tests or, more important, who fail to learn what they are supposed to learn in school are also those children of whom little is expected in school. I don't remember his response, but I remember not being satisfied with it.

Our oldest child was attending the Westside Parent Cooperative Nursery, and the following fall we were planning to send him to kindergarten at Keyser School. Zatella Jenkins (an African American parent in the nursery) and I visited Fitler (the "White" school) and Keyser (the "Black" school) at the end of January 1968. We were shocked by the inequities we saw when we compared these two schools. After our visits, I was so angry, so scandalized by what I had seen, so furious that the principal in charge of both schools was allowing these inequities, that I wrote a letter to him and sent copies of it to everyone I could think of, including the superintendent of schools, the district superintendent, the associate superintendents, the entire board of education, and the early childhood supervisor for our subdistrict (see Appendix C).

My first letter, February 1, 1968. In my letter, I first reminded Mr. Gideon that I'd heard him speak the previous fall and had asked him a question about the relationship between poor test scores and low expectations. I told him that another parent and I had recently visited the three kindergartens at Fitler and the one at Keyser. I expressed several concerns. My first concern was that in comparison to Fitler's kindergarten, which had received a variety of new math and reading materials and a newly furnished space, Keyser's kindergarten not only had no visible materials but also was in shabby condition.

My second concern, which grew out of the first, was that there seemed to be little effort to teach the children at Keyser. My evidence was that only an incomplete alphabet was hanging on the walls, no numbers were evident, and there were few books. I held the principal responsible for what appeared to be the teacher's shortcomings:

Certainly children will do poorly in achievement tests if they are not taught. Or do you have so little expectation that the children at Keyser's kindergarten will be able to learn that you did not even bother to try to have the teacher teach them? It is easy to say "Oh, those children can't learn." But it is certainly the duty of the school to show evidence of having tried. The difference in the kindergartens of the "white" and "black" schools showed clearly why the Supreme Court ruled that separate but "equal" facilities are unconstitutional.

Third, I held the principal responsible for providing equal opportunities to learn:

> Is it necessary for parents to complain before their children are treated equally? I think that it is *your* duty as an educator to be sure that children all have the same opportunities to learn even if their parents have not reached the point of feeling comfortable about complaining.

I compared the Keyser kindergarten and the work of its teacher to the parent cooperative nursery school and its teacher, using both teachers' names, writing that the nursery school teacher was given no money to buy supplies but managed to gather things in a variety of ways. Finally, I explained that I had written the letter because our family lived within the boundaries of Keyser, not Fitler, but I would not want my child attending Keyser. I pointed out that while many of the neighborhood families who were able to make choices sent their children to independent or parochial schools, and I understood why, we were not planning to do that.

The copies I sent to the administrators and the members of the Board of Education included a cover letter in which I requested that they visit the two elementary schools and the Westside Parent Cooperative Nursery to see for themselves what I described. I suggested that the Keyser kindergarten be closed as soon as possible. And I suggested three possible solutions to the unequal treatment Zatella and I had observed: Send all Keyser kindergarten children to Fitler, get a new teacher and supplies for Keyser, or start a new kindergarten class in an off-site location like a church and invite parents in to help in the classroom. I suggested they read Featherstone's (1967) series in *The New Republic*, which described the kind of teaching I believed would be effective.

A closer look at my first letter. The serious tone of my letter to Mr. Gideon establishes me as an articulate parent who wants to send her children to public schools, who is willing to take action toward improving conditions in the schools, and who is not afraid to speak out in the face of the unequal treatment of students. The letter also establishes me as a parent who is knowledgeable about the law, and in it there is a veiled threat that Zatella and I, as well as others, could sue the school district because of separate and unequal treatment of Black and White children. (This was 14 years after the *Brown v. Board of Education* decision.) I accuse the principal of having low expectations and of not doing his job with regard to both caring about all the children under his leadership and making sure the teachers are doing their jobs well. Finally, toward the end of the letter, I give Mr. Gideon an example of what I believe to be a good educational environment and a good teacher.

The cover letter to the board and administrators lets them know that they, too, have responsibilities toward the children. The veiled threat extends to them for not making sure that children, even in separate schools, are treated equally. I don't merely complain. I offer suggestions about some of the things they might do to alleviate the situation. I also try to inform them of another way of educating children by giving each of them something to read.

As I look back at the letter, I can see that I had many assumptions about children, parents, teaching, and schools, assumptions that remain with me even today:

- All children in public schools should be offered comparable opportunities, facilities, and materials. The choice of materials that are or are not placed in schools and given to children makes a difference and is an indication of expectations of and respect for children.
- In educating children, teachers' and principals' expectations matter and adult expectations should be the same for all children.
- Everyone—teachers, principal, administrators, members of the school board—should do their jobs. Everyone is to be held accountable. Everyone must show that they made an effort to educate.
- Teachers need and deserve support from administrators.
- It is the duty and right of citizens to speak out about unequal treatment and to raise questions.
- Some parents, whether because they can afford it or because they have more knowledge about schools, have more choice about where and how their children will be educated than others. Once parents with choice see positive changes, they will be interested in public schools.
- Some parents are not comfortable about speaking out, so I should.
- In serious matters, such as illegal behavior on the part of administrators, threats of further action and actually taking the action are acceptable.

Though my grandmother and mother were working-class women, I was a middle-class professional (or hoped to be) with what could be called an upper-middle-class education at an Ivy League institution. It never occurred to me that my race, my class, the suburban public schools I had attended from fourth grade through high school, and the rest of my education would allow me to have the confidence to speak out while less formally educated, and/or working-class parents might not. I just wanted to reach the widest possible audience of those in power and to let them know of the shocking inequalities that another parent and I had found in these two schools, schools that were under the leadership of the same principal. Embedded in the letter, though I did not state it explicitly, is the understanding that I am White and middle-class, and because of that I have a choice of where to send my children to school. I now think that being White and middle-class gave me an assuredness that what I was doing was not only acceptable and my duty but would also be heard.

I now realize that taking that action alone without Zatella was not wise. At the time, I certainly didn't think about the ramifications of my being the sole writer of the letter. First, though I now see it as audacious, I didn't think there was anything wrong with speaking by myself for another person. I didn't think how much more effective it might have been if Zatella and I had composed and signed the letter together. Second, I behaved as if I had a right to say what kind of education would be good for all the children in Keyser's neighborhood. I was setting out to encourage the school district to adopt an educational program that suited me and my husband and to institute it more widely in schools.

Response: My second letter. Mr. Gideon did not respond in writing to my first letter, though I did receive some polite notes of thanks from some board members and administrators. Nevertheless, the effect on the kindergarten was immediate and striking. I suspect that administrators were as shocked as I was at what they learned about the inequities, because things suddenly began to change. The associate superintendent in charge of curriculum indicated to me that he had visited Keyser's kindergarten, and he wrote to assure me that he had recommended curriculum changes there.

The principal invited my husband and me to meet with him and the kindergarten supervisor. I summarized what he told us in a second letter, which I wrote to the same audience as the first (Appendix D). At this meeting, Mr. Gideon told us of various changes and new materials that would be coming to Keyser's kindergarten. He told us of his eagerness to communicate with Keyser parents and to invite them to help in the school. The kindergarten supervisor told us that, after having spent a week working with the kindergarten teacher in her classroom, she realized that the teacher had many good ideas.

On February 15, 15 days after I wrote my first letter, the principal held a Parents' Visiting Day in Keyser's kindergarten. In my second letter, I described how the teacher had transformed the formerly dreary classroom.

> The most exciting thing that I saw happen on Visiting Day was that you asked parents to sign up to help in the kindergarten if they have time. You had an excellent list of ways in which they could help, and almost every parent signed up. One father took a rocking chair home to paint. Your open acknowledgment to them that this idea is new to you and the teacher, but that you are interested in trying it out, was wonderful. I sincerely hope that it works, and you must know that there are additional people in the community who are anxious to give time in the school.

I cautioned the principal on several matters. Parents would need the supervision and encouragement of the teacher as they worked alongside her. I warned that math and reading programs should not be compulsory for, but rather available to, all children and that a child's readiness for such programs should be taken into account. I said that parents want their children to be happy as they learn, and that would happen with a comfortable, calm teacher with high expectations. I suggested that it might be helpful for her to observe at parent cooperative nurseries. I was a parent speaking, but from my perspective as a future teacher.

In the cover letter to the administrators and members of the board of education, I expressed thanks for their moving quickly on behalf of the children of Keyser School. I gave them a list of books and articles to read, and I described and urged them to visit an elementary school classroom that I believed was an excellent example of how children could be educated effectively.

A closer look at my second letter. This letter is also written to the principal, with copies to administrators and members of the Philadelphia Board of Education. It had three purposes. The first purpose was to thank the principal directly and to indirectly thank and compliment those who were responsible for taking such quick action on the problems that were mentioned in my first letter. Many of the criticisms in my first letter were addressed by the changes in the school, changes that I described in detail. The second purpose of my letter was to mention several things a good teacher should do (audaciously, with my 1 year's experience). The third purpose was to describe my child's nursery school experience, which I believed was an excellent example of how children could be educated effectively.

Trying to Change Keyser School: The Keyser School Community Mothers' Group

While I was writing my own letters about conditions at Keyser and Fitler Schools, I was also part of a small group of mothers whose older children had attended or were currently attending the Westside Parent Cooperative Nursery.[10] We had been getting together informally as our younger children played together. I call our group the Keyser School Community Mothers' Group after the way we named ourselves in the writing described below. We mothers quickly learned that we shared an interest in education, schools, and political action. There were eight of us—African American and White. Four were high school graduates; another four had completed college, one with an advanced degree. Four had children who were already attending Keyser School, and as we talked about schools, those mothers talked about their experiences and concerns. They expressed dissatisfaction with much (though not with all) of what they and their children were experiencing at the Keyser School. We realized that we had to take action on behalf of our children and to encourage different ways of teaching them.

On January 29, the evening before I sent my first letter to Mr. Gideon, the Keyser School Community Mothers' Group met formally to talk specifically about our local school. After Zatella and I reported what we'd observed at Keyser and Fitler, I showed the group the first letter (described earlier) that I was about to send to Mr. Gideon. We immediately decided to request a meeting with him and began to plan for it. We brainstormed a list of complaints and suggestions that had grown from our experiences. They included inequalities in delivery of curriculum, especially in math; apparent different and lower expectations of the African American children at Keyser; inequality in the treatment of and communication with and to people from the community, including parents and volunteers; and worries about the safety of our children. Our list made clear some of the actions we thought the school might take to remedy the difficulties. We gave suggestions of concrete ways to help parent and community volunteers feel welcome; ways in which the curriculum could become more individualized and interesting, and suggestions as to how to make the school (especially the schoolyard) safer. In planning for a possible meeting, we drafted the following plea:

> We as parents would like to find ways of supporting the teachers
> and making real contributions to the school. We would like to meet

with them and talk with them about such things as community involvement in the schools. It is most important that parents, teachers and administrators be able to discuss such a thing together without feeling threatened.[11]

The Keyser School Community Mothers' Group met with Mr. Gideon sometime in early March, after the various changes at Keyser School had begun to take place. We voiced the concerns we'd brainstormed (Appendix E). We must not have been satisfied with the results of the meeting because we decided to take further action.

At the time, I wasn't politically savvy about how to be an effective member of a group. Though I had acted alone when I wrote my own letters, our Keyser School Community Mothers' Group's coming together seemed to bring out the strengths in each of us. For example, one of the mothers was an excellent, very emotional speaker who could move her listeners in public places to both applause and tears, but she didn't write things down. Her words and ideas were central to the notes for the meeting with the principal and to the position paper that will be described in the next section. The quick reaction to my letters by the school district and the attention they brought to Keyser School delighted and amazed our little group. Fortunately, my having written the letters on my own did not divide us.[12]

The position paper. Our group then began to write what I now call a position paper, but it did not have a title when we wrote it (Appendix F). Because we didn't want to send it to the principal, since he might not pass it along to the teachers, we mimeographed copies (no photocopies in those days) and placed one in the office mailbox of each teacher in Keyser School. No one in the office questioned us or stopped us from doing that. Today we would have had to ask for permission. We did not send our paper through or to the official representative of the parents—the Keyser School Home and School Association—because we knew that such groups were closely aligned with principals and represented the school district establishment. We typed the following note on a slip of paper attached to the front of the document.

Note to Teachers

We do not want the teachers at Keyser to feel that this is happening only to them. All over the city, in fact nationwide, parents are reassessing their role in the education process, without really being organized. We want to work together *with the teachers* for the good

of *all* the children. The verbal communication we feel is so important for children is also important for adults. With this in mind, we
hope to calmly and sensibly discuss the following points.

(Signed As) A group of mothers from the Keyser School
Community

The Keyser School Community Mothers' position paper was divided
into four sections: The parents' role, the teacher's role, discipline,
suggestions.

The parents' role. The position paper starts with a declaration of equality:

Parents and teachers are equal. Only their roles differ, and even
these only slightly. Every parent, regardless of education or background is deserving of respect from people in the school. As parents
we credit ourselves considerably with the success we have had in
teaching our children to speak which represents a far greater
achievement for the child than any other in his childhood.

We expected courteous treatment, truthful responses to our questions, and honesty about what the teacher knew or did not know. We
believed we had the right to say what we expected from schools. We
wanted to contribute directly to our children's education alongside the
teachers, which was different from supervising pretzel sales and other
forms of fund-raising. We listed ways in which this help would make a
difference for both teachers and parents, and we indicated that we recognized that responsibilities and obligations go with the offer of help. We
acknowledged that classroom practice might have to change to incorpo-
rate parents.

The teacher's role. This section begins with children:

The teacher must respect the natural intelligence and curiosity of
all children. She must have faith that almost all children want to
and can learn. And she must continually ask the question, "How *do*
children learn?" and start from that point.

We wanted teachers to treat children as individuals, to try other ways
of teaching than imparting information, and this might have meant alter-
ing the way classrooms were set up. An example was that we wanted
children to be allowed to talk with and teach one another. It was important to us that teachers demonstrate an interest in children's homes and

community by inviting them to bring things from home. We included a list of books and articles teachers might want to read and classrooms they might want to visit.

Discipline. We stated that children rarely fight or cause trouble when they are interested in what they are doing. We said that they should not have to sit still and pay attention for long periods of time, should be allowed to talk, and should be given real responsibility so that they would develop self-discipline, rather than just being told to follow orders. We made a connection between being silenced and violence: "Talking is an aid to learning. Violence is a result of a breakdown in verbal communication."

Suggestions. We continued the theme of possibly changing the way children were taught. We wanted them to be more active in their learning, rather than being told to sit and listen for long periods of time, do worksheets, or copy from the board. There were some specific suggestions, such as taking the children on more field trips, giving children interesting materials to read so that they would want to read, and taking less time with lining up and going to the bathroom. We suggested ways in which parents could help in the classroom that might cause an improvement in children's behavior.

A *closer look at the position paper.* The position paper begins with a cover note saying that it was written for the teachers. We tell the teachers that its context is the 1968 activism of parents and members of communities all over the country. We imply its local context—the dissatisfaction of the parents in our Keyser School Community Mothers' Group, whose children were attending or would attend Keyser School. Some of the children attending school were bored, some were disruptive, and their parents were not happy with how their behavior was handled. Most of us had a vision of educating that was different from what we saw at Keyser. The paper is a plea to teachers to work together with parents and to discuss the matters we raise, face-to-face, for the good of the children. We believed that open verbal communication to solve problems is as important for parents and teachers as it is for children.

The themes in the position paper are interconnected. We parents declare our equality with teachers twice in the course of the document: at the beginning with the first five words, "Parents and teachers are equal," and at the end when we say, "We want our children treated as teachers would have their own children treated." The emphasis on equality is a reminder of the unequal manner in which the education establishment treated Keyser and Fitler Schools.

Several times in the position paper we talk about changes that should occur in classrooms at Keyser. We parents recognize that our traditional roles will change and that responsibilities and obligations come with our assertion of equality. We expect teachers to change, for example, by inviting parents into the classroom and by reexamining such practices as keeping children silent and still. In every case, we give reasons for why these changes should occur.

Throughout the document and in a special section at the end, we offer many suggestions for changes in practice, for things to read, and for classrooms to visit. We back up each suggestion with reasons.

This is another audacious document—a declaration of equality, parents telling teachers what they should do, requesting that teachers question their assumptions and practices, demanding respect (the word *respect* is used six times). It is an assertion of power in a situation in which power is usually unequally exercised and felt. We Keyser mothers were well aware that schools were a potential location for political organizing activity and for people's reassessment of their roles with regard to public institutions. What we did was to question the status quo, and that was terribly threatening to the teachers.

What Happened Next

We were shocked that the teachers had an angry reaction to our position paper. In the spring following my letter to the principal and the teachers' receipt of the Keyser School Community Mothers' position paper, there was an evening meeting at a local church to introduce to the community the new principal of Fitler's and Keyser's yet-to-be-built replacement, the John B. Kelly School; to have the architect talk about the building; and to invite discussion of other plans. As members of the community gathered, we noticed that a large number of teachers from both schools were there. We later learned that, in fact, every staff member was present. Mr. Gideon, who was now the outgoing principal, called the meeting to order and before he had a chance to say anything more, Frank Sullivan, the president of the Philadelphia Federation of Teachers, Local 3, walked to the podium and began to speak. I do not have notes from his talk, but I remember his calm voice and his firm, angry stance. He said, referring to a letter (my first letter) that had been sent in February, that no teacher should ever have to suffer the humiliation that one of Fitler–Keyser's teachers had recently suffered and that there would be no more attacks on teachers. He said that if parental involvement meant that teachers would be attacked in that way, there would be no parental involvement. Now, those were not his exact words, but his intent was clear. The union would stand up to any attack on teachers, and parents had better be careful of the ways in which they tried to exert influence. He even threatened to take the letter writer to court and sue her for libel for defaming a teacher. Fortunately, that did not happen.

Until February 1968, only a few members of the Fitler and Keyser staffs had joined the Philadelphia Federation of Teachers. The principal had shown my letters to the kindergarten teacher who was mentioned in them. We ourselves had placed the Keyser School Community Mothers' Group position paper in every teacher's mailbox, and, though we had written it in order to get changes in the schools that we felt were necessary for the children, it had instead spread fear among the teachers. Though Mr. Sullivan did not mention the position paper, it and my letter became the tools for organizing the teachers. The entire staffs of both Fitler and Keyser immediately joined the Philadelphia Federation of Teachers.

I was raised in a strongly pro-union family. I knew how dangerous it was for teachers to have no due process, no safeguards against being fired. I knew that only with pressures from a union would salaries be raised beyond a survival level. As a long-term substitute at Dunbar School, when Local 3 of the American Federation of Teachers was beginning its bid to become the bargaining unit for Philadelphia teachers, I had supported the organizing of teachers in every way.

In writing my first letter to Mr. Gideon, I didn't think carefully about what I was doing when I named a teacher publicly or about the effect that would have on her. I now regret that I embodied my complaint in one teacher, saying that she made little effort toward the children's education and implying that she might have personal problems. I might have written it differently, without identifying her in any way. After I became a teacher, I realized that I would never want such a letter written about me.

But the letter was not about that teacher alone. It was about the obstacles in front of her and about the inequalities that they represented. The teacher needed to act, but she also needed action from her principal. I believed that the principal and administration were not doing their jobs, one of which was to observe teachers and help those who were having difficulty.

The Keyser School Community Mothers' position paper shows that, to us, the important issues were the separate and unequal facilities and materials, little evidence of teachers' and the principal's interest in the children, no supervision or help from administrators who were supposed to be in charge, low expectations of the children, and generally getting a better education for our kids. Sending it to all the teachers with no context or discussion was an unwise move politically.

Shortly after my letter and the position paper were shared with the teachers, I realized that fear of being spied on and then discredited was a major reason why some teachers would be apprehensive about having parents spend time in schools, especially in classrooms. Our actions fed teachers' fear of parental involvement in schools. None of us, neither I nor the other mothers, realized that both documents might undermine the trust that is essential for good home–school relationships.

And yet, good things did happen. By the end of the year, our parents' group had joined with the new Kelly Home and School Association. Parent involvement increased at Keyser and then at the Kelly School when it opened. In spite of my original criticisms of the staff of what became the Kelly School, I ended up teaching there for many years, from 1972 until 1989. In addition to the rest of the staff, I worked amicably alongside the teacher named in my letters and with Peggy Perlmutter Stone, who had transferred from the Westside Parent Cooperative Nursery to Keyser. When Kelly School opened, federal money from the Follow Through program was used to support an "open classroom" program based on English infant schools. From the day it opened, Kelly School had an unusually high degree of parent involvement for a Philadelphia public school. In part due to our struggle, Kelly School embodied some of the principles that we Keyser School Community Mothers had believed were important.

INFLUENCE OF THESE EXPERIENCES ON MY TEACHING

As a parent with 1 year's experience teaching, I had developed strong ideas about learning and teaching. I was a politically active person who believed that schools were the perfect place for people to recognize their own power and to act on it. I believed that education could change lives, could be instrumental in helping people liberate themselves. I believed, with the rest of the parents in our small neighborhood group, that encouraging children to converse in school rather than forcing them to be silent could reduce violence; that conversation in general—simply speaking one's mind—was equally important for adults. I also believed in the importance of writing—writing as a powerful tool for accomplishing one's goals, both large and small, and as a way of letting those in charge know what you want and need.

I was forever influenced by the descriptions of their own experiences by the mothers in our group whose children were already attending Keyser School; these were mothers who had to work hard to become visible. Their descriptions stayed with me for all my years of teaching, and their vision shaped my practice. I didn't want the parents of children I was going to teach to feel dissatisfied about the way I treated their children and them. It is no accident that I managed to save my letters and the Keyser School Community Mothers' position paper. Those words continued to speak for my beliefs about education throughout my teaching life.

❧ 2 ❧

Learning About Parental Concerns,
Interests, and Issues

PARENT ENGAGEMENT was integral to my classroom and woven into my practice. Because I had been involved in my own children's early education and, along with other parents, had struggled with some resistance to such involvement, as a teacher I wanted to learn what was important to the parents of children I taught. I wondered what the similarities and differences between my parental concerns and theirs might be.

I discovered parents' concerns and interests in a variety of ways. Of course I talked with individual parents when I met their children in line at the beginning of the day or when I dismissed them at the end of the day. I made occasional telephone calls, and I put handwritten notes into homework books. When I wanted to communicate with the entire group of parents, I did it in several ways. I spoke with them at parent meetings and at report card conferences. I wrote explanations as part of homework (see Chapter 3). And I sent a newsletter to parents.

MY NEWSLETTER TO PARENTS:
AN INVITATION TO INFORM ME

I started writing a newsletter for parents during the spring of my first year of teaching on a full-time basis. In 1967 the federal government funded the Follow Through program, in which grades K–3 in certain Title I schools implemented various teaching methods to attempt to maintain the gains children had made in Head Start (Kennedy, 1977).[1] Philadelphia had eight different Follow Through models in place, each with a different sponsor. The government planned to track and compare the success of each. An advisor to Follow Through teachers visited my classroom and, during our conversation, told me about a school in which the teachers regularly sent newsletters home to parents. She suggested that I do the same. I immediately began to send a newsletter once a week. Over the years, according to how much time I had, I sent it weekly, biweekly, or monthly. I love writing and was an avid letter writer at that time, and so it was natural for me to begin communicating with parents in that way. From the beginning, I made the newsletter as conversational and as clear as I could, with as little educational jargon as possible. I used the first and second person to speak directly to parents, just as I did in my letters.

I felt it was important to communicate in this way for several reasons. In the Introduction, I described some of the ways in which my classroom was different from most first- or second-grade classrooms. I wanted the parents to know that even though it might look like their children were "merely" playing (and they were playing), they were also learning; that learning takes place through play; and that I was teaching and would continue to do so. I was telling the parents before they asked, taking a posture of offense.

I believed my job was to educate parents as well as children, and I thought the newsletter would be a good vehicle for doing so. It was a place where I could help parents help their children by telling them what we were doing in the classroom (as a model) and also by telling them things they could do at home. This would give parents opportunities to learn a variety of ways of working with their own children.

Like my journal, the newsletter was also a way for me to later recall what had gone on in the classroom—an important record of curriculum. And it served as a way to let my principal know not only about my classroom (curriculum, for example) but also about the valuable contributions the parents made to the children and to me. Again, this was important because my way of teaching was different from a traditional teaching model. Thus, the newsletter had educational, curricular, accountability, and (perhaps) political purposes.

Over the years, I've become aware of complicating issues involved in sending newsletters home. Though I wouldn't have sent e-mails unless every family in a class had a computer at home, when I began to send my newsletter home (just as with homework), I unfortunately didn't think much about whether or not all parents would be able to read English. I didn't think that communicating in writing might leave some families out. A possible reason for that (though there is never an excuse for leaving even one family out) is that I taught few children whose parents didn't speak or read English. An additional complicating issue was that the newsletter told parents what they could be (and by implication because a teacher was writing it—what they *should* be) doing at home to help their children. While there was the danger that parents could have interpreted my giving advice as my trying to intervene in their lives at home or as my saying that they were not doing enough with and for their children, I certainly didn't mean it that way.

I'm not certain those two things would have stopped me from keeping parents informed in this way. Though some of my assumptions changed over the years, when I began to send newsletters home I assumed (as did educational policymakers) that parents wanted to and should help their children at home so that they could "succeed" at school. I assumed that it was possible to show parents how to help their children achieve academically, that it was good to do that, and that it was my job. I believed that to have kept this knowledge secret would have been unethical. I assumed that parents had the right to know what their children were learning, what and how the teacher was teaching. I assumed that parents would read the newsletter. Since I assumed that because most of the parents would be able to read it, it was worth doing. I assumed that I would learn from the parents and that every parent could be a teacher in the broadest sense of the word. I assumed that some parents would respond to me, would let me know their thoughts about what we were doing in school, and that even if I did not agree with them, it was important that I pay attention to what they were saying.

A glance at the newsletters through the years shows them to be quite similar (Appendix G). The format remained the same—three columns wide, border at top with the title and date, border at the bottom with announcements and reminders. As computers became more available and ultimately saved time, I stopped writing by hand (which continues to appeal to me). I continued to hand-draw decorations, which made the newsletters more personal. I sent them home regularly.

I recognized children's birthdays, parents who helped and what they did, and parents or children who sent or brought things to school. Most of the newsletters didn't have student work in them. I wrote from my teacher point of view. I informed parents about classroom curriculum and sometimes about school policy. I explained why things were done in certain ways in my class. I included examples of ways in which parents could help their children with learning and schoolwork at home, and I sometimes modeled how they could do that. Most of all, the newsletters were my invitation to parents to enter into the school lives of their children, both in school and at home. Because I wanted parents to be involved with and in their children's school learning, I had to make sure that my invitation was gracious and sincere.

As part of my analyzing the data for this book, I reread the newsletters; I noticed that in the first and second newsletters of the year, I tried to establish the warmth and openness of the classroom and to set the tone of welcome to which I hoped parents would respond favorably. I introduced myself and told the parents exactly what they would find in each newsletter. Even though most of the families in second grade classes were familiar with the newsletter, I repeated welcomes and invitations to remind them. I also did this to include newer families whose children had not been with me in first grade. Here is an example from a first newsletter:

9/11/98, Newsletter (first grade)

WELCOME TO 209

I'll introduce myself briefly. My name is Lynne Strieb (say "Streeb", not "Street" or "Streem"). I have taught kindergarten, first, and second grade. I have also taught four-year-olds in England as a Fulbright Exchange Teacher. I have three married sons, and one three-year-old granddaughter. My husband teaches physics at LaSalle University.

I am especially excited because we are in a class that has four walls and a door. In my thirty years of teaching I've worked in classrooms with four walls for only five of those years. For the rest of the time, at John. B. Kelly School and at Greenfield, I've taught in shared rooms and open space classrooms. This is wonderful!

Please watch for this newsletter at least once a month. I have been sending class news home for at least 27 years. I welcome your comments and suggestions. The newsletter will include news of classroom activities, important announcements, recognition of parents' involvement, some of my observations of the children, the ways in which I think about teaching and education in general, and other items of interest.

ALL NOTES, INCLUDING NEWSLETTERS WILL BE SENT HOME IN A POCKET FOLDER. PLEASE CHECK YOUR CHILD'S BOOKBAG EACH NIGHT FOR THE FOLDER. PLEASE SIGN NOTES AS QUICKLY AS POSSIBLE.

I invited parents to attend class meetings; to contact me; to talk with me about their children; to give suggestions and ideas, to ask questions, to make comments. I believe that it was in response to these invitations that so many parents wrote to me to inform me of their concerns, wishes, and interests with regard to school. In the rest of the chapter, I focus on parents' communications to me.

PARENTS' COMMUNICATIONS TO ME

I found that the contents of my journal entries about parents and the notes and letters from parents shared certain themes. They informed me about their children and families; they showed attempts to make sense of school policy in a variety of areas; they expressed concern for the well-being and happiness of their children.

Children, Families, and Lives at Home

I received many communications from parents in which they gave me information about their own children and many in which they shared information about themselves and their families. The variety of such informational notes was great. Parents informed me about things that were on their child's mind, sometimes complying with their child's own requests to do so. Parents told me about their separations and divorces and the impact of those on their child's life. They made requests on behalf of their children for music lessons and art lessons within the school day. For instance, one parent wrote me about her son's accomplishment.

3/16/99, Note

Ms. Strieb
    Anthony read the whole book Lon and Pon by hiself tonite. (He asked me to send a note to you. For some reason he loves when we communicate.) Thank You, Arlene

Parents let me know about their child's health. Notes about health were usually sent for three reasons. The first was when they wanted to inform me about a health condition that might affect the child in class in some way. Thus, Mrs. Davis wanted me to know that her daughter should be seated close to the board until she received her new glasses, and Tabitha's parents let me know that her cut hand might make it hard for her to do some of the written schoolwork.

The second reason was when parents wanted me to send their child to the school nurse. This happened if the child had to take some kind of medication (which only the nurse was allowed to dispense) or if the child had been sent to school although not feeling well because he or she was not ill enough to be kept at home. The third alerted me to a condition of some sort or another—for my own information, for example,

4/7/97, Note

Ms. Strieb, Just wanted to let you know that Tommy's eyes are red from his allergies. We went to Cape May this weekend and he really got a bad case of it. His eyes were swollen shut on Saturday. The reason I am letting you know is because the last two times it happened he was sent to the nurse for pink eye and he explained it was his allergies. Thank You, Tracey Manno

Parents sometimes wrote to me so that I could get to know about their children's activities and interests at home. Daniel's dad told me that not only was Daniel reading well at home but that he'd also learned to ride a two-wheeled bicycle and was proud of his accomplishment. They told me of activities they did with their child, such as cooking something for the class or reading a book that was not part of the homework. They did this to inform me, to impress me, or both, and they knew I would be interested.

I received requests from parents, requests that usually concerned only their own child or family. They asked me to allow the child to do something outside my classroom during the school day, such as buying something in the school store, auditioning for a talent show, going to an enrichment class, or searching for a lost item. They asked for some kind of special attention or recognition of their child (recognition for bringing something, an opportunity to perform a musical piece for the class). I was asked to check on books ordered or to fill out forms for admission to independent schools. There were many notes in which parents expressed a desire to celebrate a child's birthday by providing a party. Quite often they asked me to follow up on a problem, such as stolen pencils.

1/29/97, Note

Dear Mrs. Strieb—Mattie insisted I write this note to you but I'm not sure there is anything you can do. Mattie says that her pencils keep getting taken from her desk so she never has any. She feels it may be a particular classmate. I had no idea until yesterday anything was happening, but she says it's been going on for some time. Whenever she buys pencils at the school store, they're gone the next day. She has 2 pencils with her today and I warned her to be careful. It may be that she's just losing them on her own, but I'm not sure. Maybe you can check it out. I know this is rather trivial, but it seems to be upsetting her. Thanks, Pam Kaye

Usually the notes were pleasant, but occasionally parents got angry. Once, I was required by the school district to send home a note about federal welfare reform. This made one set of parents quite angry:

2/26/99, Note

Mrs. Strieb, We received the first note about welfare reform two weeks ago. Now Larry has come home with a second note about the same thing. The first note had his name on it and was in an envelope but the second came in his note folder. We are aware about welfare reform. We would appreciate it that no more notes about this subject be sent because we find it insulting as we are not on welfare. Thank you, Mr. and Mrs. MacDonald

I received many notes that had a dual purpose. On the first Monday of the school year, while waiting for my first-grade children to arrive in line in the schoolyard, I noticed that Casey and her father were conversing in Spanish. I'd collected many children's books written in or translated into Spanish and French during my years of teaching, and I was delighted that I would once again be able to send them home for a parent and child to enjoy together. Later, during that first week, I sent home *Osito*, the Spanish translation of *Little Bear* by Else Holmelund Minarik, for Casey to enjoy with her parents. I received the following note, which, as usual, started with words of thanks and included a compliment to me, and then apprised me of some important personal family information.

9/11/96, Note

Dear Ms. Streib—
　　I want to thank you for your thoughtfulness in sending home the Spanish book for Casey to read. Unfortunately, however, I am unable to assist Casey in cultivating her Spanish language skills, since mine are very weak. Casey's dad, Alberto Avillo speaks to her exclusively in Spanish. Since we are no longer together during the school week Casey spends every Monday night at his house. I know he would be able (and very willing) to help her with Spanish reading. So it might be best if Spanish books went home with Monday night's homework.
　　Please know that I was thrilled to see that you've picked up on her dual language skills. Also, I've already noticed an improvement in her reading this year. Thanks!
　　Sue Minton
P.S. We read *Clifford's Manners* instead tonight.

Parents also informed me about:

A ruined book (the dog chewed the pages, the thermos bottle leaked
　　and pages stuck together)
A child upset to miss a day of school because of an automobile accident
An invitation to First Holy Communion and party
A father taking his child to visit a member of the city council
Permission to send silkworms home

A child filling out an official form for parents
Halloween (family doesn't celebrate, allow to leave during scary
    stories)
A child's happiness about his visit to his mother and grandmother with
    whom he does not live, and a request that he be allowed to write
    about the experience
A child sent to the wrong place after school
Condolences because of supposed death of my grandmother

Sometimes a parent was concerned or worried about her child and
sent me a note to inform me of the concern. Such notes usually began
with a positive comment or a compliment, followed by the real purpose
of the note—the concern.

6/83, Note

Dear Mrs. Strieb,
    I really enjoyed *The Children's Own Workbook*. It was both clever
and practical and I would like to keep John's copy. Unfortunately,
he made a mess of it and he's driving me crazy. When we started
working on it he, as usual, turned the drawing part into a major
chore. That is why I asked him to do just the math equivalent.
Alice Trainer's story was a problem for John. (Take a look.)
    His reading has improved greatly but his interest is very
minimal. I feel he can handle a much higher level of reading in
school but his attitude is holding him back. Working with him at
home is very difficult. And in fact, living with him is the same.
Lately he has been extremely restless and bored and I thought that
he's being a pain in school as well. I thought that I'd let you know
that I sympathize with you (smile!!) and I am seeking possible
solutions.
    If you can, please try to schedule our conference late in the
day as possible. See you soon,
    Lauren T. Friend

At the report card conference that followed, both Lauren and I addressed the concerns she expressed in this note about John's approach
to math problems. I was glad she raised the concern—something I had
not noticed in class. We also discussed both his outstanding ability in and
his deep interest in reading during his time in school—so different from
what she described as happening at home. I suggested that she give him

a flashlight and tell him that he's not allowed to read in bed after the lights are out. Parents found this advice humorous but often told me that it worked.

Finally, parents simply sent notes to introduce their children to me. Amy Cabot was entering my second-grade class after having been home-schooled while most of the children were starting their second year with me. The first note I received from her mother, Brenda, was brief, but it alerted me to Amy's reaction to the first few days of school:

9/15/99, Note

Ms. Strieb, You were right—this was a challenge for Amy—but she persevered—and enjoyed it! I didn't know that her sister helped her [with her homework]—and I did #5 with her—I wasn't sure how much to do with /for her but decided to take her through each step or she'd never have gotten it. Do you want me to do as much as necessary or do you want to see just what Amy can do herself? Thanks, Brenda Cabot p.s. Can't believe her reading ALREADY!!! . . .

A few days later, Brenda took time to write me a longer letter introducing Amy to me in more detail. She believed that describing her child, and the things she and her family did at home would not only help me know Amy better but would also help me understand the choices the family had previously made to "home-school" their children. I was grateful for this note, if only because I had been concerned about a possible tension between Brenda's teaching methods at home and mine in school. This note calmed my worries.

9/21/99, Note

Ms. Strieb,

Although by now you're getting to know Amy, I wanted to tell you a few things about her especially since she—and our family—is new to Greenfield.

Amy is the third of our four daughters. . . . All have been in school (or pre-school) some years, and home-schooled the rest.

Amy has been at home for the past two years, and she has already taken part in some organized group activities—Hebrew School, ballet, sports, etc. and asked to try "real school" last spring. She led the way for her sisters, Molly & Carla, & so all three ended up [in public school] this fall.

Although she has made amazing strides in the last two weeks (!), Amy had not shown much interest in reading, and has resisted any effort I made to help her along. This was fine with me, but I was concerned that in school, her non-reading would be a problem. I'm glad we were steered towards you, as your approach seems to accommodate her and encourage her at the same time. She has made a smoother, faster transition than we expected!

Amy loves to be challenged. She is fearless, gregarious, energetic, and daring—but until now has been uninterested in learning some of the basic skills many children her age have already mastered. She learns easily by *doing*—works hard & loves piano, gymnastics, ballet, anything physical or kinetic. . . . I was concerned that she wouldn't be able to sit still long enough to do what she is asked to do in school, but, again, she has surprised us.

Amy is working hard on her homework and taking it all very seriously. Please let me know if there are things she needs to work on or ways I can help her "catch up." On the one hand she is very concerned about how her writing compares to others in the class, for example. On the other, she doesn't worry at all about "fitting in"—when I told her early this summer (after she came home embarrassed from gymnastics having been unable to read a checklist she was asked to fill out) that although a lot of those kids were older, & knew how to read well, many kids her age also don't know how to read. She just looked at me and said, "really?!"—she just hadn't thought about it as a deficit. She knows that her sister Sally learned to read very early, but Molly was much later—and only recently had become focused on her own not-yet-reading.

So, without blathering on, I just wanted to point out her sensitivity, which is coupled with determination and new found enthusiasm—she is already blossoming. Thanks for taking the time to read this, and please let me know if there's anything more I can do to help Amy in her new endeavors. She is very happy at school!

Thanks, Brenda Cabot

It was clear to me that parents believed that these little windows into their children's lives would interest me and that by giving me information about them, their children would be helped in some way. They were correct. I found the letters informative and fascinating, and they helped me to know the children. I always responded to their notes: with telephone calls, with a conference, with notes, sometimes with only the word *thanks*—but always with an assurance that I'd noted the concern and information and would follow up if necessary.

My Confusion

Forty-five years ago, in 1962, when I arrived as a long-term substitute teacher at the Dunbar School, with its all African American teaching staff and student body, it was a highly regarded school. Many parents who had attended the school as children sent their own children there even though they lived outside the school boundaries. More than 20 years had passed since Drs. Kenneth and Mamie Clark had done studies showing African American children's preferences for White rather than Brown-skinned dolls. Nevertheless, it wasn't until the fall of 1962 that Dunbar's first Brown-skinned dolls were purchased for the kindergarten class, and they arrived when I did. The early 1960s were important years for the civil rights struggle in Philadelphia. Though in 1962 I had participated in protests led by the local branch of the NAACP against employment bias in the construction industry in Philadelphia, and though I considered myself knowledgeable about racism, like many White people, I knew nothing about the Clark studies.

As the only new teacher (and the only White teacher) at Dunbar, I also didn't know much about school culture. I was grateful to be invited to eat lunch with a first-floor group that included the two White school secretaries and two Black first-grade teachers. One had ancestors who were freedmen during colonial times; the other had, as a child, attended desegregated demonstration schools in Philadelphia, where she was one of a few African American students. Another lunch group on the first floor was made up of younger African American women, closer to my age and more politically radical than the group with which I ate. I was not invited to join them. And I quickly learned from their coldness toward me—when I once tried—that a new teacher didn't just barge into groups of teachers who ate lunch together, especially when not invited.

I thought things were going pretty smoothly that year. The parents of my 70 children (35 in the morning, 35 in the afternoon, no assistant) seemed satisfied, and the first-grade teachers with whom I ate, and the principal, Marcus Foster, seemed to feel that my kindergarten children were making excellent academic progress in spite of my lack of formal training.[2]

Among the children I taught were twins—Maureen and Mack Peters. They were tall, slender children. Maureen had long, wavy hair, which her mother fixed in braids or pony tails. Adults often noticed her and commented on her beauty when they visited the classroom. I felt that I had an excellent relationship with Mrs. Peters. During the spring, I became concerned that there might be some difficulties at home because the children began coming to school in an unkempt condition. Particularly noticeable was that Maureen went for many days without seeming to have had her hair combed. In my innocence, and not thinking about the bound-aries of my work, because I wanted to express my concern and care, and because if the family needed help, I wanted them to get it, I decided to speak to someone on the staff who I thought might be able to help.

There were two women on the staff to whom I might have spoken. One was Mrs. Battle, the home and school coordinator.[3] She lived in the community and was hired by the principal because of her community connections. She was the official representative of the school, a liaison between home and school, and her job was different from that of a truant officer. The other woman was Miss Chambers, a former teacher at the school who was forced to retire because of poor health but who had been hired by the principal to work part time. She found winter coats for chil-dren, raised money for families in need, collected and distributed food at Thanksgiving, and helped families when there was a fire or a tragedy. Both women were African American. The distinction between the work of Mrs. Battle and Miss Chambers had never been made clear to me. As it turned out, I should have gone to Mrs. Battle, but I spoke to Miss Chambers. I told her how worried I was about Maureen and Mack and that I hoped there was nothing wrong at home.

The morning after I spoke to Miss Chambers, Connie, one of the young teachers from across the hall who was part of the other lunch group, who rarely spoke with me—and who seemed unhappy with my presence in the school—stormed into my room and began to yell at me in front of the children. "How *dare* you think you can teach our children! What makes you think you have a right to come in here to teach our children?" She was furious, and I was stunned. I began to cry, and the only response I could think of was, "You know, my family was poor when I was little, too."

At that time I had no idea what had brought on this expression of anger. Later, when I spoke to Mr. Foster to explore what I might do about this unhappy situation—and I thought that perhaps it might even mean my leaving the school—I learned that Mrs. Peters had received the fol-lowing note from Miss Chambers: "Dear Mrs. Peters, How dare you send your child to school with her hair uncombed." When she received this note, rather than speaking with me, Mrs. Peters showed it to Connie. Connie, justifiably angry about the tone of the note, blamed me and came to yell at me. I believe it was Connie who had shown the note to the principal.

A few days later, Mr. Foster invited Mrs. Peters and me to a meeting in his office. He asked me to explain what had concerned me and why I'd spoken to Miss Chambers about the matter. (I don't know if Miss Cham-bers was reprimanded for the tone of her note.) Mrs. Peters then explained why she'd been so upset with the note. She was not neglecting her children. She was pregnant and hadn't been feeling well and was not able to do everything she was used to doing.

Then she said, "I didn't know what Mrs. Strieb was talking about. You know, my Maureen has *nice* hair." I was puzzled. Mr. Foster must have seen the puzzled expression on my face, stopped her, and said, "I don't think Mrs. Strieb knows what you're talking about when you say 'nice hair.'" And I didn't.

Though Mrs. Peters did not directly inform me of her distress with the way I handled the situation, her confronting me (through Connie) raised my consciousness and I learned a great deal from the experience. What I learned the day we met with the principal—that to some African Americans, the longer and straighter a person's hair, the "better" or "nicer" it is—completely surprised me. I'd not been aware of such thinking.

I believed that because our family had been poor when I was a child, I had something in common with the children at Dunbar that enabled me to understand them and qualified me to work with them because they were also poor. But I was not African American, and that seemed to be more important. I suspect Connie thought I was ignoring what she must have seen as a racial slur or at least insensitivity. Like many White people, I'd had no idea that hair was a sensitive topic within the African American community.

Concerns with School Policies

Confusion about school district and local school policies often disturbed parents. Occasionally my own policies added to the confusion because they clashed with official ones. Sometimes parents didn't know about a school policy and I had to inform them. The stories in this section illustrate some of our interactions regarding policies.

Report cards and grades. Teachers in Philadelphia were required to give children in first to fifth grade report card grades of A, B, C, D, F, along with brief comments. Children who were progressing slowly in reading in first grade, according to book level and end-of-book tests, were to be given an F—even during the first report period. I hated giving grades and wanted to avoid giving them, but that was not allowed. Many first-grade teachers refused to give beginning readers a failing grade. This had nothing to do with "self-esteem"; we just thought that it was not sound procedure to fail a child who was beginning to learn to read. After many teachers' complaints, the school district allowed us to give no grade in the first report card of first grade.

In spite of my wish to not focus on grades, some parents raised questions about academic progress and their child's grades. This was only natural in a system where grades are given. A few parents were interested in more than grades.

3/94, Note (first grade)

Dear Mrs. Strieb,

After reflecting last night, I have changed my mind and decided to ask you to change Matthew's B in spelling to an A, which you offered to do. My reasons are as follows:

1. Matthew has had 100%s on all of his spelling tests.

2. As you stated, a B is not a bad grade. However, it doesn't reflect his achievement or his improvement this year. His mastery of spelling far exceeds expectations for a first grader. To hold him to other standards of spelling accuracy is unreasonable. He is improving constantly and consistently, and he has done so since the beginning of the year.

3. I am concerned that an out-of-proportion perfectionism will stifle some of his creativity. We have struggled for 3 or 4 years to get him to relax a bit and not worry so much that a drawing or story is not perfect the first time. Oftentimes, an adult is not immediately available for the frequent spelling checks he asks for, and he is not yet comfortable with a dictionary. We have encouraged him to go ahead and try, which he is now doing. Your classroom and teaching style have supported this, and his output has exploded this year, as his confidence has increased.

Please feel free to call me or make an appointment to discuss this. Thank you for your patience.

Norma Kelly

4/10/97, Note (first grade)

Dear Mrs. Streeb,

I am sorry I was not able to attend the conference on Jason's report card and progress in school, but I was unavoidably scheduled to be at a meeting out of town on April 8. I would appreciate it if you could schedule a time for us to meet to review his work.

I am always interested in identifying where his strengths and weaknesses are and how he can improve his grade. But I am now very concerned because his reading grade has deteriorated from a B, which was barely acceptable, to a C, which for me means he has a problem that deserves special attention. Emma recounted to me that you described his ability as improving, and your written report did make suggestions for reading, but did not stress the risk that he is getting worse, not better.

My telephone number during the day is _____ and after 8 PM is _____. If you can find time to see me to discuss this, again, I would appreciate it.

Rodney Stedman

12/14/99, Note (first grade)

1. What is Harriet's reading level? MATH?
2. How and at what rate is she progressing overall?
3. Does it appear that her spelling has improved?
4. How is she doing regarding her behavior with and toward peers, staff?
5. Listening to adult supervision and requests?
6. Attitude toward learning? [Mr. Sinicki]

All three notes are similar in that they come from parents who want their children to do well in school. All three parents want me to know they are informed and care about the well-being and the grades of their children. All three parents speak to me as if I were an understanding equal in this relationship in which their children are central.

There are differences, however. The notes about Matthew and Jason were written after report card conferences. Harriet's parents wrote in anticipation of their conference with me. Mrs. Kelly shows that she knows a great deal about standards and grading and the effect that holding too high standards might have on children. Grades are of great concern to her, even though Matthew is only in first grade. She believes that I had not recognized Matthew's achievements.

Jason's father is already worried, during the second report period of first grade, that his child will not achieve as he thinks he should. He is determined to do something about it. I knew that Jason was learning to read. I knew from years of experience that children learn to read at different rates and in different ways. I also knew that the tests I was required to give the children to determine their letter grades did not accurately show their abilities and that those tests (in which a child had to circle the correct missing word beneath blanks in sentences that were visually difficult to read) did not tell the whole story, even though the school district said (and probably those in charge believed) they actually did.

Harriet's parents let me know what they think is important in their daughter's education, not only academically but also socially. (And they, too, are concerned about spelling.) By writing questions before our report card conference, they let me know that they care not only about Harriet's academic progress but also about how she treats other children and whether or not she respects the adults who work with her.

As usual, I responded to these notes. I spoke with Mrs. Kelly, explaining to her that not only did I not like to change grades but also that parents rarely asked me to do so. I was not happy about what seemed to me an extreme concern with grades, but I finally agreed to change her son's from a B to an A for two reasons. It mattered much more to Mrs. Kelly than it did to me. Furthermore, I'd not warned parents and children that I based spelling grades not only on spelling test results but also on correctness when actually using those words when writing stories.

I immediately held an additional conference with Mr. Stedman. I assured him of Jason's progress in reading and also that we could count on his grade improving for the next report card. In Jason's final report card of first grade, I wrote:

> Jason has really progressed in reading. He has begun to read easy "chapter books" like *The Mouse Tales*. He tried *The Boxcar Children* and, though it was difficult, he liked the challenge. He benefited from reading some of the easier books for a while, which gave him practice. Now he is moving along more quickly. Please be sure he joins the summer reading club at the Free Library. It's fun and good practice. And I will send home some of the basal readers he enjoys. Reading them will give him practice with letter sounds and word families. Please return them in the fall.

Finally, at Harriet's report card conference, I held the list of her parents' questions in front of me as we spoke, responding to each question in turn and thanking them for raising them as a guide to the conference.

Curriculum. Another area of elementary school parental concern was curriculum. The following story about one parent, Linda, illustrates how she expressed her opinions about social studies over the course of 2 years and my reaction to them. She did this not only in letters to me but also in face-to-face contact.

Linda, a working mother who was also politically active, expressed three concerns to me and what she wanted with regard to them. She wanted to be sure that her children (and all children) were taught about African American history and culture; that they understood that many African American women are intelligent, strong, and independent; and that parents and individuals from the community surrounding the school be invited into the school as an advisory voice. Linda knew me because I'd taught her older daughter. She had chosen to have her second child,

Atiya, placed in my class.[4] I taught Atiya for 2 years, in first and second grade, and Linda and I had powerful exchanges about curriculum.

At the first parent's meeting of first grade, Linda asked, "What famous Americans do you teach about?" I told her about the many biographies in our class library, mentioned some names (Martin Luther King, Harriet Tubman, Frederick Douglass, Susan B. Anthony), and asked for suggestions of others. In addition to the books I read to the children, Linda contributed books. She knew I would welcome them because I always thanked parents publicly in my newsletter for anything they contributed.

Several times during that year we teachers took our classes to theater performances for children sponsored by a university in Philadelphia. For February's performance, a play about President Teddy Roosevelt, I explained in a note home what we'd be seeing and asked parents to sign the permission slip. I received the following note from Linda:

2/6/81, Note

Dear Lynne,

Atiya has my permission to go to the play, but I am distressed that the excursion planned during Black History Month is not about a Black American.

I've always believed that a major portion of my child's education around her heritage has to come from home. I see that I am correct. I would like to discuss this further with you.

Linda

I responded immediately:

2/6/81, Note

Dear Linda,

I'll be glad to discuss this with you. I also feel that this is true, [that education around heritage has to come from home] not only for Atiya, but for all kids.

I have already expressed my distress about this play (especially at this time) to the people at [the university theater]. I hope that they will think a little more about the plays they present to kids and will take some of the suggestions I've made to them.

Lynne

I'd had the same unease as Linda—that during Black History Month, a play about a White historical figure was not appropriate. I, too, was not too happy about taking first-grade children to see a play about Teddy

Roosevelt; I was very conscious of the all-White production and it upset me. I wrote a letter to the organizers of the event in which I lodged complaints about some minor issues (early starting time and ways in which they made it difficult to arrange the trip). I also complained about this particular choice of a play about a famous White man during Black History Month and about the fact that the plays we'd seen so far were all-White productions. I told them that, at least in Philadelphia (but actually everywhere), all-White productions were unacceptable. Yet, to me, the theater experience was the important thing—for the children to see live drama and to understand the difference between television, a movie, and a play and the behavior that would be expected of them in a theater. I jumped at the opportunity whenever possible.

Linda had written in her note to me, "I've always believed that a major portion of my child's education around her heritage has to come from home. I see that I am correct." Over the years, I grew to see that Linda was correct. At that time (the early 1980s) there was no national holiday in honor of an African American hero, and the history of African Americans the children were learning in the early grades, if at all, was limited to two or three people and to a period of 4 weeks. When schools celebrate only White male heroes, when the history children are taught deals only with the accomplishments of White people (mostly men, few of them poor), then a parent who complains about people being left out is correct. I knew something was wrong because in my journal, following Linda's note and mine, I wrote

2/6/81, Journal

> I feel really badly because I know I can never do enough. But in
> discussing difference as strength, I know I'm doing a lot. In our
> class we never hide the differences, I try to help the children to
> take pride in their backgrounds and celebrate them, and the
> children are not invisible.

At a parent meeting in November of Atiya's second year with me, Linda again spoke out about what she felt was the lack of teaching about Black history and culture in the entire school. She wanted the school to develop a set curriculum for teaching and wanted a parents' curriculum committee for our class. I offered to give such a committee a try in the classroom, and I suggested that Linda also make an effort to set up such a committee through the Home and School Association (though, to my knowledge, nothing ever came of this). I told the parents, however, that I sometimes wondered about kindergarten, first-, and second-grade children "studying" history. In particular, what aspects of history and the past are they able to understand? I told them I'd noticed over the years that many young children (first and second graders) have little sense of time, especially historical time. Even though I usually developed several time-lines with the children (personal, school year, and 100 years), they usu-ally placed Martin Luther King Jr. at the same time as slavery. Some of the White parents at the meeting felt that little if any history was taught in the elementary schools. Like me, these parents were part of the domi-nant culture of our country, and they couldn't see that White male his-tory was all around us and taught without much effort in the schools. I noted that children are fascinated by biographies and that using them is a good way to begin to teach history. I said that I would tell the children about my own participation in the struggle for civil rights during the 1960s. I would teach freedom songs to the children, but I would still be a White woman doing it.

Throughout second grade, Linda continued to send me books to read to the children. A favorite was *Aiesha's Crowning Glory*, a book about a child who wanted to have her hair braided in cornrows. In sending this book to be read in class, Linda was teaching all of us about several important as-pects of African American culture—attention to hair, mother–child relation-ships, and the help and support for children by adults in the community.

Linda was concerned about more than curriculum in schools. She was also concerned about how policymakers—in this case, the Philadelphia Federation of Teachers (the teachers' union)—could gain the support of parents. She was a strong member of a union at work. She spoke in public about our school and how the teachers there had the support of the par-ents, including her, even throughout the terrible 2-month strike during the fall of 1981. She knew that that support had been influenced by some of the communications from the union, which contained information (fact sheets) about each school showing how cuts in funding would affect the children. She talked about ways in which individual teachers made par-ents feel either welcome or unwelcome as well as about how important it was for schools to make parents feel welcome.

I grew comfortable with Linda and able to laugh with her when dis-cussing cultural issues and differences.

3/12/82, Journal

On the bus home from [a class trip] . . . all the girls were playing clapping games. I love the sound of the claps and the rhythms of the chants. It reminds me of tap dancing. Maria and Anita (two African American girls) tried to teach Jane and Belinda (two White girls), and it was very hard for them to learn. Linda tried to teach me a game, and although I was able to learn the clap and rhyme, Linda said, "Your hands are so stiff and tight. Relax." I laughed and said, "Linda, that's what they mean when they say 'culturally deprived.' It's a lifetime of deprivation for me. I just don't have it in me to loosen up. If I had learned in kindergarten from good peer teachers, then I might be able to loosen up. But it probably won't happen at forty-two. I'll just be glad if I can keep up the pace."

Linda, always thinking about curriculum, suggested that we do an assembly in which the children demonstrate clapping games and jump rope or circle games as a way of us showing that the school values their culture. I realized that I should be putting those rhymes into homework books for reading homework. And I want to be sure that Jill, Jane, Belinda, and Susie [White children] are taught these clapping games this year. It's important for the Black girls to teach them some of their culture. Why else would White parents want their kids in integrated classrooms?

Though sometimes Linda's contributions led me to feel that I wasn't doing enough, I could usually convince myself that one person can't possibly do everything or know everything—and how lucky the children were to have more than just me to think about these things, how rich her contributions made our lives together. Linda's concerns about the ways in which her own child was and would be taught about Black history and culture in 1980–1982 had an impact on my many years of teaching that followed. When we went to performances, I always checked to see if African Americans and themes from various cultures were included. I made certain that children went to appropriate plays during Black History Month. I made sure when I taught social studies that I continued to include information about more than White males. Though in my later years of teaching I wanted to give an honest picture of the struggles of the 1960s and 1970s, which of course included some aspects of the harsh treatment of civil rights activists in their struggles, I tended to concentrate more on accomplishments and important personages who were still alive and on ideas that engendered hope. The children would see the more violent events in documentaries on television. Unfortunately, they continued to be fascinated by the violence and to remember more about the violence than about the accomplishments.

In the spring of 1982, when we took a class trip to the Wagner Free Institute of Science, Linda accompanied us. During the lesson, she added to what the teacher was saying. The teacher graciously included Linda's comments. Later, when we were about to visit the vast upstairs 19th-century museum with its collection of insects and bones, I prepared the children for acceptable behavior. Linda added, "You have to be careful because the objects in the museum are no longer available; they can't be replaced." Linda not only wanted parents to be welcomed into the schools and informed by the teachers, she also believed it was important for both White and Black children to recognize Black parents as knowledgeable, as teachers, and as equal contributors to the school experience. Whenever possible, I invited parents to teach the children in my class about their own cultures. Parents, White and Black, often commented favorably about the ways in which I taught social studies. In large measure, I owe that teaching to Linda.

School boundaries. If children were discovered to live outside the boundaries of the neighborhood school, they could be transferred to a school closer to home. An investigation was more likely to occur if a child had excessive absences, was considered to be a "behavior problem," might lower overall test scores, or might add to an increase in the number of children retained.

Corey's mother, Ms. Wallis, may have been older, but she looked to be in her early 20s, which meant that she had had Corey's older sister when she was quite young. She arrived for the report card conference angry, seemingly ready for an argument. I said, "Do you remember the note you sent me?" I'd saved it and showed it to her. It said, "Please don't talk to Corey about his absences. He has parents. . . ." I said, "Please don't send me notes like that. I like Corey and I'm on his side. I *have* to tell him he must come to school. If I don't have a note from you that explains why he's absent, I have to mark him truant—that means he's illegally absent. That's not *my* rule. That's a state law, and the principal really checks these things." I told her that on occasional mornings I met Corey and his sister going to school on the trolley, which meant I knew they were coming from outside the school boundaries. I told her that I was happy to be teaching Corey and it didn't matter to me if he was coming from another part of the city. "But if these absences keep happening," I said, "someone is going to try to find out why, and they'll find out where you live. I won't tell them, but they'll find out. So when I ask you to send notes, please do it." I told her how Corey was working hard at learning to read, reading any time he could, and how thoughtful he was about math. After I said that, it was as if she and I had a secret together, and her anger disappeared. I was able to continue the report card conference.

My feeling was that if a parent felt strongly enough about her child's education to choose a school outside their neighborhood, I was not going to do anything to exclude that child even if rules were broken. But I felt that I had to warn Ms. Wallis that the many absences were going to alert the principal that something was amiss.

Well-Being and Happiness of Their Children

Children's worries. Many parents sent a range of notes to me alerting me to their child's worry and anxiety about school matters. Dan was concerned because he brought the wrong book home. Ned's mother asked (10/21/96) that "as Halloween approaches, would you please excuse Ned from any 'scary story' time? He becomes *quite* scared." Frances's mother reported that when her child chose a book to read at home, she'd made a mistake and chose one that was too difficult. Molly was worried about forgetting her words in a class play and her mother asked if I could suggest anything to calm her. Mattie didn't have time to do her homework and was worried that I'd be angry. Carly couldn't find her reading record card. Susan's mother was concerned about her child's nervousness.

10/20/99, Note

Dear Ms. Strieb:

   I am writing this letter because I am extremely concerned about Susan. She has begun to bite the skin on her fingers *off*. She did this before so I know it is because she is anxious and nervous in the classroom. She has explained to me that the class knows some multiplication tables and she does not. Susan feels embarrassed about her lack of knowledge in this area. She also feels unable to grasp some lessons quickly when called on and subsequently she becomes overly anxious, nervous and then begins to bite her fingers. I am asking for your *HELP*! Please communicate to me what areas I could help Susan with at home and try to help her overcome her anxiousness in the classroom. She wasn't clear, but it seems other children laugh at her or don't give her a chance to think about what is being asked of her.

   Susan is a bright child and very enthusiastic about school and learning. Please help me help her remain this way. Together, I am sure we can help her overcome this anxiety that results in her biting the skin off her fingers. Take a look at her hands, you'll see.

   I would appreciate a response, by letter, over the phone, any way you choose. I am extremely upset but I trust that you can help me help Susan.

   Sincerely, Rachel

Notes from (as well as face-to-face communications with) parents about their children's worries alerted me to things I would never have known but that had an effect on their children's learning.

My yelling: Reactions and help from parents. No, I wasn't a perfect teacher, if there can possibly be one. I was not a calm and quiet teacher, and I envied those who were able to communicate displeasure to the children with the lift of an eyebrow or a quiet reprimand. Unfortunately, I have a loud voice and throughout my teaching life I often yelled, especially if a child repeatedly did things that disturbed the other children or me. I am not making excuses when I say that I recognized that there were conditions that kept me and the children from remaining calm. Working in an open-space classroom didn't help because there was always noise from the other three rooms (there were four rooms in a row, and only the rooms at either end had more than one wall.[5] Thirty-four children were too many, and moving them as a group—through the halls, to the lavatory (some years it was required by the principal that the teacher take the entire class to the lavatory)—made them restless. There were other times, too: when I was anxious about the children's progress and discovered that they hadn't learned what I thought they knew; when I had to do things I didn't think were good for children (such as giving standardized and math levels tests that didn't test what they purported to or covered material that was inappropriate for the children's age); when children behaved in ways that were unkind to one another or made things unsafe for themselves and others; when I was trying to teach a whole-class lesson to all 34 children and some of them were talking at the same time; when the noise from neighboring classes became loud; when an enormous number of interruptions occurred (messengers, other teachers, or announcements from the office on the loudspeaker); when the administrators made unannounced changes in our schedule. Facing even one of those conditions, I was likely to yell, and often two or more of these conditions were present at the same time.

My yelling was something I hated about myself. It was when I knew that particularly quiet, well-behaved children thought I was yelling at them that I felt especially bad. Yet no matter how hard I tried, I was unable to stop for very long. I tried a variety of methods: inviting children themselves to signal me, asking student teachers to write observations that included the circumstances during which I yelled, promising the children that I would stop, counting to 5 before bursting out (that never worked), keeping a tally with a slash on the board each time I yelled. I would ask the children and colleagues in the adjoining room to help me. One of my kind colleagues, who was at the other end of the open space, once told me that the words I used when I yelled were helpful to her in dealing with children. I couldn't take that as a compliment. I knew that there was simply no excuse for yelling.

There was the time in 1989 when I was yelling at a child who was flitting around the room, telling her to choose an activity and stick to it. I looked up and saw the principal standing at the doorway with a visitor (another principal). The principal later told me she'd just finished describing to her guest the wonderful teacher whose interesting class they were about to enter when my loud voice shocked both of them.

Often I got feedback from parents who didn't like my yelling, but their children saw it a different way. There was a parent who worked in the classroom weekly. When I yelled when she was there, she said nothing to me but left the room until she thought I'd calmed down. Occasionally parents treated my yelling humorously because, though their children noticed and even remarked on the yelling, they didn't seem especially disturbed by it. At a parent's meeting in November 1981, Ben's mom told a wonderful (if embarrassing) story: "Every night Ben sings the songs you put into his homework book on Monday nights. Last night he said, 'C'mere everybody. Listen to this.' He started to sing: 'Did you feed my cow? <u>Leonard, sit down.</u> Yes, ma'am. Did you know just how? <u>Leonard, be quiet.</u> Yes, ma'am.' And he went through the whole song doing a perfect imitation of you leading the singing and yelling at Leonard because of his many interruptions." I appreciated Ms. Corbett's kind way of telling me that I yell too much, and I was relieved that her child wasn't overly upset by my yelling. But hearing that story in front of other parents was a kind of warning.

Janice, a parent who was helping in my classroom, commented to me about my yelling and about how much it disturbed her. The next day, she told me that she was going to transfer her son Conrad to another class because of the yelling. I spoke honestly. I acknowledged that I knew it was a problem, and I told her I'd often thought about what caused me to yell and described those times. I told her that in spite of my yelling, there were other things in the class that might make her keeping Conrad with me worthwhile. Of course I apologized and told her I'd try to stop. I solicited her help—asking that on days when she was helping in the room she give me a signal that would make me conscious of what I was doing. I have no further notes about Janice and her concerns about my yelling for that year, and Conrad remained with me for 2 years.

Throughout my teaching life, this inability to moderate my voice when I was angry made me feel terribly guilty and made me believe that I would never be a really good teacher. As a parent, I'd wanted my children to have decent, kind, and firm teachers and to be happy with and love school. I tried to be honest with the students, to let them know that when I made a mistake and yelled it wasn't their fault. For the most part, children in my class loved school. I knew that there were other reasons for parents wanting their child in my class and for wanting me to be their child's teacher. My yelling was a problem I never fully resolved, but I was grateful to parents who recognized my honesty just as their children did, who realized I was serious in my desire for their help, and who had the courage to help me with goodwill and, occasionally, with humor.

In the fall of 1998, the semester after a child sent me the following end-of-year note, I was finally given a classroom enclosed by four walls. Though I was never able to completely stop, the number of times I yelled during the course of a day was considerably reduced.

6/15/98, Note

Dear Mrs. Streib,
   thank you for being my teacher for two years.
   You have taught me alot.
   I have learned a lot from you.
   Can you teach me again?
   You make me happy except for the yelling.
   I will always remember you.
   Love, Shira

A Complex Example

The story of Mrs. Collier and Tonya[6] illustrates all the concerns discussed in this chapter: absences, curriculum, grades, and the safety and well-being of a child. Added to those concerns were those of promotion, attending report card conferences, and making up missed work. I've chosen this story because Tonya's mother expressed her concern and disagreement with my judgment regarding Tonya and school district policy. This is a story of anger and misunderstandings and, possibly, not enough information. It is a common story about a teacher who has certain expectations for parents and becomes impatient because a parent can't seem to keep up with the teacher's expectations or the requirements of the school district; it is about a teacher who wants to teach all the children but believes a child's mother is undermining her work, a mother who may have felt threatened by the school and school policies. Just as with yelling, I'm not proud of this story, but I'm including it because, first, I think it illustrates a difficult instance where policy almost doesn't matter, and, second, perhaps readers can learn from this experience. I wonder—how could I have handled this situation differently?

I have always believed and still believe that it is the work of teachers to teach children during school hours and not to depend on their parents and others in their homes to help them (though it might have made my work easier); that is, regardless of a child's home situation, I am responsible for the child's academic learning. Even if children have no academic support at home, it is my job to teach them without judging their parents or them. In spite of this strong belief, problems sometimes arise. First, it's easy to set aside these beliefs—much easier than I prefer to think it is. Second, sometimes parents don't get their children to school and as a result a teacher can't fulfill her responsibility. What happens when a child is kept home and is falling behind as a result?

As I understood it, the school district's promotion policy had two criteria for elementary students. Adequate progress in reading and math was the first. Progress in reading was based on book tests. For math, it was based on criterion-referenced tests developed by the school district. Second, regardless of progress, if a child missed a large number of the 180 days of school, the teacher was required to retain that child. In practice, if a child missed many days but was making adequate progress in reading and math, that child was usually promoted. I did not like to see the policy about absences rigidly enforced in elementary schools, since some children did well even when they missed a lot of school.

In June of second grade, I was thinking of recommending Tonya for retention for two reasons: excessive absences and doing poorly in math. She had missed 70 days of school in first grade, but because the class was going to continue with me the following year, the principal and I both felt she should remain with the children and teacher with whom she was familiar. In second grade, she missed 60 days. On the days she did come to school, she usually arrived late, having missed writing workshop and, often, math. Her mother always brought her directly to the classroom, rather than signing her in at the office (which was school policy).

In spite of Tonya's many absences, I knew that Mrs. Collier did not neglect her in any way. She was a devoted and conscientious parent who cared about her child's progress in school. She worked with her at home. I knew that Tonya suffered from stomach cramps, but that was not always the reason given for the absences. I had observed that Mrs. Collier sometimes had trouble allowing Tonya to do certain things independently. I also noticed that when Tonya was faced with something she had forgotten or didn't know how to do, she often froze. For example, once, when the class was ready for our meeting circle, Tonya stood still in front of a group of already seated children who had not left room for her assigned space. She seemed unable to ask them to move back to make room for her. I told Tonya that she would have to tell the children what she wanted them to do. It took her a long time to get the words out. Mrs. Collier had observed the incident and expressed anger with me for insisting that her daughter speak for herself.

Tonya was able to do the rote math expected of first and second graders. She had difficulty with certain concepts involving decreasing number (such as fewer than and less than, counting backwards, subtraction, naming numbers that come before), dividing objects and numbers into equal parts, understanding our money and measurement systems and using them in practical situations suitable for a second grader. She also had trouble with what I could only call "reasoning." Tonya was not alone in having these difficulties. Many parents, including Mrs. Collier, believed that if their children were able to do vertical addition and subtraction, they were doing well in math. Though I tried in my newsletter and homework and at report card conferences to make clear that more was required for children to be fully competent, parents usually ignored this as long as their children could mechanically add and subtract.

I attributed Tonya's difficulty in math in part to her having missed instruction because of absences and lateness in first and second grades. I often said to Mrs. Collier, "I can't teach Tonya if she's not in school." I realized that I could do nothing to force Mrs. Collier to send Tonya to school (after all, she was the mother and was in control). I did care. And so I did what I could to help her help her child to catch up and progress, in spite of the many absences. I was not the most organized teacher—keeping even everyday papers in order took tremendous effort. Usually, if children were absent for a day or two, even a week, I was able to help them make up the work missed through an extra lesson and extra practice in class, without having to send extra work home. But Tonya's many instances of absence and lateness made it difficult for me to catch her up during the school day. I tried to keep track by putting the work she missed in class into a folder and then sending it home. I went over lessons with her mother. But I found myself angry and confused about the extra work and time her mother seemed to expect from me in order to fulfill my obligation to teach Tonya when she wasn't there.

Throughout the year, I often alerted Mrs. Collier to the fact that many absences could trigger automatic retention. I was required to do that, to have her sign a paper saying I'd told her, and to tell her that if she did not want her child to be held back, she could send the principal a written protest that would be considered by the school's Promotion and Retention Committee (made up of the reading and math teachers, the counselor, and the principal, with each child's teacher advising). In late May, I finally warned Mrs. Collier about Tonya's possible retention and had her sign the paper acknowledging that I had done so.

There were still more school district policies that caused difficulties between Mrs. Collier and me. I was required to develop standards on which I based my report card grades, which I did according to school district guidelines. However, when a child had missed more days than she attended during a particular marking period and there was not enough work on which to base report card grades, I did not have to give report card grades for that period only. In the spring of second grade, I was unable to give Tonya a complete report card. Because of her many absences, there was not enough student work to base it on.

As part of reporting a child's progress, parents were expected to attend a brief, face-to-face conference. I loved these conferences because they gave me a chance to look at each child's work in the presence of the parents, to discuss the child's strengths as a learner, to go over ways parents might help their child at home, to hear what the parents felt about their child's learning. I adjusted my conference schedule to accommodate parents' work schedules and gave most parents at least 20 minutes rather than the allotted (and ridiculous) 10. Furthermore, my open-door policy for parents at other times was well known throughout the school, as were my many ways of letting parents know how to contact me. I was frustrated that Mrs. Collier missed appointments she'd made with me. I knew all the possible reasons: She was overwhelmed by caring for two children; she didn't trust me; she didn't want to have an argument face-to-face; perhaps she was fearful of school because of past personal experiences. But that knowledge didn't help me to have patience or keep me from getting annoyed. Mrs. Collier's failure to attend agreed-upon report card conference dates both disappointed me and upset me. I had the following exchange with Mrs. Collier soon after I'd warned her about Tonya's possible retention.

6/2/82, Journal

This morning Mrs. Collier came in *furious*! She said, "You never gave me Tonya's spring report card."

I replied, "I *told* you that I could not write a report card for Tonya since she's missed so much school this report period."

"You never gave me her report card conference either."

"Just a minute. I made *several* appointments with you, but you never showed up. You know when my planning time is. You know that I'll meet with parents whenever they request a meeting with me. Why haven't you asked for another appointment? I'll be glad to meet with you. If you can't stay today, come tomorrow."

"Okay, I'll be here tomorrow."

Once again I made an appointment with her, and once again she did not keep the appointment. I attended a meeting of the school's Promotion and Retention Committee. Mrs. Collier had written an angry letter to the principal stating her belief that the decision to hold Tonya in second grade had already been made. Still, she suggested that Tonya be promoted this year, and she promised that if Tonya didn't do well by the end of third grade, she would agree to her being held back. The principal, after looking over Tonya's records, said that regardless of what her mother wished, the number of absences required retention. The reading teacher and I suggested that we do as Tonya's mother requested: Promote her and wait to see what happened at the end of third grade. He agreed and told me to speak to Tonya's teacher in the fall, letting her know about this agreement.

I called Mrs. Collier to tell her three things: that Tonya would be promoted to third grade as she had requested, that I would still like to have the spring report card conference we'd never had, and that there was a summer program I thought Tonya would enjoy.

The conference, which finally occurred 15 days before the end of school, was cordial. I was able to let Mrs. Collier know about Tonya's progress in learning to read, her growing ability to talk with and initiate activities with other children, and her unusual ability in drawing. I also told her about all the things Tonya had missed and needed to learn. I showed Mrs. Collier many ways in which she could help Tonya in math, especially examples of problems Tonya should have been able to solve. I explained that computation was only part of what Tonya was expected to know. It was not unusual for me to describe to parents in detail ways in which they could help their children academically if they wanted to do so. I realized that Mrs. Collier recognized that Tonya was lagging in school when she asked me if there was a tutoring program that might help Tonya catch up. I also suggested children in the class with whom Tonya might enjoy getting together during the summer. Finally, I apologized for my anger and sometimes harsh words to Mrs. Collier.

6/82, Journal

I said, "I didn't want our two years together to end badly. I really only want Tonya to do as well as I know she can. I *did* make report card conference appointments with you but you never came." I couldn't possibly apologize for trying to get her to send Tonya to school. That school district policy was out of my hands. Mrs. Collier apologized for her anger about that.

Though I never asked Mrs. Collier why she was finally able to keep this appointment, I believed that once the decision was made to promote Tonya, Mrs. Collier could let down her guard. Perhaps she felt she could now trust me; perhaps she was happy that now we would not have an argument when we met. From my perspective, I was relieved that we had worked out an amicable agreement. There's an old expression, "Never go to bed angry at someone you care about." That had relevance in my teaching. Though it didn't happen often, I didn't like to allow parents' bad feelings to go unaddressed. I believed that unless I addressed parents' concerns we would not be able to establish trust with one another. I was unsettled until we reached some common ground on disagreements. I saw this as one of the strengths of my teaching.

Throughout this incident I felt that I had to defend my actions, though it was school district policy that had put me into that situation. I felt embarrassed and defensive as I wrote this story, mostly because of my anger. I was not certain that promoting Tonya when she hadn't learned that math was the right thing to do. On the other hand, I knew that holding a child in grade might not help either. One could say "the parent won." But I didn't see it as a battle.

COMPARING DOCUMENTS

During the 1960s and early 1970s, both local and national groups like the Keyser School Community Mothers' Group struggled to have their own knowledge recognized and included in schools. Our political involvement in schools (and that of parents around the country) during the late 1960s may have encouraged shifts in policy that made schools more welcoming to parents. Unlike the Keyser Mothers' position paper, in which we were addressing matters that affected the entire school, most of the parents of my students expressed concern for their own individual children and only occasionally wrote about policy or what they believed would be good for all children. Mrs. Carson's letter to the superintendent of schools in February 1984 was an exception.[7] There is another letter from her to me, written at approximately the same time, in Chapter 5.

Mrs. C. Clayton
I am praying that this letter reach your desk and it is not ignore or push aside. I notice that since your administration the school board is going through a lot of good changes. I would like to bring another good change in your school board.

I am a mother with six children all of whom has attend and still attending the Phila's school. But, the last of my six children is in the second grade at John B. Kelly School. Her teacher, *Mrs. Lynn Strieb*, Room 214. My daughter process is unbelievable and I will speaking for quiet a few mothers who feel the same as I. For a small example. My daughter couldn't read, now she can read and sing to me the Harriet Tubman song. She can tell me more about the Art Museum, famous people, arts and craft, cooking, math, etc.! Her way of learning or rather her teaching is more ~~like~~ different but enjoyable. The children is so well manner and *organize* than anything you can imagine. You would have to see for yourself. But, you need to look into this teacher and her way of learning—if you like to see an improvement in the *elementary school system*. Sometime we close our eyes an a open door. She is an asset to the Phila. School System.

Concern mother

Hattie Carson

P.S. I thank God that my Charlene Carson had an opportunity to have such a teacher.

By 1970, when I began to teach full time, I had incorporated into my teaching many of the suggestions that we had made as parents in the 1960s. By that time, the school district policy had begun to change enough so that parent involvement was recognized and encouraged. I cannot speak for other schools or other classrooms, but the parents of children in my classes did not have to fight for changes in policy. I trusted that parents wanted what they thought was best for their children. They did not have to struggle with me to be heard or to become involved. I was (usually) not threatened by parents' comments and critique. If I felt threatened, I tried to communicate further about the matter. I welcomed parents' notes (and other communications) to me, I read them, and I knew it was important to respond to them.

It is certainly because of my political involvement during the 1960s, and teachers' reaction to that activity, that the parents of the children I taught for 30 years did not have to fight for my recognition or for their inclusion in my classroom. My association with the Keyser School Community Mothers—sharing our stories and wishes, interests, and concerns about our own children—made me more attentive to parents when my role changed and I became a teacher.

ɞ 3 ৶

Homework: The School at Home

EVERYONE—children, parents, and teachers—knows what homework is. It's schoolwork that is to be done at home by students. But is that all? Whenever it is given, homework is a site where parents and teachers regularly come together. Homework can be a bridge, a meeting ground, or a battleground. It is a major point of parent–teacher contact—an opportunity for communication. A great many of the notes that parents wrote to me, many of the questions they asked at meetings concerned homework, and tensions often arose about it.[1]

I lived in Philadelphia until I was 9. Even when there were 30 to 45 children in my classes, we didn't have homework. After school, I roller-skated or jumped rope or played hopscotch outside; when it got dark, I came inside to eat and then to read or listen to the radio. After we moved to the suburbs when I was 9, I played outside on the street after school in all weather until it got dark; then I came inside and read or watched television. Through sixth grade, with the exception of a memorable project about American history, we rarely had homework—or at least homework that was a burden to me. I read and read and read.

WHY I GAVE HOMEWORK

The work teachers give children to do at home may be the result of district and school policies, teacher beliefs, and/or parent and student expectations and influences.

School District Requirements

During my 31 years of teaching first and second grade in Philadelphia, I experienced a change in school district policy with regard to the emphasis on homework for elementary school students. When I taught kindergarten for a year in 1962–1963, teachers were not required either to give homework or to teach reading formally to kindergarten children. Parents certainly didn't expect their 5-year-olds to have home assignments. When my own children went to elementary school during the late 1960s and early 1970s, I think they did have homework starting in first grade, but it didn't take a lot of time for them to complete it, and we never helped them with it, perhaps with the exception of memorizing spelling words.

When I began teaching full time in 1970, I noticed that many parents wanted homework for their first-grade children, but the principal didn't require it; rather, it seemed to be a tradition or custom. Something changed during the next 10 years. By the mid-1980s, school district policy required elementary school teachers to assign homework related to class work Monday through Thursday nights, to place it in homework books, and to check it daily—a policy that continues to the present day. Many principals examined teachers' lesson plans and occasionally the children's homework books to be sure this policy was carried out. In 1997, late in my teaching career, we teachers received the following directive from the principal:

9/97, Note to teachers from principal

You are requested to share the following with your parents tonight [Back to School Night] . . . Homework
    Effective October 13, homework for all students will include 15–30 minutes of mathematics drill nightly. Teachers will be provided with materials to assist in this effort to improve computation skills in addition, subtraction, multiplication and division

My Expectations Changed

During my early years of teaching, I not only disliked giving and checking homework, but, because it wasn't required that I do so, I didn't make an effort to comply with parents' expectations. Sometimes I did and sometimes I didn't give it, and homework was a minor matter to me. I believed that children should do all the work they needed to do during the school day. Some parents raised questions about this, but there were few complaints. I realized that because of my casual attitude toward homework, along with the fact that my classroom didn't look like the traditional classrooms in the school, parents might be questioning whether or not I was teaching with enough rigor and whether their children were learning. Even children expected homework, and I began to wonder if they and their parents thought I cared as much about their learning and if they thought I had expectations of the children as high as those of the other teachers in the school, for whom giving homework was both natural and essential. It was evident that teaching, learning, and homework were closely aligned in the culture of Philadelphia schools. Even today, in spite of a current movement among progressive educators to require less or to stop assigning it altogether, homework, like teachers standing at the front of the room to teach, seems to be embedded in most Americans' visions of the way public schools should be.

I understood the urgency many of the parents felt. I understood that they couldn't wait for the results from standardized testing or until June or even until the next report card period to find out if their children had learned what they thought was enough. They seemed to feel that homework was a way to check on the teacher and their children's learning.

I gradually became more serious about my assignments and made my peace with the homework policy, especially because it seemed so important to parents. I learned the kinds of homework that were acceptable to most parents, which often varied from year to year. I knew that the best homework should be individualized, but with at least 30 children in the class (sometimes more), I usually couldn't do that. I came to use homework for a variety of purposes: for children to follow up at home on certain things I'd taught during the day with practice and repetition; to help the children become stronger readers through practice at home; to inform parents of the academic work we were doing in class; and to encourage conversation between children and parents by providing topics to talk about at home (trips, science activities, books, things that went on in the classroom).

INFORMING PARENTS

With these purposes in mind, I then had to develop homework that made sense to me and that seemed appropriate for the children's ages and interests. When I taught first grade, I tried to give homework that could be completed in 10 to 15 minutes; for second graders, 20 minutes for each of the four nights. The following entries show how I communicated to parents my way of giving homework. We discussed homework at meetings at the beginning of the school year; I wrote to them about it in notes that our principals required us to write at the beginning of the year and in my newsletter to parents.

9/13/99, Note (second grade)

Dear Parents,
        A note about homework
        Homework in 210 will be mostly practice—practice of things I've taught, practice of things the children have learned, review of things we've gone over during the school day.

Children will receive homework four nights a week, Monday through Thursday. I expect all the homework to be done each night, though of course I know there are times when that is not possible. I will keep a record of whether or not homework is completed and it will affect grades.

The children have two homework books—one specifically for reading and one book for all the other homework.

Directions for homework will be in the regular homework book.

There will usually be math and reading homework each night.

Children will be able to do most of the homework by themselves, but will probably need help with reading math "word problems." It is important for you to check the homework every night, even if your child does the homework at the after school program. PLEASE SIGN THE HOMEWORK EVERY NIGHT

It will also help your child if you talk with her or him about the homework. Any conversations you have about the work will help your child in school.

In addition to written homework, children are expected to read for at least 15 minutes each night, including Friday, Saturday and Sunday. I am happy to lend books from the classroom library. We will also take books from the school library and the Free Library.

[In the first-grade letter I also wrote:] If the homework isn't hard enough, children can copy writing on cereal boxes, cans, in newspapers, books and magazines. They can make books—drawing the pictures. They can memorize the poems and songs in their reading homework book. And, most important, YOU can read to your children. That's the BEST homework.]

If you or your child don't understand the homework, please send me a note in the book.

REMEMBER: YOU PRACTICE READING BY READING. IF YOU WANT TO BECOME A GREAT READER, YOU HAVE TO READ.

Although I am firm about homework, I am also quite understanding if a child misses a night once in a while or has trouble doing all of it. I only notice when there is a pattern of a child not doing the homework or doing only part of the homework. Just write me a note and assure your child that it's okay to miss every once in a while.

Warmly, Lynne Strieb

SOME EXAMPLES

I began to realize that most children don't have time in their lives for reading at home, whether because of after-school schedules filled with daycare or lessons or television watching—and now computer games. I knew that many of my students didn't belong to libraries or have a variety of books at home. I also knew that the only way for a child to become a fluent reader is by reading and the only way for a child to become a voracious reader is to be given books that "grab." Though children had ample time for reading in my classroom, with its library of thousands of books, I wanted to help them both to get practice at home and to develop a habit of reading at home. I encouraged them to borrow books from my large class library every day. On Mondays, I also placed various kinds of reading homework such as songs and poems in a special homework book. I asked the children to read these with their parents and to try to memorize the poems and sing the songs at home. We practiced them in class during the week, and I based brief whole-class lessons on them. I believed these materials would give first and second graders some of the practice they needed to become fluent readers.

I also placed typed transcriptions of discussions that we had in class into their reading homework book. I liked these transcribed discussions because they provided all the children with a common experience, regardless of ability. In addition, the vocabulary came from the children's own speech and offered the kinds of repetition many of them needed. Finally, they were interested in reading the words they had spoken. As with other reading assignments, we read these discussions together during the week as a play, each child proudly reading his or her own words. The following note to parents appeared at the top of a reading assignment, based on a class discussion, from the beginning of first grade:

9/13/94, Homework (first grade)

Note to parents:
   Ms. Strieb read *When Will I Read*, by Miriam Cohen, to the children. We talked about learning to read. Children should try to read this by themselves, but if they need help, that's fine. Ask your child to find her or his own name without your help, and to read what they said. Then they should read about what other children like to do. They can read along with you. It will help if your child points to the words as you say them.
   I told them that some children learn to read when they are only three years old. Some children don't learn to read until they

are ten. But most people learn to read. Some children in our class
already know how to read, while other children are beginning to
learn. We never say, "I can't read." We say, "I'm learning to read."
I asked the children if they can read anything at home: signs,
labels, cereal boxes, other boxes, books. Here is [an excerpt of]
what they said:

MATTHEW T.: I can read "Corn Pops".
LONNIE: I can read "stop".
CAROL: I can read books. My favorite is *The Lion, Witch and the
Wardrobe*. My father is reading it to me.
SHARON: I can read my mom's name.
TODD: I can read the word "yes".

When the same children were in second grade, I gave them a book
report as a homework assignment. School district policy required students
to do 10 book reports during the course of the year. Beyond book reports,
I rarely asked children to do projects at home because they so often became parents' work. I had a discussion with the children about why adults
require children to write book reports. I said, "It's important to understand
and remember the books you read. What ways can you think of to remember the books you're reading? How can you let me know that you
understand what you're reading?" I took notes as the children stated their
suggestions and sent these suggestions home for reading homework.

11/1/95, Homework

SOME SUGGESTIONS FOR REMEMBERING THE BOOKS WE READ
These were wonderful suggestions and I'm going to put them
on a poster. I do want the children to have a purpose for recording
what they read, and not merely to please me. . . . I'd appreciate
your suggestions, too—something the kids can do fairly quickly and
often, not a home project like book reports.

HUSSEIN: You could write some of the story and the characters.
HALLEY: After you read the book, write the story and draw a
picture. (LYS: The whole story?) No, just some of the story
BARBARA: Fold a paper into three sets. Write the beginning, middle,
and end and then draw the pictures, like we did when Ms.
Strieb was absent.
JORDAN: Write the title and author and some things the books said,
not the whole thing.

LING: Use a paper and try to remember the book. Write the title.
     Write the story in your own words.
MATTHEW T.: We could take another homework book and use it for our
     reading record and we could write at least two pages each day.

DO THIS TONIGHT: Pick the three suggestions you like best for
helping you remember what you read in a book. If you have a
different idea you may write that. Write below on this paper.

Work that involved talking with adults at home was very popular with
both children and parents. Sometimes the assignment was as simple as
telling someone at home what they did in school that day or teaching the
family a math game they played in school such as Guess My Number.
Sometimes there was a common topic that was tied to a book we were
reading or to another activity or experience in school. I'd give an assignment that involved my asking a question and the children writing one to
three sentences about it. Some particularly popular topics over the years
were: When I Was a Little Baby; Once My Parents Were Worried About
Me; A Story About When My Mother/Father/Grandparent/Guardian Was
Little. The sighting of a mouse in our classroom led to both the reading of
Arnold Lobel's *Mouse Soup and Mouse Tales* and to our own homework assignment about experiences we'd had with mice at home. All of these
homework assignments led to the creation of class books, with each child's
story on its own page, accompanied by a drawing. These books then became part of the class library.
     A topic that held great interest was the children's names. Occasionally
I had a class in which children were teased about their names, and sometimes I learned that there was a child who disliked a first name. I gave classes
the assignment of learning about how they got their names. Because everyone has a name and because there's a story behind everyone's name, children and parents enjoyed this homework. Parents talked enthusiastically
with their children about this topic and told them how they chose the
child's name. One year, each child, the classroom assistant, the social studies teacher, even the principal, and I participated. When the children read
their stories to the class, there was the kind of silence in the room that lets
a teacher know that something important is happening. That homework
assignment led to a class book, which included the following introduction:

About the Names of 214, May 1985

How did you get your name?
Where did your name come from?

Do you like your name?
Do some names sound strange to you?

If you ever hear names that sound strange or unusual, don't laugh at them or tease their owners. They didn't choose their own names. Their parents chose their names and they couldn't help it.

Some parents named their children after people who are alive. Some parents named their children after people who are dead. Some parents chose a name that sounded nice to them. Some parents chose a name that means something nice in another language.

When your parents chose your name, they thought you would like it too.

If you think a name is unusual, you *could* say, "What an unusual name. How did you get it? Where did it come from?"

And that is exactly what we did in Room 214.

Every participant had a page in the book where they wrote their name in fancy letters. I typed the stories about how children got their names, stories that came from discussions with their parents. This book, too, was placed in the class library, was well loved, and became worn from use.

Practice was an important component of homework. I could never understand the amount of time many teachers spent during the school day on handwriting practice. I did do some lessons, but at the beginning of first grade I gave the children the simple assignment of practicing hand-writing on sheets I made up for homework; they included copying lines, then circles, then letters.

Mathematics homework took three forms. There was often practice, or "drill," on things I'd taught in class. This work was often but not always in torn-out pages from (required) math workbooks. Sometimes I asked children to make up number stories or to make up equations for the date. I also gave "word problems" for the children to solve and then to explain how they figured out the answers to those problems. Some assignments had children counting or measuring large and small objects at home. I always encouraged them to discuss mathematical topics with their parents.

PARENTS' RESPONSES

In general, parents understood and enjoyed the kinds of work their children were asked to do at home. Even when the assignment was unusual, I often received supportive comments. Occasionally a child would tell me that her parent enjoyed the poems and stories in the homework book. A parent wrote in a note:

6/26/96, Note from parent

Your enthusiasm for the literary arts & your capacity to communicate it in the classroom are compelling. We also appreciated the organized way homework assignments and projects were presented.

Whose Work Is It?

In spite of general support, all the emphasis in Philadelphia on homework, and the fact that parents felt quite strongly about it, created tensions for parents, children, and me. The tensions involved who should be doing the homework and how much help parents should give; the anxiety it caused children; my expectations for careful work; content; and the amount of time it involved for children, parents, and teacher. One thing was certain: I could not please everyone, including myself.

I wanted children to be able to do the homework assignments on their own, but my notes to parents and entries in the newsletter told another story. In written directions, I told parents that they would probably have to read homework directions to the children and sometimes would have to write the children's words, that the best way to help their children would be to work with them on homework each night, that they should check work completed if children did it without help or at after-school programs, and that they should sign homework every night. I urged them to talk with their children about the homework, which I said would help their children in school.

10/6/98, Newsletter

MOST IMPORTANT—Even if you are unable to volunteer in the classroom, the greatest way to help your child is to work with him/her on homework each night.

1. If children do homework by themselves, it is important that an adult checks it. Please sign the homework each night.

2. A big part of learning is following directions. Even if you read the directions to your children because they are not yet able to read them, getting children to explain what they are supposed to do in their own words is an important learning experience that will help them in the future. The only way to do that is by practicing

every night. Read the directions, then say "What are you supposed to do? Tell me in your own words."

3. I give reading homework every night. If I have not listed it in the regular homework book, please be sure your child reads at least one of the poems, songs, chants or discussions in the reading homework book. If your child is just learning to read, pointing to the words is very important.

4. If your child already knows how to read, she/he should read every night, and the flashcards could be used for spelling.

5. If your child is just learning to read, please go over some of the flashcards every night. Make sentences using the flashcards.

6. Remember—the more you read, the better you get at it. And children whose parents read to them every day do better at school than children who have no one to read to them.

YOUR CHILD NEEDS YOU TO TALK ABOUT THE HOME-WORK AND TO SUPERVISE IT, EVEN IF HE/SHE GOES TO AN AFTER-SCHOOL PROGRAM WHERE THEY DO IT. THAT TIME TOGETHER WILL HELP IN THE FUTURE.

This need for adult help or supervision made homework a problem for children whose parents felt that the work should be done without such help, and it created a dilemma for children whose parents were unable to read English.[2] Whenever teachers give homework that involves reading, they assume that either the children or someone in the home can read English. That is a major assumption and is sometimes unjustified. I always said to children and parents that if they didn't understand the work, they should let me know. In addition, I expressed my willingness to help children in school if they couldn't do the work at home. Over the years, only two parents told me they couldn't read English, though there may have been others who didn't tell me.

With the exception of book reports, I rarely assigned major projects to be done at home—no dioramas, no science projects, no posters, no research projects. I wanted children to do such projects in school because I had observed that when other teachers gave such assignments, the strong hands of parents were evident. My second-grade children worked in small groups to learn about various topics, often animals or insects. After doing research in books from the class library, they taught the class what they had learned.[3] A volunteer videotaped the children teaching the class, and I sent the videos home for parents to see what the children had done in school. Parents appreciated being informed in this way of the serious manner in which their children treated their research and reporting responsibilities.

Often the children didn't listen when I explained homework assign-ments, though parents generally expected their children to be able to tell them what they were supposed to do.

10/13/92, Journal

Miranda told me that her mother said she would be angry if Miranda doesn't understand how to do her homework. I told her I agree with her mother and that's why I'm explaining the home-work to the class now. I said, "I can see that some people aren't listening. When your parents are angry because you can't explain how to do your homework, don't blame me. I've been telling you what to do and you're not asking any questions. When I asked you to raise your hand if you understand, everyone raised their hand. That means you know what you're doing." Miranda certainly understood. I'm not sure about Diane, who was playing with things in her desk, reading or talking with Mariel. . . . I told them . . . "I'm doing my job. If you weren't listening, you weren't doing your job." It was not a pleasant conversation. . . . It's difficult.

Parents sometimes let me know when directions were not clear. Questions about whether or not they should correct developmental (to them, incorrect) spelling arose every year.

The following note represents many sent when a parent didn't under-stand my directions and felt responsible for their child's not doing the as-signment the way I wanted it done. I'd wanted the children to bring a newspaper or magazine article that they either read or had had someone read to them. Then they would be able to explain what the article was about.

3/16/00, Note

Dear Ms. Strieb
     Susan and I both misunderstood your directions for yesterday's homework. I thought she had to bring an article "OR" a picture that she could talk about. That's why I didn't practice reading the words with her. She was prepared to talk about the "picture".
Please give her another chance with this page.
     Thank You. Rachel

Expectations for Careful Work

I didn't like to be harsh about homework that wasn't done in the ways I expected, but as the years went on, I became more caught up in the formalities around it. I wanted the children to take care doing their work, to not be sloppy, to give it some thought. Teachers in my school insisted that parents sign homework daily as a signal that they'd checked to see what their child had done. It was late in my teaching career when I began to request parents' signatures. When I started doing so, I didn't check for signatures every day. If the work got done fairly competently, it didn't matter to me whether or not the parent signed the homework. But occasionally I made a big deal about it, and this sometimes had larger consequences. One day I noticed that Mick had worked carelessly on some problems. I'd asked him where he did his homework, and he told me he'd done it at the after school program. He also told me that his mother never checked his work. I wrote the following note:

2/18/98, Note to parent

Dear Sarah, Mick needs to do his homework at home, under supervision. Thanks, L. Please sign the homework each night after you check it. Thanks.

The next day, underneath my note, on the same page of the homework book, it said, "I check his homework every night. The 33¢ problem— I read it wrong—my fault." Mick then handed me a much longer note.

2/19/98, Note

Ms. Strieb—
    I saw your note about homework—except for last night, Mick + I always go over his homework every night, and do a lot of it together—just as I do with Daniel. Start to finish, I spend at least 45 minutes with Mick on his homework, then we add 15 minutes reading. We diligently do our homework together, and I definitely supervise it, without doing it. I am gravely concerned that you do not think that I am doing MY PART as a parent; You called into question if Mick's behavior had been a problem when we were in Virginia, and I told you no, it never was. I am extremely unhappy and dissatisfied with the influences to which Mick has been exposed at [this school], but I have attempted (every day) to address each problem with Mick and people [there]. Now, you are asking me to sign his homework as if somehow I am at fault and not doing my mothering role properly. I don't appreciate that insinuation.
    Sarah Morris

I immediately realized that my brief note in the homework book represented much more than a mindless reminder about doing homework.

It was clear that Mrs. Morris believed I was overstepping a boundary, insulting her, and raising questions about her competence as a mother. I wrote back,

2/19/98, Note to parent

Dear Sarah,
        Is there a chance we could talk together at 8:15 on Tuesday in the classroom? I never meant to insinuate that you are not mothering properly. That never entered my mind. Both of us want Mick's behavior to improve and I, too, want to work together. It's the only way. Please let me know if Tuesday is O.K. Thanks, Lynne Strieb

Mrs. Morris and I met and discussed the issue. I reminded her that at the beginning of the year I'd asked parents to sign homework and told her it was a school custom. I tried to make her understand that my concern for Mick was not only about homework but also about his general demeanor in school.
        Following the meeting, she seemed calmer, and 3 months later, when Mick had not done his homework, she wrote to me,

3/6/98, Note from parent

Ms. Strieb, Mick left his homework book at After School Care—we will complete last night's and tonight's homework for tomorrow. I apologize for any inconvenience. Thanks, Sarah Morris.

This note showed me that Mrs. Morris understood my expectations and was willing to work with them—or at least was willing to do things on my terms.

Favorable Reactions

Occasionally I received a note or heard a comment that indicated parents liked the homework I sent home.
        In October 1995, I asked parents to let me know how they felt about a "take-home quiz" about fairy tales. I received a variety of responses that helped me know whether I could give such an assignment again.

10/95, Notes

I thought the exercise was very good. Nora really enjoyed it as well as I did. Jean Darymple

I think the Fairy Tale take home quiz is a really good idea. It gives me a chance to see if Robert is really paying attention to the story while it's being read. Robert also said he liked it, so I hope you continue to send them home.

Thank you,

Gayle Dickenson

This quiz was very challenging and helpful in preparing them for future work in higher classes. I personally feel, this being the first of its kind for many of these children, it was too difficult for them. I feel it would have been a lot better if the children were given this in class so they may be able to use the books in question to help them, until they are able to get the hang of this type of work. Then after being (getting) used to this type of assignment they will be ready for a take home quiz of this type.

Harold Rossiter

Complaints

Sometimes parents wrote notes to me that indicated their displeasure with something about a homework assignment. I gave the following assignment for homework in April 1990.

4/1990, Homework

The United States has many people. The first people were Native American Indians. Three hundred years ago people started to come here from other countries and continents. Three hundred years ago, Black people came from Africa. Some of those people were your great, great, great, great, great, great, great, great, great, great grandmothers and grandfathers. They are your ancestors. You probably don't know their names.

Please write a list of other countries that other American ancestors came from.

4/1990, Journal

Mrs. Horton objected to my choice of the word "came" in the following sentence in yesterday's homework assignment: "Three hundred years ago, Black people *came* from Africa." Unlike other immigrants, Africans had no choice. She wants that distinction kept in mind. They did not "come." They were brought here against their will. She was right. The words one chooses to use matter.

I received complaints about content in other areas. Emma Stedman wrote the following note to me after I sent home two math problems that confused her son. The first problem asked, "Is the ball inside or outside the closed curve?" An amoeba-shaped closed curve was depicted along with a large black dot. The dot was outside the curve, but partially surrounded by a portion of the curve, like the ball before Pac-Man eats it. The second problem pictured four objects (a ball, a bat, a pair of ice skates, and a car) and asked "Which one does not belong? Explain your answer."

10/17/97, Note

Dear Ms. Strieb:
      The difficulty of explaining what's inside and outside was so great that Rodney [father] had to lead Jason to his answer but he doesn't understand it.
      Even Rodney, with a couple of post-graduate degrees to his name finds the concept so difficult to articulate because it is a relative one.
      If this is what you need to teach to the [standardized achievement test] I'm not sure Jason *can* achieve on this test. I don't think I get it.
      With a *lot* of prompting, Jason said, "Outside was ground." He *could see* that the dot was outside, at least he believed that.
      Also—by the way the thinking problem from Tuesday, he also didn't get. I didn't either. I thought only the bat and ball went together because you could play with them—unless the car was a toy, in which case you could play with it. The skates don't belong anywhere because they are more like apparel for the sport rather than the playing equipment. If you had shown a hockey stick or a puck maybe I would have understood the connection.
      This is not a criticism of you. I *want* you to teach whatever problem-solving skills that Jason will need to do well on the [test.] But he doesn't get it and I can't help him because I don't get it either. Help!
      Emma

I didn't give these daily problems merely because of the tests. It was my job to try to get the children to think about problems, to explain how they solved them and why, and to discuss solutions with the class. I knew that the importance of those daily problems lay in the conversations we had about solving them. I noted in my journal that perhaps the problems were too difficult for some of the parents and that maybe I shouldn't send them for homework. I realized that if I were to continue sending them as homework, I'd have to write about my reasons for doing so in my newsletter.

Creating Appropriate Homework

It took a lot of time and effort to create homework that reflected what children were learning in school and contained activities appropriate for first- and second-grade students. It was the habit of many teachers in Philadelphia to have children copy homework from the board. Each morning when the children arrived, the homework would be on the board and the children would immediately go to work. Those teachers believed that copying from the board was good reading practice and that it taught the children good handwriting. Though every now and then I tried to have children do this, I could never get it to work because it always took too much time. I preferred having the children read books to having them spend half an hour copying something. Commercially prepared homework sheets were also popular. Of course I occasionally found a prepared worksheet that fit perfectly into what we were doing in class, especially in math, and I used it, but that was rare. I didn't want to spend time searching for commercially prepared worksheets that both matched what I was teaching and appeared in a form I thought was appropriate. In addition, I always had trouble keeping track of worksheets.

Instead, I created the homework, typed it on the computer, photocopied it, and pasted it into each child's "reading" and "regular" homework books. The copying, pasting in, and checking of homework took a long time, and I had trouble finding time to keep up with it on a daily basis. I believed, however, that if I gave children work to do at home, and if parents took the time to make sure they did it and, sometimes, to help them, then I had an obligation to check it. I occasionally missed a day and sometimes received a complaint like this one:

10/28/98, Note

Ms. Lynn . . . Please check Shirin's homework. Some homework has not been signed by you or no check marked.

Fortunately, throughout my teaching life many parents came to my aid by helping. They both pasted in and checked the homework, notifying me if a child seemed to be having a problem.

I gave children little role in deciding what I would give for homework. Occasionally they suggested that a discussion I'd recorded should or should not be placed in reading homework books to be shared with parents. An example of this was when we had a discussion about some children creating "clubs" and excluding others. Children spoke honestly about being mean to others, and they requested that I not send the transcribed discussion home. When I asked them why, those who had done the excluding said that they were ashamed of their behavior and didn't want their parents to know about it. I didn't send it.

Sometimes children complained that homework was too hard, and we often had discussions about why I give them homework.

10/19/92, Journal (second grade)

The discussion was about homework. It came up because Nancy, Frank's mother, told me that he complains so much about doing homework that she doesn't know what to do. She doesn't want it to turn into an unpleasant experience. I told her it might be a good idea for me to have a discussion with the whole class rather than to have it with just him. I asked the children, "Why do I give you homework?" Many of the children said that I give them homework so that they can learn, so that they will get jobs, so that they will be able to go to college, so that they won't watch so much television.

I then began to talk. I said that I give them homework for many of the reasons they stated: so that they can learn; so that they will remember the things I've taught them in school; for practice; because my boss tells me that I must give homework every day with Friday Optional, (what's optional?).

I asked "How many of you like homework?" Though they were not in agreement about how much homework they preferred, most of the children raised their hands. That surprised me. I told them that they really had no choice; that they would keep getting homework and they might as well enjoy it. I asked how many of them complained to their parents about their homework. Many raised their hands. I asked them what kinds of things they say. "I can't do this" "It's too hard." "I want to watch television." . . . I told them that I don't think the homework I give them is too hard, since so much of it is what they've learned in class. I read tonight's homework to them and said, "You see, there's nothing too hard there." I promised to tell them when they could ask for help from their parents. I told them to stop trying to trick their parents and making them think they are not able to do it. I said, "You can't trick them any more."

These discussions always made me more aware of the need to create homework whose content would be suitable for as well as interesting to the children.

Some parents complained that the homework was not challenging enough, while others felt that it was very challenging. Parents complained that there was too much homework or that there wasn't enough. Following a second-grade parents' meeting at the beginning of the year, I wrote in my journal about a discussion we'd had about homework, begun by June, Violetta's mother.

9/24/97, Journal

At the meeting last night Violetta's mom said there's too much homework. Pia's mom agreed. Theodore's mom agreed. Today quite a few people came to me to express support for the way I give homework and to ask that I not change the way I give it. They feel it is a parent problem and not a child problem. I need to talk to all the children about this.

Violetta, whose mom raised the issue, has her own agenda both at home and at school. She doesn't like to read when I want them to read or to write when I want them to write. I'm torn because I can appreciate the rhythm of a child who really "covers" everything, but not according to schedule. She's quite creative and becomes involved in projects at home. Homework distracts her from those projects. . . . June complains because a) she is a single parent with limited time for her kid; b) she doesn't see the purpose for homework; c) she can't even turn the TV off without running into trouble with her kid, who throws a fit when she tries.

Following the meeting, I received a series of communications from parents that illustrate this tension about the amount and difficulty parents saw in the homework. Two parents responded specifically to June's plea to change my homework, which they both liked.

9/25/97, Note

Dear Mrs. Strieb,
    Parent's night was enlightening. You gave an informative presentation. Thank you. As one of the concerned parents I am in favor of homework as we had before. You might consider a lighter load towards the end of the week; but I would not mind the

assignments as given earlier. Please continue to challenge our children and to strengthen their skills via homework review. Cherise Gilmore

9/26/97, Note

Dear Mrs. Strieb:

It wasn't until I returned home on Tuesday evening that I had time to mull over what the group was discussing regarding home-work and how long it takes to do it. Frankly, until Wednesday, I never timed Mattie's homework. Thankfully it has never been an issue for us. She brings it home, she does it & it's over. As I men-tioned, I don't have the luxury of sitting with her through every moment of homework time. I have an extremely supportive husband but, still, we have 2 other children. Mattie has had to learn to deal with this responsibility, for the most part, by herself. She knows we are always there to help if necessary and, of course, to remind her it it's not done or to correct it when it's not quite right.

Dan and I don't find this to be a chore but,—actually an integral part of the learning process. She gets reinforcement for what she has learned during the day plus a subliminal lesson in responsibility and action/consequences. On those rare occasions when she doesn't want to do it, I suggest that she not do it and just write you a short note explaining why she didn't do it. That brings a groan from her and she quietly goes back to her work.

I'm sorry for rambling on but I say all this to preface my real point: PLEASE DON'T BACK DOWN ON THIS ISSUE. Please don't reduce the amount of homework.

I can't believe that the homework takes a hour to do. But, what if it does? What's wrong with spending an hour with your child doing something truly constructive? Won't kids take school more seriously if their parents do? How are kids going to feel about school & homework if their parents think it's a pain? This sounds like a classic case of parents expecting the school & teachers to do everything—it's got to be a group effort.

I also don't buy the "I'm a working mother" routine because I am, too. And, yes, it's a pain to come home & do all the home stuff & supervise homework, too. But that's life—grow up.

I just wish we could hold the kids to a higher standard. If we pander to the lowest common denominator, everyone suffers. What's going to happen when these kids are in 4th & 5th grade &

there's serious homework? It's only going to get harder so they might as well learn to buckle down & do it now.

This letter doesn't require an answer. I just wanted to let you know how one mother feels. Excuse the handwriting and paper but . . . a blank sheet was staring me in the face. Thanks for letting me vent. See you in the schoolyard.   Regards, Pam Kaye

Not surprisingly, I didn't change the homework, though I was always concerned about not demanding an unreasonable amount of time for its completion.

MY CURRENT THINKING

I believe that in general the homework assignments I gave the children were fair and appropriate. They reflected and related to what was going on in school and kept parents informed. Along with my newsletter to parents, homework was a bridge between school and home. And I came to feel that the parts that were self-explanatory and didn't need parental help gave the children practice that they needed.

Nevertheless, after looking through entries about the theme of homework in my journals, newsletters, notes from parents, and in the homework itself, I'm not completely satisfied. First, homework created tense moments both for children and for me. Children became anxious if they couldn't get the work done for some reason, such as not understanding the assignment, having to do another activity at home, or forgetting their books in school or at home. I became tense when I believed I was being pushed to give assignments that I felt were inappropriate. I became tense because I was in a constant rush to get homework done and into the books on time. It was always on my mind. And because I wanted the assignments to be interesting to the children and up to date and related to what we were doing in class, I sometimes waited until the last minute to write them. I knew teachers who assigned homework for the week. When I tried that tactic, my assignments became the same week after week—and quite boring.

Second, it is never possible to please all the parents with the assignments. Some felt they took too much time, they weren't challenging enough, they were too challenging, they weren't like the assignments they had when they were in school.

Third, as I said in Chapter 2, I still believe that young children (say children up to third grade) should not have to follow up school learning with work at home, that it's the school's job to teach the children as if parents didn't provide help or support. However, even when volunteers helped children complete unfinished homework during the school day, even though I allowed time for children to read or to do lots of practice in school, there was never enough time.

Fourth, after school is not always the best time for young children to do schoolwork. Many children are in schools and daycare from early in the morning until almost dinnertime. When they get home, both child and parent are exhausted. As some progressive educators have suggested,[4] educators and parents must examine their basic assumptions about homework. Are there better times and places to do this kind of work than after school or in the evening, when children and parents are often tired?

Fifth, teachers often say that they give homework to help children develop responsible behavior early in life. Does homework do that when parents must help children with it? I was rarely able to create homework that could be completed without parent help. I wonder if it's even possible to create such assignments for first and second graders (and in Philadelphia kindergarten teachers are now expected to give homework).

If it is not possible to create work that can be done independently, what if parents are unable to help or believe that a child should do the work on his or her own and won't give help? What if parents can't read English? Homework puts the children of these parents at a disadvantage. This seems to me to be the biggest problem with creating homework that demands parents' help. It not only exposes inequities between those who receive the help and those who don't, but it can also create further inequities. Children who get help at home already have a "leg up" over those who don't. I was torn between my desire to give homework that was interesting and important, and the demands it made on parents, demands that parents are not equally prepared to handle. And I had no control over what went on at home. Parents who may have been taught differently in school might not have understood what my homework assignments requested. This might have made doing the work more difficult for their children.

I assumed (and still assume) that it should not matter whether children are "well prepared" or "ill prepared" for school, or whether they have a great deal of or little help at home. It is the work of schools to educate all children (and to educate them in all ways, not to merely do well in standardized tests). In the history of this country and my own family, even though parents didn't prepare their children for success in school, many "unprepared" people have been educated in outstanding ways. I've heard teachers say, "How am I supposed to teach 'them' if their parents don't care?" In my experience, most parents do care about their children, so that is not an acceptable excuse.

Even though I wanted and helped parents to be involved in their children's education (and homework was one of those ways), for the most part I assumed that I was the one primarily responsible for the children's learning and that if the children didn't do well (say, if they didn't learn to read during the 2 years they were with me), it was my fault, not the fault of their parents. In other words, I wanted parents to help their children if they wanted to and were able to; I did everything I could to help them do that; but if they didn't, I knew it was ultimately my job.

❧ 4 ❧

Children's Behavior and Parents' Reactions

The boundary between the creative and destructive is a shallow one. When children are out of control, giving evidence of noncompliance— that gives us evidence of their humanness. It's not merely being "bad."
—Patricia Carini[1]

THROUGHOUT MY TEACHING life, I made an effort to let parents know that I cared about helping their children take responsibility for their behavior in school. I often spoke with or wrote to parents about their children's behavior, whether acceptable or unacceptable. It was something that also concerned them, as shown by their many conversations with, telephone calls to, and notes to me. I have chosen to use the words *behavior* and *behave* because those are the words most teachers and parents use. Many teachers' relationships with parents, whether good or not-so-good, are built on the common ground of a child's behavior. Though most children behaved appropriately, this chapter is mostly about how I worked with parents to address children who didn't.

In most classrooms, the teacher is the judge of whether a child is behaving or misbehaving and whether or not the behavior is acceptable and suitable. Though often children call attention to bothersome behavior, the teacher determines if a child lives up to the standards, acts according to the rules, and does the right thing as well as whether all the children are safe or unsafe because of another child's actions. Because behavior is tied to judgment, it is based on the teacher's and parents' values, expectations, and standards, and the rules that codify them. In schools, behavior has come to describe a child's relationship to those values, expectations, standards, and rules, and to the teacher and the other children. "The right thing" or "good behavior" is generally what I, the teacher, expect. (At home, "good behavior" is what parents expect.) At home or at school, adults are in charge, and that gives them power. At the same time, one child's negative behavior can affect the tone and atmosphere in the classroom, can distract the children from concentrating, can interrupt the teacher's ability to teach, can cause other children to feel unsafe, and can cause disruptions that hinder the formation and continuation of community. Children can resist, disrupt, and refuse to comply. That gives children power. In many classrooms, appropriate behavior can become an issue of power and control.

MY CLASSROOM AND SCHOOL

I start with the school and my classroom to sketch the context in which my students and I functioned. This is important since the acceptability of anyone's behavior is not absolute but is context dependent.

From the mid-1980s to 2000 in the Philadelphia public elementary schools where I taught (and I think the practice continues), classroom teachers were required to create, with children, a list of class rules regarding behavior. These rules were to be displayed where they could be easily seen by teachers, children, and adult visitors. Then, the theory went, when a child disobeyed one of those rules, it would be easy for the teacher to remind the child by merely pointing to the display and saying the number of the rule violated.[2] The rules were to be stated in a "positive" way. They were not to begin with words such as "do not" or "don't," even though those were the words that came naturally to the children (like "Thou shalt not . . ."). It was always easier for the children to say what they shouldn't do than what they should do, and so the children and I had difficulty formulating these rules. In the end, the wording was almost always mine, not theirs. Nevertheless, discussing and creating the rules gave us common understandings about appropriate and inappropriate behavior. Once we decided on the rules and understood them, the children were supposed to follow them. It was assumed that they would be monitors of their own behavior. For the most part, however, it was I who decided whether or not a child's behavior was acceptable.

I had many expectations related directly to children's behavior that turned out to be implicit in my documents. I came to an understanding of my own expectations, my responses to children's behavior, and how I worked with parents on these matters as I prepared to write this chapter. As I read my journal entries, narrative records, newsletters, and notes to and from parents, I created a list of all the behavior I had considered to be inappropriate. I then grouped the items on the list into the expectations listed below. As I worked, I realized that even though I had not written down these expectations while I was teaching, they had been part of my practice. I expected that the children would:

Feel and be safe and happy in school
Use words rather than fight when they had disagreements
Talk about and explain things that bothered them
Solve problems on their own with the help of other members of the class

Work for sustained periods of time, whether by themselves or with
   other children, without disrupting others
Help one another as needed
Choose associations and friendships that would be supportive
Be courteous to me and to their classmates by paying attention to
   whoever was talking, adult or child
Follow my directions when I first gave them
Not curse, hurt, kiss, pinch bottoms, touch someone's private parts,
   or use suggestive gestures to annoy or disturb others

When children's actions disturbed me and I had to let their parents
know, it was usually because of a child's not meeting one or more of the
above expectations. I hoped that parents would understand and agree with
my expectations, though I knew that was not always possible. I hoped that
parents would be happy with the classroom and with my teaching. And
as I had hoped with the children, I hoped they would approach me about
things that concerned them and that we could solve problems together.

I worked my own expectations into the rules the children and I wrote
together. When we finished creating the class rules for behavior, I displayed
them on a poster at the front of the classroom for the children and visiting
adults to see, and I included them in a newsletter to parents early in the
year so that they, too, knew the rules.

10/2/95, Newsletter

HERE ARE SEVEN IMPORTANT RULES FOR ROOM 204 . . .

1. Follow directions the first time they are given.
2. Listen when someone is talking (to the whole class).
3. If someone does something you don't like, tell them what they did,
   then say, "Stop doing that. I don't like it." Say it loudly.
4. Keep your hands and feet to yourself.
5. If you accidentally do something to someone else, say "I'm sorry,
   it was an accident."
6. Use quiet voices in the classroom.
7. Make the circle larger, then there will be room for everyone.

INFORMING PARENTS ABOUT BEHAVIOR

I usually informed parents about their child's and sometimes the entire
class's behavior. I often complimented children who "did the right thing"
in person, in notes, and in the newsletter, but more often, I informed

parents about behavior that was disruptive, unsafe, or unusual and disturbing to other children or to me in some way.

Why I Informed Parents

I informed parents for a variety of reasons. First, I felt it was important for the record—so that they would know if anything unacceptable was happening. It was my habit to write daily records on all the children in my class for teaching and for report cards, and if I noticed a pattern of behavior that was unacceptable to me, I felt it was important to note it. I'd learned early in my teaching that parents want to be told immediately if their child is causing trouble. They don't want surprises at, say, report card conferences, if their child has been doing something unacceptable throughout the term, nor do they want to be called into school for an emergency when they haven't been told about things that had led up to the emergency. Many parents seem to view a teacher's honesty about their children's behavior as a measure of a teacher's caring. I also had to make sure there was a written record of serious disruptive behavior in case of future problems. I felt that keeping a record and informing parents showed that I hadn't ignored serious incidents, even if school counselors and administrators didn't follow through.

Second, I wanted to solve problems, to improve things, to stop disruptive or disturbing or unsafe behavior. I believed that the child's behavior in school would improve if the parents worked on in-school behavior at home. I also thought that in some way, children's awareness of their parents' knowledge would be another layer of support and enforcement for following class rules.

How I Informed Parents

I informed parents by writing notes and placing them in the homework books or by making a telephone call in the evening. Rarely, in the event of more serious incidents, I immediately called parents from school. Until the 1990s, there were no mobile telephones, and making a telephone call during the day was difficult because it meant getting someone to cover the class and interrupting teaching. I usually wrote after a situation during which another child was hurt, after the child continually interrupted me or other children, or after a series of daily disruptions that were frustrating to me.

11/1/90, Note

Dear Ms. Marshall,
    Dontay was very angry, disruptive and disrespectful today. He has forgotten that the teachers are the ones who make the

daily schedule. Dontay was furious today because there was no Project Time. He kept *loudly* talking about it even when I was trying to teach the entire class. I told him to move to the back of the room. He picked up his chair. I told him to put it down. He slammed it down and hit George's arm. (Hitting George was an accident, but he was *so* angry he didn't [have] control over what he was doing.)

Dontay *has* to learn that the adults are in charge.

Thanks, L. Strieb

P.S. He got into a fight with Daniel early in the day. (We couldn't determine the cause) and he joined Jimmy and Tom in making noises and not listening to the substitute and student teacher. L

Dontay's behavior continued in this manner, and I continued to inform his mother by sending her notes. I often wrote them when I was angry, which can be surmised from their tone.

1/3/91, Note

Dear Mrs. Marshall,

I hope you are feeling better. Dontay was extremely rude and fresh today. As I write this he is saying "I don't care what you say to my mom." He talked when I was talking. He argued with me when I told him to do things. He answered me in a rude, fresh way. He refused to sing when everyone else sang, holding his ears. When he finally sang it was in a silly, mocking way. This is the start of a new year. I hope Dontay will behave better.

(He also didn't listen when I was teaching the whole class at the board, though things did improve after I threatened to take away his Project Time.)

Please speak to Dontay about talking in a fresh way under his breath when I am speaking to him. That kind of talking will get him into *a lot* of trouble one day.

Thank you,

L. Strieb

When I read this note to him he said, "I won't listen because I'm going to hear it at home." That's the kind of talk I mean must stop. When I asked Dontay what would happen when his mother read this note, he said, "Nothing." L

Occasionally the whole class was difficult over a long period of time. In those cases, I wrote about the entire class's behavior in the newsletter I sent home to parents. Before I wrote a finished version of the newsletter, it was useful to me to use the journal to "vent" by writing a draft, as shown below.

3/4/98, Journal first draft

My biggest concern right now is behavior. Some days it seems like just a few children can take the teacher's attention from (most of) the class. Last week was very difficult, but I think we're back on an even keel again. I'm telling you this so that you can talk to your child about her or his behavior.

Lunch behavior—throwing food, dropping papers on the floor or on the table and not picking them up, running around, making noise. I ask the children to behave as they would at home. That doesn't always work.

Misuse of materials—this is a new problem for me: throwing clay, taking pins that are to be used for sewing and bending them, playing with rubber bands, getting paint everywhere. When children do these things, it's hard for me to keep those materials available. If it should happen that a child misuses a material enough for me to remove it, I will make clear to the rest of the class who is responsible. I've never experienced these things before in my teaching in other schools because children have valued Project Time and its activities so much.

Threatening others; trying to get others in trouble: I suspect children do these things to get my attention. To be honest, I can't tell who's telling the truth when one child accuses another and the other denies it. I'm getting really frustrated with this. I'm going to have to tell them to stop coming to me with such tales. I want to go back to the policy of having children say "Stop doing that" or "Stop saying that" and not telling me.

Talking during writing and Quiet Reading Time: Many children are not getting enough work done (especially writing) because of all this talking. Talking while someone else is talking to the class: This is just plain rude.

Not following teacher's directions; being too noisy when getting into line. With 29 children, all transitions and class movements take a long time.

It is very few children who are doing these things. Most of the children are always productive and well-behaved. I am trying to ignore the children who are being naughty, but it's very difficult. Please speak to your child about her or his behavior. I want to thank everyone for their help and patience. I want to thank the parents whose children are not being disruptive for all their hard work.

Writing in my journal allowed me to gain some perspective, and between the draft and the actual writing of the newsletter, I had calmed myself. Thus, the tone and content of the original journal entry changed, and I explained why in the newsletter.

3/4/98, Newsletter

When I began to write this newsletter, I was pretty upset with the behavior of some of the children in the class. But before I wrote it, we seemed to have turned the corner, and they are back on track, with everyone trying to be good. I decided not to list all the different kinds of disturbing behavior that only a very few of the children are exhibiting. I just want to thank the hard work and concern of all the parents, especially those whose children have been difficult. It's upsetting to everyone when a few of the children are able to disrupt things. As for me, sometimes I have more patience and sometimes I have less. It goes in waves, and the past few weeks have been difficult. I apologize for that.

PARENTS' REPORTS ABOUT THE BEHAVIOR OF OTHER PEOPLE'S CHILDREN

When I wrote about children's behavior in the newsletter, it opened opportunities for feedback from parents about what they might be hearing from their children at home. Sometimes parents were so disturbed by what their children told them about other children's behavior that they felt it was important to inform me. Two examples follow.

4/12/84, Note

Ms. Strieb,
    Ron has told me a number of things regarding incidents with his classmates. I've basically been telling him a lot of the behavior he is enduring is due to ignorance, parental neglect, and just general childhood insensitivity. Today I was brushing his hair and I found a

small abrasion that he says came from a kid throwing a cup at him in Ms. Shapiro's class. He says this is where the bad boys are kept.

1. Has he been misbehaving and is he being disciplined for it? If so please make me aware.

2. I realize that a number of the children in this area suffer from a lack of attention and somewhat poor self-images. As a result the 'bully' is born. Be that as it may I do not want Ron reaping the brunt of their frustrations. Either these children are better restrained or I'm going to start telling Ronald to start defending himself with my *full* blessing.

R.L. Tierney

In February of 1991 I received a note from a parent who accused me of not enforcing school rules against fighting, hitting, and kicking. He gave me some examples of how his daughter had been hurt by other children, including being hit, kicked, and pushed. He felt that she was not being protected from exposure to serious harm and that "her caretakers" had ignored her reporting of the incidents. He said that was unacceptable and that he wanted to talk about the matter with me.

Both the note and its contents disturbed me, especially the accusation that I was allowing violence toward a child. I again wrote a draft in my journal, this time of a response to the note. I wasn't certain I would send it but it calmed me to write it. I wrote that his own daughter was sometimes the first to push or hit another child and described some of those incidents. I continued:

There is NO lack of enforcement of school rules against fighting, hitting and kicking in room 205. It is something that I CONSTANTLY work on with the children. . . .

I am truly concerned about the safety of ALL the children. I am TRYING to create a world in the classroom where children don't tease and bother each other to the point of no recourse except hitting. Carol needs to protect herself by not bothering other children to the point of their frustration. And I will NEVER condone hitting, pushing or kicking as a reaction to being bothered. Children who do so have been and will continue to be reprimanded, then punished.

After I drafted the letter, I wasn't sure about its tone and decided to ask the principal to read it and to advise me about whether or not to send it. He did not want to read my draft response and did not want me to reply to the note, nor did he want any further background, which was available in my narrative records. Instead, he said he would call the parent and take care of the matter. The principal didn't tell me what happened, but I did not receive further complaints. Following this incident, I still had to occasionally remind my students to stop annoying others. The struggle against children harming one another continued throughout my teaching life.

Parents' information about problems influenced what happened in the classroom. In the following incident, Nayomi didn't tell me about behavior that was disturbing her and others, but rather reported it to her parents. Mrs. Bodin had observed Nayomi writing a note to me about what a group of boys did to her and to a few other children in the class. She sent me Nayomi's own note in its unedited, uncorrected form. She knew, from observing my pleasure with children's own spelling, that I would appreciate its being sent that way rather than revised and perfect.

11/14/97, Note

Ms. Sterb Theeo. S. and Donald. J. and Shwn.
is massing with me.
I told them to stop.
they ceep doing it.
Can you tell them to stop.
they hit me and One time kicked.
they call me name's.
they do it after school.
they call it Beet up gril time.
they do it to more peppol to
it gets on are very
latst norv.
my dad said get them I try to
the name's they call me:
fatso: fat moma: fat: chubey: ugly: freak:
Nayomi Bodin

Can you reemind me to
Sty away from Donald
And Theeodor[3]

Mrs. Bodin added a note of her own on the same piece of paper:

Mrs. Strieb
       Could you please check into this for me please. I figured it
must be pretty serious for her to write this out and ask me to talk

with you. She didn't want to tell you in person because she said everyone would be listening. This is supposedly also happening to Austin Blake and Mattie Kaye. I know that the school doesn't allow the kids to fight, but my husband and I have taught our kids to defend themselves if needed.

Thanks, Mrs. Bodin

Please send me a note or call me [telephone number].

Mrs. Bodin wanted to support her daughter in the face of the teasing. Nayomi conveyed something that meant a lot to her, which she showed by taking time to write. Mrs. Bodin didn't merely tell me verbally that Nayomi was being bothered but rather accompanied Nayomi's note with her own. She recognized that there would probably be a difference in the way she and her husband might tell her daughter to handle this situation (defend herself by fighting) and the way I would handle it. (Use words, tell them to stop. If they don't stop, tell an adult.) In other words, she was depending on me to take care of this matter in a way that would satisfy the family or else they would tell Nayomi to defend herself physically.

As soon as I received the note, I called Mrs. Bodin. I thanked her for letting me know what was happening after school. I told her that all children have the right to feel safe and protected against teasing and bullying. I said that if Austin and Mattie were also being teased, we could be sure that it was happening to even more children who were also not speaking up. I said that I would do my best to take care of this matter without mentioning Nayomi's name. I told her that rather than confronting Theodore, Shawn, and Donald alone about this, I preferred to bring up the matter of teasing to the entire class. I asked her if she thought that would be all right and she said it would be okay.

I settled the children into a circle for a whole-class discussion and said to them, "I got a note from a girl in our class and she's very upset. Does anyone know what it could be about?" Everyone knew immediately what I was referring to. As usual, I took notes as the children spoke. Donald, Theodore, and Shawn contritely, tearfully, and immediately described what they'd done without having been accused, and their confessions were amplified by the many witnesses in the class. I learned that they had teased the girls and Austin more than once and did so either because they thought teasing girls was acceptable or because none of the children would fight back.

The three boys apologized spontaneously, without urging from me. I wrote in my journal:

11/14/97, Journal

It seems that the time to find out the true ways boys treat girls, or rather, the way children treat one another is to observe at recess and after school. But of course, my presence would change behavior, since the children know my values. I need to check to see if everything is okay on Monday.

I checked with the children the following day, and they said there had been no more teasing at recess or after school. I reported this to Mrs. Bodin and asked her to let me know if and when there were any more problems. I thanked her for letting me know because we teachers can't remedy such situations if children don't tell us about them. I also thanked her for letting me handle the situation.

PARENTS' VARIED RESPONSES

Parents responded in a variety of ways to my communications about children's negative behavior: helping in the classroom, writing notes, taking the matter into their own hands, refusing to do anything about the matter, and joining me in addressing the difficulties.

Helping in the Classroom

Juan was becoming resistant to working on reading and math, and he was bothering other children, especially a few of the girls. His mother, Mrs. Perez, thought that volunteering in the classroom would be a help to both him and me. Whenever a parent offered to help, whether or not their child was difficult, I accepted. In Juan's case, I believed that, at least while his mother was present, he would not disturb other children. It didn't work out that way. Juan continued to be unpleasant to children, even though his mother was helping in the classroom. However, being in the classroom did make a difference in terms of Mrs. Perez's knowledge and awareness of her child.

Writing Notes

Jonathon was in my class for 2 years, and during that time I wrote many, many notes to his parents about his disruptive behavior. I was often frustrated when I wrote. If I made a telephone call, which was rare, it usually meant that I felt an urgency to speak directly to his parents. Each time I wrote a note (and there were many), his mother, Mrs. Callen, wrote back to me. And each time she did so, her responses were respectful and polite. She always thanked me for informing her about the problems and often told me what punishment Jon had received at home as a result. Home punishments ranged from talking with him to revoking the privilege of playing video games to depriving him of drum lessons.

I once called the Callens to report a quite serious matter, and his mother said angrily, "What do you want? Do you want me to take Jon out of your classroom?" I told her, "Mrs. Callen, I don't give up on children. No, I don't want Jon out of my classroom. As far as I'm concerned, each day is a fresh start. I just think I have to let you know when there's a problem." The following day, I received a response to the telephone call that surprised me. I was reminded that sometimes parents rethought their angry reactions to something I said or did.

2/7/97, Note

Dear Ms. Strieb:

Please forgive me for lashing out at you as I did on last evening. I truly did not mean to hurt or upset you in any way. Please know that I am very appreciative and grateful for your concern about our son Jonathon.

My family and I are trying so hard to help him. We really thought that we were getting through. Jonathon's attentiveness, ability to follow instructions, and listening skills have increased so much at home that we assumed things were going great in school as well.

I should not have let my personal feelings of failure interfere with your actions of wanting to help my child.

We will continue to work hard at home with him. We will never give up on him because we realize that change will come if we be very persistent that it occurs.

Again, I thank you for your help and support and pray for your forgiveness.

Sincerely,
Mrs. Callen

Taking Matters into One's Own Hands

Mrs. Collier, about whom I wrote in Chapter 2, took matters into her own hands when she believed I was not handling a discipline issue the way she felt I should. One Thursday afternoon at the beginning of June 1981, after dismissal, she came running back into school in a fury, after I'd sent the children out. She was irate! "You know that little boy with brown hair that sticks out and glasses? Well he punched Tonya in the stomach as hard as he could!"

"Are you sure it was intentional?"

"Yes! He's the boy who said to me one time, 'Your daughter doesn't have any friends,' and then stuck his tongue out. He's been bothering her for a long time."

I told Mrs. Collier that I would talk to the child, Bob, the next day. I also said I'd had no idea that Bob had been teasing Tonya and that it was hard for me to remedy a situation like that if Tonya doesn't tell me about it. (I'd meant to call Bob's house at night, but forgot.) Anyway, Mrs. Collier was very upset.

The next morning, when I got out to the line to pick up the class, David's mother and a few other parents were standing outside. The children told me that Bob had run away. Henry had Bob's homework book. Tonya's mother had yelled at him. Atiya said, "You should have seen when Mrs. Collier started running after Bob. And she hit him with her pocketbook too. She said if he ever hit Tonya again she would lay him flat on the ground."

I was upset, of course, but I had to get the children inside and settled into working. I also felt that I must find Bob. I knew he had a house key because when I'd asked the kids the day before where they would go in case school was closed early, he had said that he had his own key. I didn't want him to be alone in his house.

Mrs. Collier came up to the room with the class. She told me that Tonya had hardly slept Thursday night, that she had vomited, and that she had pain from stomach cramps. I told Mrs. Collier that I felt Tonya was upset because she (her mother) was so upset—that if Mrs. Collier had been calm, Tonya would have been calm. Mrs. Collier assured me that she had now decided to let me handle the situation.

I got permission from the principal to go across the street to Bob's house, got a neighbor to open the front door, and found Bob locked in the bathroom. I managed to talk him into opening the bathroom door and coming out. He sobbed all the way back to the classroom. Mrs. Collier was waiting there as I'd asked her to do until I returned. When I was back in the room, I spoke briefly with Mrs. Collier before talking with the children.

I told the children how upsetting it was to me when I heard that children tease children. I said that I'd try to find out exactly what happened. Then I reviewed the steps they all knew they should take if someone hit or continually teased them.

"If someone hits you or teases you, what should you do?"

"Hit them back."

"No"

"Tell the teacher."

"No"

"Tell them, 'Stop doing that (stop hitting/teasing me). I don't like it!'"

"Good. And suppose they keep doing it. Suppose they keep on bothering you?"

"Then you can tell the teacher."

"Right. You must tell me. You may also tell your parents when you get home. But I can't help you to stop others from bothering you if I don't know they're doing it. Tonya, what should you do if children bother you?" (And I went over it with her.)

The conversation with the children continued with Mrs. Collier present. Bob admitted having told Tonya that she didn't have any friends, "But that was a long time ago." And he said that he had not hit Tonya on purpose, that it was an accident that happened when he turned around to call for his friend Henry. I told him that Mrs. Collier definitely thought he wanted to hit Tonya. "Well, I didn't," he responded. Well of course I didn't know the truth but among the things I said in front of the class was, "Bob, Mrs. Collier believes that you hurt Tonya on purpose. She doesn't believe it was an accident, and that's because a long time ago you teased her. (Pause) Now, everyone—no more teasing! And remember, you don't have to like everyone. But you can't go around hitting, hurting, or teasing the people you don't like. You should just kind of keep it a secret."

In the afternoon, Bob's mother came to find out what had happened. She wondered what to do with him on Monday, when he probably wouldn't want to come to school. (He hadn't wanted to come that day, either, and she knew something was strange when he wore his house key again.)

Tonya's mother came up to the room once more and I told her I understood how upset she was, but that she really mustn't go hitting children who bothered her daughter.

On Sunday night, Bob's mom called to talk about what to do. She'd decided that she and the school couldn't allow parents to take matters into their own hands like that (and I believed she was right). She was concerned about the lack of supervision in the schoolyard that would make such an incident possible. She was going to speak to the principal. She would bring Bob to school on Monday. I asked, "What if Mrs. Collier were there?" She really didn't want to argue with her. But she believes her son. He never lies, even when it means a punishment for him. "He's the kind of kid who would say, 'Yeah, I hit her. And I'm sorry I didn't hit her harder.'"

I said that she should do what she felt should be done, that Mrs. Collier would never believe it was an accident; and that when there are two different stories about the same incident, it's impossible to know who's telling the truth.

Monday morning I spoke to the principal and told him the story. I wanted to warn him of what might be coming. I described what nice people both mothers were, how much Mrs. Collier helped both me and one of the kindergarten teachers, how shy she was, and how protective of her daughter.

He blew up! "That parent needs to know she could be sued! I could call the police!"

"No. Please. I don't want her scared off. And I don't want either mother to feel I'm calling her a liar. Maybe you could just listen to what Bob's mother says. Maybe you could send a general note home to parents saying that they can't go around hitting children in the schoolyard. Something general, not specifically directed at Mrs. Collier."

Mrs. Collier volunteered in one of our kindergartens. She had told the teacher about the incident, and the teacher and I had talked together. I told her about the principal's reaction, and she immediately went to speak to him. He'd calmed down and agreed not to be harsh with Mrs. Collier.

Later that day, Mrs. Collier showed me a note she'd written to me:

6/5/81

Dear Mrs. Strieb,
    I'm sorry about all that happened last week. Tonya is sorry too. She said that now she thinks Bob and her can be friends. She promised to tell you if anyone bothers her. She wanted me to write you this note. Sincerely, Mrs. Collier.

Then she said, "You know, I really do like this class, and I'm glad Tonya is in it. They really were good on Friday when I was here helping them write. They write good and they kept busy without talking or fighting." And I told her how glad I was that Tonya was in the class, how much less shy she'd become, and how talented she was. "She's a *very* special girl. And the children know it."

Mrs. Bodin (who had sent me the note from her daughter Nayomi) and Mrs. Collier (who had told me herself that her daughter was being bothered by one of the children) were both concerned because their daughters were unhappy and felt unsafe. Neither child had told me that she was being harassed. Both parents were willing to handle the situation themselves if I didn't do so. The Bodins allowed me to first try to solve the problem before taking action; Mrs. Collier didn't wait and immediately took matters into her own hands.

It is never acceptable for another parent to yell at, hit, run after, or threaten other people's children, no matter how angry. My experience with Mrs. Collier illustrates how important it is for schools to provide adequate adult supervision in schoolyards. It also shows how important it is for schools to inform parents of the procedures they should follow when they believe their child to be unsafe because of another child's actions.

Resisting

Sometimes there were children who were disruptive but whose parents, perhaps frustrated with my repeated notes home, didn't want to work with me in any way to try to solve these problems. For example, Jalil Howard's father quickly lost patience with my many reports to him and, at least according to his son, ignored them.

I had already asked Mr. Howard to meet with me about Jalil's difficulties in class. Jalil had trouble sitting still, made noises that disturbed the other children, often did something different from what I asked or told the children to do. When unsupervised, he verbally or physically threatened, started fights with, punched, or pushed other children. Sometimes this behavior was provoked, but at other times he lashed out when he merely thought another child was going to hurt him. Sometimes he used the excuse "It was an accident." Sometimes he said, "Well, he hit me," when the other child had accidentally bumped into him. He had difficulty telling the difference among joking, accidents, and purposeful hitting by other children.

Early in the year, I invited his father to meet with me so that we could talk about Jalil's behavior. Mr. Howard brought both Jalil (age 6) and his younger son (age 4), and he expected both boys to sit still while we talked. Though I offered to give the two boys pencils and paper, books, or toys with which they could play, Mr. Howard wouldn't allow them to do anything. He insisted that they sit still and not say a word. It might have been a way of modeling the kinds of behavior he expected children to exhibit in school at all times—behavior that would demonstrate to me proper respect for the teacher. It seemed to me to be unnecessarily harsh. It was evident that we had different expectations for children.

When I first spoke with Mr. Howard, he was willing to try to help as long as I sent home a daily report card. Though finding time to do so was always difficult for me, I had learned from past experience that creating a report that broke the day into segments and grading each segment could be a little easier for me to do than giving a child a grade for a whole day. For one thing, it would allow me to let the parent know about times when the child was cooperating. Mr. Howard insisted on one grade for the whole day, which didn't allow for letting him know if anything good had happened. "I don't need the details," he said. I felt that that was exactly what he needed. But once, when I told him that if I were to give Jalil a grade for that day, it would be a D, he asked me what Jalil did that merited a D. I wrote in my journal, exasperated:

11/20/09, Journal

> Yesterday he'd said that he didn't want the details, just a grade. Now he's asking for details, which I find hard to give. I can't remember the details unless I write them down immediately. I didn't write them because I didn't think I needed them.

Jalil told me that in response to hearing about the grade of D on his daily report, his dad beat his feet with a cord. I spoke with the counselor about this, and the counselor said I had to report it to the school nurse. The nurse and counselor then spoke with Mr. Howard about inappropriate punishments. He yelled and screamed at the nurse and counselor, accused me of exaggerating what he did to Jalil, and said that he would continue to do the same if he needed to.

I knew that I could not continue to inform Mr. Howard about Jalil's behavior and that that was the end of my working relationship with him. I felt disillusioned. However, once in a while I wrote a note home, reporting on Jalil's behavior. Once, when I asked Jalil what his father had said when he saw a certain note, Jalil said, "Nothing." "Nothing?" I asked. "Well, I'm afraid to tell you." "You don't have to be afraid to tell me. You can tell me." Jalil said, "He said, 'I hate that teacher.'" I replied, "Well, I don't hate your dad. And—I like you very much." At another time, after Jalil pushed a metal bookcase so forcefully that some mugs on it fell to the floor and broke, Jalil promised, "I'm gonna buy you another cup." I said, "I don't know where you're going to get the money to do that. Besides, you know you're going to have to tell your father how you broke my cup. And I don't think your father would buy me another cup." "You're right," said Jalil. "He won't buy one for you."

Working Together

The most satisfying parent reaction to my reports of disruptive behavior was when, at my suggestion, a parent and I worked together to find a way to support the child.

Like many children, Denise Booker, who was in second grade, demanded a lot of attention not just from me but from whatever adults were in the classroom—parents, other teachers, visitors, student teachers. She often asked for praise and expressed frustration when I praised others for things she'd also done well. She had stormy relationships with other children; they often got angry at her because she teased them or because she told them what to do. The word they used to describe her was *bossy*. For all of these reasons, she often seemed unhappy.

This description leaves out all the other things about Denise that were strengths. It leaves out other aspects of her behavior, such as her awareness of others' accomplishments, which motivated her to work harder; her attention to the activities in the classroom, with the potential to teach others and to help me; her great interest in class discussions about science and about cultures and languages other than her own. Denise contributed many important questions and comments to these discussions. I spoke with Denise's mother, Mrs. Booker, about Denise's behavior. Mrs. Booker seemed concerned about similar things at home: her need for attention; her easily hurt feelings; and her need for praise, which seemed to her mother to be excessive.

I told Mrs. Booker that I was a member of a group called the Philadelphia Teachers' Learning Cooperative (PTLC) and that I thought if she and I could together present a Descriptive Review of Denise to this group at one of our regular Thursday meetings, we might both gain some insight into our concerns and some suggestions about how to approach them. Mrs Booker agreed to join me, and we met before the meeting to plan.

At the PTLC meeting, Mrs. Booker and I presented a Descriptive Review of Denise using the headings listed in the Introduction to this book as a framework.[4] We also described Denise's strengths and vulnerabilities, both at school and at home. Our focusing question was, "How can we help Denise make more friends and enjoy her relationships with other children?" We added, "She's very comfortable with adults and looks to them for company and praise."[5] As they listened, many of the teachers in the group were reminded of similar children in their own classes.

As part of the Descriptive Review process, following our description and participants' questions, the group gave both Mrs. Booker and me suggestions about supporting Denise's strengths as a leader and as someone who sees other children and events from an adult perspective. They noted that Denise related well to people who could teach her, which was described as a strength. They recommended activities that would foreground her competence and ability as a teacher, such as reading with younger children. They also suggested titles of books whose characters might help Denise understand the dynamics of interaction and power-sharing—especially if there were an opportunity for her to discuss such books with an adult. They recommended reasonable ways in which both her mother at home and I at school could give her the attention she needed. They suggested ways that Mrs. Booker could connect Denise with children on weekends, through drama or art classes or singing in a choir.

During the critique at the end of the Descriptive Review, the participants, including Denise's mother, agreed that no one—neither the child nor her parent nor the teacher—was a problem or at fault. Someone said, "We teachers often say 'It's the home' or 'It's the child's fault,'" but at the meeting we noted that rather than trying to change Denise, some things in her life at school and at home might usefully be changed. It was a powerful experience to have a group of people focus on one child. Mrs. Booker and I learned much more than if either of us had tried on our own to consider ways of supporting Denise.

During the months following the Descriptive Review, I noticed that Denise stopped telling other children what to do. She sometimes still asserted herself in ways that made the children unhappy, though not as often. I supported her interest in and concern for two children who had been born in another country and who were learning to speak English, and I encouraged her interest in languages other than English. Planning and presenting the Descriptive Review together with Denise's mother strengthened our relationship. We became partners in trying to support Denise. Doing a Descriptive Review is a wonderful way for parents and teachers to work together for the benefit of the child.

WHAT I LEARNED, WHAT I WONDERED

I believed that informing parents about their child's behavior was part of my work as a teacher, my responsibility, a way of showing that I cared about their child. However, I wonder if it is possible for parents to influence their child's behavior in school when those parents are not present in the classroom at all times. I had assumed that if parents dealt with school behavior at home, it would help the child in the classroom. It didn't occur to me until I'd retired from teaching that there might be problems with this. It was then that I realized that often, when the disruptive behavior continued, sending home notes day after day (or calling night after night) did not foster change at all. It's only since I've stopped teaching and have looked back on this issue that I realize I was asking parents to do something that might have been impossible for them to do. For parents whose children constantly did not follow rules, the effect of my repeated notes left them more frustrated than anything else.

A second problem about informing parents about in-school behavior might have been my lack of knowledge about or disagreement with ways in which parents handled children's negative behavior at home. I realized late in my teaching that I could have enlisted more parents' help if, early in the year and at the two report card conferences, I had asked them to compare behavior I was describing in school with behavior at home and in other settings. I could have asked specifically about how their child behaved in church, another place where some of the children I taught spent many hours. I could have asked them how they disciplined their children. I could have asked them for suggestions. Perhaps if I had gained these insights, I might have been able to work better on behavior at school, and this might have resulted in my writing fewer notes.

Perhaps my way of teaching, which included choice and the ability to move around and talk as part of the structure of the day, was confusing to children, some of whose time or activities everywhere outside of school may have been strictly determined by adults. Often children's behavior improved when I taught them a second year and as they became more used to the structures and expectations of my classroom.

A third problem was the kinds of punishments parents gave at home. Some parents spoke to their child about the behavior. Some denied privileges and beloved activities. For example, when Jonathon's parents denied him drum lessons as punishment for continued infractions, I felt sad because I knew how talented Jon was and how much playing drums meant to him. Nevertheless, I didn't stop informing his parents, and I regret that. After Jon had a series of good reports, his parents would allow him to resume taking lessons and playing the drums, and I'd feel much better. Punishments were sometimes dangerous to children. Occasionally after I'd written a note home, a child came to school with a mark on her or his face or a report that there had been a beating. At that point, I stopped reporting to those parents because no matter what I said about appropriate punishment, they were probably not going to hear what I said and the child would continue to be victimized.

I noticed that in my journal I often raised the question to myself about how to teach children who seemed stubborn or disruptive. Sometimes I felt almost desperate:

2/27/98, Journal

I am frustrated by the behavior of some of the children. Four or five of them can keep the rest of the class (29 children) from enjoying the day because it takes so much of my time to deal with them. I know that I'm not doing it right; that I'm paying attention to bad behavior not good behavior, but I feel that I have to stop the disruptive behavior when it happens. There must be another way.

I sometimes felt I should admire a child's stubbornness. I *sometimes* believed it was that child's way of asserting who he or she was. I think particularly of Connor, a child who refused to go to the room to which he was assigned in second grade, even though he had to face the daily humiliation of being forced into school, crying, by his puzzled and distressed parents. His classroom was next to mine, in a two-room open space. We realized it was possible that he wanted to be in the classroom of the teacher who had taught his brother, but couldn't say it. After a meeting of Connor's parents, the counselor, his teacher, and me, he was transferred to my class. After the change, he came to school more willingly and seemed happy in school.

I also think of Alice and Larry, two children who usually ignored what I wanted the class to do. These were children who had strong wishes, who were difficult when I gave the whole class directions and assignments as well as during transitions when they were not closely supervised. But they thrived when the class was given choices during Project Time and they were involved in activities that interested them. Choice Time or Project Time offered opportunities for children to follow their interests, and it also made demands on them to follow the class rules—working on a project to a satisfactory completion, being engrossed in reading a book, respecting their own and other children's work, for example. The children behaved appropriately because they wanted to participate. That indicates to me that sometimes it is not the children who must change, but rather, the classrooms and schools. Perhaps parents can play a role in helping to bring about those changes.

❧ 5 ❧

Opening the Classroom Door: Inviting Parents and Preparing to Work Together in Classrooms

IN MANY schools, parents are invited to work in the cafeteria, halls, or library to help maintain order and safety; to organize, shelve, and repair books; to do fund-raising for the school; or to chaperone class trips. When I first taught at Dunbar in 1962–1963, despite the fact that I could have used it, I was reluctant to request parent help in the classroom. In addition, it wasn't the custom in the school for parents to be invited in.

Then, as a young parent, while working for 3 years alongside Peggy Perlmutter Stone in my children's classrooms at the Westside Parent Cooperative Nursery and at Keyser School's kindergarten, I promised myself that when I again became a teacher, I would value the parents of the children I taught, just as I felt Peggy had valued me and the other parents.

When I began to teach as a fully certified teacher, I recognized that the invitation to parents must be serious; that both parents and I had to prepare for the experiences; and that there might be tensions, which I was confident could be overcome.

THE PARENT SCHOLAR PROGRAM

In 1967 the federal government funded the Follow Through program, in which grades K–3 in certain Title I schools implemented various teaching methods to attempt to maintain the gains children made in Head Start (Kennedy, 1977).[1] Philadelphia had eight different Follow Through models in place, each with a different sponsor. The government planned to track and compare the success of each. In the mid-1970s, the School District of Philadelphia formally inserted parent involvement into all the Follow Through models in the city. In Philadelphia, these parents were called Parent Scholars, and they were trained to work in all Follow Through classrooms in the city. Though in some parts of the country parents also worked with other parents in their homes, in my school they worked only in classrooms. This Parent Education/Parent Scholar program was one of the first examples of formal, national, institutional recognition that parents who work with their children make a difference in their school success. In Philadelphia, parents were paid a stipend to work alongside teachers for 10 weeks. They received a small amount of training, had to attend meetings, and then worked with the teachers and children in classrooms.

Parent Scholars were expected to work with Title I–eligible children only. They worked for one 10-week period, had to skip the next 10-week period, and, if there were not enough new people to take on the work, could work for another 10 weeks. In 1981 I was not certain that I would be allowed to have a Parent Scholar in my classroom because at the time only nine of the thirty-two children in my room were eligible for Title I–funded assistance.[2]

WHY I INVITED PARENTS

Although some of my assumptions matched those of the Parent Scholar program (such as that parents would learn from my modeling), and though I appreciated its goal of including parents in classrooms, educating them was not my only goal. I had important reasons for wanting parents to join me in teaching in the classroom whether they were Parent Scholars or not.

I Needed Help

I taught in a less traditional manner, in a more informal way, in an "open" classroom. Such classrooms, though sometimes seemingly lacking in structure, actually require a great deal of planning and structure. That's because some of the time students work in smaller groups or individually, with a variety of materials and choices. The presence of additional adults (such as parents) in a class of this kind with a large number of students (30–35) can be of enormous help. These adults can help prepare the materials and can also increase the adult-to-student ratio so that small-group and individual work become more feasible. They can help with the academic work in the classroom: reading with small groups of children or individual children, working with those who are having difficulty with math, playing games that give the children practice with important concepts, holding writing conferences.

Parents made it possible for me to have cooking and art activities (including clay, sewing, and painting). These were activities that either needed an adult to make the materials accessible, to keep them orderly, and to supervise their cleanup, or needed an adult to supervise the actual activity while another person watched out for the well-being of the rest of the class. For example, for sewing, children often had trouble threading needles. If I'd had to thread all needles, that alone would have caused children who needed help in other areas to interrupt me many times. A parent's presence alleviated those interruptions.

An entry from my journal shows how beneficial a parent's help could be for the children.

5/5/81, Journal

If it weren't for Marcy, I'd never have finished the clay for firing. She's Isaac's mom and she owns a wholesale ceramic supply business. She really gets upset when she comes in and sees the mess the clay is in. So she helps. The kids work on it but I don't seem to find the time to do the things I like to do—give the guidance that kids need, fire the clay and have them glaze it. She is very tactful. . . . She's stayed and worked with the kids a few times and each time there's been an improvement in the care and quality of their work. I know from working so hard on the children's writing, how much they are helped by contact with adults and by conversations about their work.

A Calming Presence

Parents would be able to attend to individual children when it was sometimes difficult for a teacher with 33 children to do so.

More than occasionally, I seemed to lose control of the tone of the classroom. The afternoon of November 19, 1992, for example, couldn't have been more chaotic. It was late in the day. I insisted that the children complete some exercises on odd and even numbers before they went home, without giving them enough time. When I told them to prepare to pack up to go home, I realized I'd forgotten to have them glue the homework into their two homework books. And the children wanted me to keep my promise to share with them a small piece of the candy that one of the children had brought for me. To top it all off, it had begun to snow. The children became excited. Two very understanding parents, Wendy's mom and Karl's mom, walked in and, instead of being upset by the noise, just took over helping the children put homework into their books, which calmed me. They knew from previous conversations with me exactly what they could do to help. I managed to deliver a piece of the candy into each open mouth as the children left the room, feeling like a priest distributing the wafer at a communion. Those two parents saved the day.

Talents, Interests, and Cultures

Parents could add richness to the classroom with the clothing they wore, the languages they spoke, the literature they brought to us, the foods they helped us cook. With the exception of my Fulbright teaching year in England (where I taught many children of immigrant Indian Sikh and Hindu, Pakistani and Bangladeshi Muslim, and Afro-Caribbean parents), I had taught only about 15 children or children of parents who were born in countries other than the United States (China, Colombia, Yugoslavia, Finland, Denmark, Argentina, India, Malaysia, Japan, Russia by way of Israel). When I did, I tried to include their cultures, knowledge, and languages, whenever possible, in the curriculum, just as I tried to include the knowledge, language, and cultures of children and parents from various U.S. ethnic and racial groups (African American, Hispanic, Irish American, Jewish, European American, Asian American). One way that I did this was to display posters on the wall that contained the words for colors, parts of the body, and numbers, written in all the native languages of parents in the class. All the children and parents enjoyed seeing this variety of languages.

Among other ways home culture was brought into the classroom: Chinese and Chinese American parents taught about the Moon Festival and Chinese New Year as well as how to make steamed dumplings, to stir-fry string beans, and to use chopsticks (with popcorn). They described what it was like to be a first and second grader in China. An African American mother taught about how her family celebrates Kwanzaa; an Indian parent taught about the Hindu Festival of Divali and demonstrated traditional dance. Jewish parents taught about Hanukkah and Passover, and an Irish American mother taught about how her family celebrated their Irish heritage with food and singing and learning about famous Irish Americans. Inviting parents to speak to the class about their families' celebrations of their cultures and religions had much more meaning than when I did it, even if I was describing my own family celebration. I encouraged parents to keep their descriptions of their holiday practices close to what the family did and why and to downplay religious aspects. I also made sure that either they or I stated clearly that different people have different beliefs and ways of celebrating those beliefs. I don't remember any objections to these parent presentations.

The following three stories further illustrate ways in which parents' cultural knowledge enhanced my teaching.

Sub-Saharan Africa: Samantha. Samantha Green had danced in Philadelphia in a nationally known African dance troupe. Even before she did that, she had begun to adopt many traditions from various African countries in her dress and her way of life. She eventually married a man from Ghana. She brought objects, her interests, and her expert knowledge of some cultures of sub-Saharan Africa to the children and me.

Her visits started when she asked if she could talk with the children about her work as a graphic designer. She talked about having wanted to be an artist since kindergarten. She showed them some of her drawings, stating that she especially liked to draw pictures that have African Americans and people from Africa in them. Our discussion of why she likes learning about people from Africa led to a discussion about the meaning of the word *ancestors*. Everyone in the class told from which continents or countries their ancestors had come to the United States.

When the children went to lunch, Samantha and I had some time to talk. Her daughter had not been in my class during first grade, but she knew from my newsletter to parents that I welcomed parents to join me in the classroom on a regular basis. We both felt that her first visit was very successful, and I invited her to follow up with more visits. I was delighted when she said she would come back once a week for the next few weeks. She offered to share some of her knowledge about culture in various regions of Africa, and, knowing that she was much more of an expert than I, I encouraged her to return as soon as she could.

As promised, Samantha brought artifacts from and about sub-Saharan Africa. Like a wonderful teacher, she had planned ahead of time. She brought a map of the continent and pointed to various countries: Nigeria, Ghana, Senegal, and Gambia. As she prepared to show the children photographs in a book about Ghana, she first reminded them, "Remember— no laughing at people's names, at their clothes, food, or the words of their language." It was obvious to me that she'd done this before. Anyone who works with children knows that they often laugh at or deride things that seem strange to them. Each photograph elicited talk about its contents. She explained that in Ghana the language spoken is called Chree, and she introduced some words. When Malik said, "These words are hard to say," Samantha told the children that as they practiced and learned the words, it would become easy. She showed them a picture of a funeral and taught them a dirge. Thien asked, "Are they sad that someone died?" And she replied, "African people believe that the person is just gone. They believe good things will happen to the person who died and that the soul will go to another place."

Samantha's lessons and knowledge made me want to know more and made me want to help the children to learn more. Here was a person (a parent) who could guide us in our studies. I was grateful. I began a list in my journal of some things that I needed so that we could do an extended and deeper study of aspects of various cultures on the African continent.

12/86, Journal

1. Find a good, large map of the African continent.
2. Choose from among the African sculpture the school purchased with money from our arts grant (currently in the storage room) [and] display the sculpture in the main classroom. With string, link photographs and sculptural objects to the place of origin on the map.
3. Ask the children to write captions for the photographs that will be hanging near the map.
4. Take advantage of Samantha's knowledge of various African dances, and see if she will help us with some sort of culminating activity or performance that I'm now thinking of doing later in the spring.
5. Talk to the teachers at Powel School who'd received funding for books and artifacts about aspects of African culture and about their experiences teaching about it to the children.
6. Collect and make available books containing tales and stories from various regions of sub-Saharan Africa. I have an excellent collection in my class library but the school's good collection could augment it.

During the year Samantha worked in the classroom, I had a student teacher, Gwen, who I felt could be responsible for carrying out the activities related to this theme. I knew that collaborating on curriculum with a parent would be an unusual experience for a student teacher. I knew that she was interested in drama, and I saw the potential for that in our work with Samantha. I supervised but left the details to Gwen and Samantha. Samantha led the way. She read tales from Ghana and Nigeria to the children during various visits. She and Gwen determined that the children would enact a story about Anansi the spider. The children and Samantha chose a mask from a book about African masks to re-create in papier mâché. Starting with newspaper and window screening, they made a large mask, painting the surface with gesso that Samantha sent from home. Samantha painted the mask, and the children glued beads, shells, and straw onto it. Each of the children used a balloon as a form and made a small mask to take home

The performance was more spectacular than any of my other classes ever did, previously or in ensuing years. I generally kept performances and culminating activities fairly low-key because in general I became tense when preparing elaborate performances and rehearsing them. Because of Samantha's guidance and help and the student teacher's efforts, I was able to stay reasonably calm. It was elaborate! We tie-dyed cloth for tunics and head wraps for the girls, and for daishikis for the boys. Samantha designed the simple patterns, and all the children sewed their clothing by hand. She taught the class several songs, both in Chree and in Swahili, to accompany dances that she choreographed. She invited a professional drummer, a friend, to accompany the children during the performance. Gwen supervised the performance of the story about Anansi, the mischievous spider. The children performed all of this for the K–1–2 assembly and for their parents. I certainly didn't have the expertise Samantha had as a visual artist, as a professional performer, or as someone with a deep interest in and knowledge about African heritage. We were fortunate that she wanted to share all of this with the children and me.

New languages and literature: Marya. Igor's mother, Marya, had been in the United States for only a few weeks when she began to help in the classroom. She was a graduate student in the school of education at a local university. Though her son was only beginning to speak English, Marya was fluent. As did most parents who volunteered, Marya worked with children both individually and in small groups at reading, writing, and playing games. But I also wanted to learn about Marya's and Igor's home language and culture, and I was certain the children would be interested in that, too. One day when Marya was in the classroom and Igor was teaching us some words in Serbo-Croatian, I asked the children, "Is it easier for Igor to learn English or for us to learn Serbo-Croatian?" Many of the children said it would be easier for him to learn English. Leslie agreed and said that's because English is easier. Penny said, "More children in this room speak English, so it will be easier for him to learn English." When Marya saw how interested the children were in learning her language, she offered to teach it in a more formal way. So on days that she helped, we always set aside time for a lesson in the Serbo-Croatian language. Marya taught us greetings and farewells as well as parts of our bodies (by playing Simon Says). She taught us children's songs, and poems by Yugoslavia's famous poet Dushko Radovic, and she translated the poems for us. She wrote color words in Cyrillic letters, which we added to our bulletin board of color words in many languages. She used Cyrillic letters to label a child's drawing of a person with the Serbo-Croatian words for parts of the body. Sometimes she just talked to us—saying sentences whose meanings were fairly obvious—and we were pleased when we understood her.

In her second year of working with the same group of children, Marya came with different ideas about what she wanted to do with them. She taught Easter egg dyeing the way she did it when she was a child in Belgrade. Although she continued to speak Serbo-Croatian to the children, she particularly wanted to read some classic English books to them—books she had loved as a child in translated versions. She started with the original versions of *Alice in Wonderland* and *Through the Looking Glass*. We worked through the difficult parts of the books, and the children loved them, looking forward to listening once a week. If the only reason for thinking of this as an excellent experience had been the number of math discussions the books led to (such as size and scale, bilateral symmetry, mirror images, quantity), it would have been enough to have made the experience outstanding. But the children grew to love the books—everyone, that is, except Tony, who said, "I liked it the *real* way I saw *Alice in Wonderland* on HBO." I told him that what Marya was reading was the *real* way, which led to a very interesting discussion about movies and TV shows made from books. When we were finished with *Alice*, Marya read Kipling's *Just So Stories*. Though the language is rhythmic and captivating, we had to watch for racism and stereotyping, and together, we either changed the stories slightly or addressed the issues raised. Those were books I never would have read to the children because I thought the language might seem unfamiliar or difficult, but they thoroughly enjoyed them. Marya showed me the way.

The Jewish New Year: Sandra. It was my 21st year of teaching in 1990, and I was new to a school where parents were not accustomed to working alongside teachers. They were, however, an active presence in the school. They volunteered and supported teachers in a great many other ways, including running a school store, holding various fund-raising events, and working in the office and library. In contrast, Martin's mother Sandra helped in my second-grade classroom once a week.

Sandra asked if it would be all right if she brought some objects and told the children about the Jewish holidays of Rosh Hashanah and Yom Kippur, which comprise the Jewish New Year. School would soon be closed for 3 days. I always explained the various cultural and patriotic reasons for school closings because I felt that sometimes reasons for holidays were mysterious to my young students. Whenever possible, I preferred parents to explain what these holidays meant to them.

Sandra and I met to plan; in this case, planning consisted merely of her telling me what she'd bring and outlining what she would say, and my offering to buy any food she needed. I let her know that sometimes during her presentation I might interrupt to be sure the children understood a point she was trying to make. I also wanted to be sure that she would tell the children that she would be describing her own beliefs and that she should acknowledge that some of them might have different beliefs.

I was pleased the next day when not only Sandra but also her mother, Mrs. Weinstein, arrived, carrying shopping bags. "I've come to talk to you about Jewish holidays—the New Year holiday," she said. One of the children spoke out, "I have Jewish holidays."

Sandra told the children, "Jewish people have 10 days to think about whether or not they've been good, to apologize to people whose feelings they've hurt. There's supposed to be a book where it's written whether you've been good or not, and that book is closed after these 10 days." We also talked about what a synagogue is (a word Sandra had used) and what the phrase *New Year* means. We spent some time talking about how people of other cultures celebrate the New Year.

She said, "You know, my favorite subject is food. I just love to eat. And when we Jewish people celebrate our holidays, we eat foods special for each holiday. Martin's grandmother and I have brought some food things to show you and to eat." And as she spoke about each item, she pulled it out of the shopping bags. First came apples and honey. She explained, "We eat apples and honey because they are sweet, and if you eat them you're supposed to have a sweet year. There's a special bread that Jewish people eat on Friday nights called challah." She took a braided loaf out of her shopping bag, saying that for the New Year Jewish people eat a round challah to make them think of the whole year 'round. Sometimes that challah even has raisins mixed in. She showed the children a picture of a round one.

"Many people eat fish that's made a special way—chopped, then shaped into oval pieces and cooked with carrots and onions. It's called gefilte fish, and we eat it at other holidays, too." She showed the children the wooden bowl and *hoch messer* (chopper), along with the large pot her bubi used for making this special chopped fish. She told us that the recipe she uses has been in her family for about 100 years.

Sandra pulled one more thing from her shopping bags. It was a shofar, made from the horn of a ram. She demonstrated how to make a sound by blowing into the narrow end, similar to making a sound on a trumpet. "The horn has to be curved," she told us. "They blow it in the synagogue just about the time that book of the year is closed—you know, the book I was telling you about where it is written whether you were good or bad."

After Sandra finished speaking, she and her mother stayed to help the children cut the apples into quarters to prepare for dipping them into honey. I posed two math problems for the children: (1) "If you cut an apple into halves, how many pieces would you have? What about cutting it into quarters? How many pieces all together?" (2) "I brought 15 apples. If we cut them in half, how many pieces will we have?" Project Time followed the discussion, and the children took turns cutting the apples using real knives, supervised by Martin's mother and grandmother.[3]

After we cleaned up, the children sat in their places at the tables and we adults joined them. We waited until everyone was ready and holding hands around the table. We thanked Sandra and her mother for teaching us about the Jewish New Year. And then we sang the song we always sang when we sat down to eat together. Years ago at the Parent Cooperative Nursery, a parent had liberally translated a Hebrew song, *heenay ma-tov oo ma-na-yeem shevet achim gam yachad* into the words: "Oh how very nice it is to sit and eat with friends."

Another Set of Observant Eyes

Parents would bring another set of eyes into the classroom, but from a perspective different from mine. Listening and seeing from a parent's point of view would teach me valuable things. Gayle, whose three children I taught, worked alongside me for 5 years, usually one or two mornings a week. Once, I remarked to her about how purposefully the children were working at writing/reading time. She said, "What I notice is the caring feeling that the children have for one another." As a teacher I was very hard on myself, so it was always helpful when a parent told me that the behavior I valued was actually happening or that a lesson they had observed while helping in the room or had heard about from their children was an effective one.

In 1990 I found myself having difficulty with some of the children in my new class. I felt a little better when I learned that a previous teacher had had difficulty with many of the same children. I didn't see that as an excuse to give up. Mr. Hadley, Malcolm's father, came to tell me that his son had lost his homework book, to complain about the homework I'd given (lack of clarity in the directions), and to say how concerned he was that his son was being teased. He decided to stay that day to help while the art teacher was in the room during my planning time. It was always difficult for the art teacher to handle the children on her own, and I usually stayed and worked in the back of the room rather than work elsewhere and return to chaos and very unhappy children. Mr. Hadley resolved to help the art teacher every week. One day when I did leave the room for a few minutes, I came back in time to hear and see Dontay yelling that Jordan had been bothering him. I tried to stop him from yelling. Mr. Hadley, who *had* seen the whole thing, intervened on Dontay's behalf. He told me that while I was gone, Jimmy had been constantly needling Dontay, that Jordan and Walter had been running around cursing. The art teacher had been unable to stop them. Mr. Hadley offered to work with the three boys so that the art teacher could work with the rest of the class. When I spoke with Mr. Hadley later, I told him that Dontay often got into trouble because his loud voice always drew my attention. For that reason, I was grateful for his observation.

Seeing Children Learning

Mrs. Carson had been coming to the class one afternoon a week. At around the same time she wrote a letter to the superintendent of schools (see Chapter 2), she wrote this one to me, letting me know that she could see that her daughter was learning.

2/22/84, Note

Dear Mrs. Strieb
    I am really amaze with my daughter learning process. Charlene was cover her words and breaking down the spelling of words she didn't know. I am over joyed by her reading the song of Harriet Tubman. You make a parent like me appreciate a oustand teacher such as you. You are an asses to the public school of Phila. I thank God that Charlene had an opportunity to have you.
    I have been working 8 hrs for the pass month and on Saturday for the pass 2 weeks. So our library day has stop and I can't come in for at least one more week. Then, I'll be back to normal. Maybe soon I'll have a phone. But, you can still reach me between 6 a.m. to 10 a.m. at work, [number] or write.
    Thank you
    Hattie Carson

    P.S. I'm sending a ck to the library for a loss book!

Parents Learn, Too

At times as a young parent, I had used Peggy Perlmutter Stone's words and actions as a model for relating to my own children. Perhaps parents of the children I taught would do the same with my words.

MY NEWSLETTER: AN INVITATION
TO WORK IN THE CLASSROOM

In addition to inviting parents to let me know their concerns (see Chapter 2), the newsletter was also the place where I invited parents to be an on-going presence in the classroom; to teach the children alongside me; to help me in other ways; to be an occasional presence (for trips and celebrations); to contribute from home; to bring children's siblings to the classroom; to visit, stop by, or drop in; to send things to school with their children or to bring things themselves. My newsletters to parents were my invitation to them to enter into the school lives of their children, both in school and at home, and to offer their own ideas.

I wanted the parents to know that I was sincere about inviting them to join me, so I gave specific examples of what they might do and actually did to help, both at home and at school. I also included their suggestions and comments. More important, when parents helped in any way, I thanked them in the newsletter for each thing they did. This recognition served two purposes: It let them know that I valued what they were doing for the children and for me and, more important, it gave other parents ideas for things they could do to become involved in the life of the school with their children. It was an attempt to give parents inspiration, encouragement, and an invitation to join in. It also told parents why I invited certain kinds of help.

10/25/98, Newsletter

A GREAT BIG THANK YOU to all of you parents and volunteers who have helped in the classroom:

Tina, Harriet's mom, has been in with Roman every Wednesday. We observed and described the baby and have talked about the important things a parent does to make the baby safe and comfortable. Roman is a most pleasant baby, which makes it possible for Tina to also work with the children. She helps with homework, she works with children who need extra help with reading.

Gayle, Johnny's mom, has worked with the class during formal lessons. She will be working with children at Project Time, playing games, reviewing work, hearing children read.

Debbie, Mark's mom, has listened to children read their own stories and other books. Mark's dad, Burt, has delivered two rugs to our classroom. He and Debbie donated the rug in the class library which makes our meeting times so much more comfortable. He delivered the one for the block corner. We haven't been able to use blocks because it would have been too noisy without a rug. Now we can.

Gene, Peter's cousin and guardian, volunteers when he can. He is studying at Community College and wants to learn all he can about teaching. He is a wonderful young man who hears children read and talks to them about their behavior. He went on the farm trip with us. Whenever he comes, we really enjoy it.

The night of the Parents' Meeting, Albert Carroll's parents came early and helped me set up the food.

Miriam Snyder's mom found us a praying mantis and brought it to school.

Esther Benton's mom went on the trip to the farm.

AND OF COURSE. . . . Teacher Kathryn has been in most Monday and Thursday mornings. She does so many things for the children and me. She works on homework, files papers, and most important, helps the children with writing and reading. She's been doing this for about five years, so she's quite experienced. She notices a lot of things about the children, and tells me about them. That really helps. She is also another sympathetic ear for them. The children LOVE Teacher Kathryn.[4]

WE ARE VERY GRATEFUL FOR OUR IN-CLASS VOLUN-TEERS! WE ARE ALSO GRATEFUL FOR THE PARENTS WHO HELP US WITH SUGGESTIONS AND COMMENTS AND FOR THE GIFTS YOU'VE GIVEN THE CLASS. THE CHILDREN GAIN MORE BE-CAUSE OF YOU.

Assumptions underlay my inviting parents to work alongside me in the classroom. I assumed that parents had the right to see firsthand what their children were learning, what and how the teacher was teaching. Though parents and children who were unable or reluctant to work in the classroom might be unhappy, I assumed that the value of having parents participate in a variety of ways and my mentioning their contributions in newsletters overshadowed possible bad feelings.

PREPARING TO WORK TOGETHER

I taught in five schools. Some teachers with whom I taught were not enthusiastic about inviting parents into the classroom to work alongside them with the children. When considering inviting parents into classrooms, it is important to address teacher concerns. Here are some of the concerns I heard from teachers: Parents might not be well educated enough. They might become anxious or upset if they saw that their child wasn't performing as well as another child or as well as they thought he should. Parents might pay too much attention to their own children, and if they did, others would be jealous of that special attention. A child might be unhappy if her parents were unable to help in the classroom. Parents might think that teachers want to have help from parents because they are unable to do the job on their own. Furthermore, if parents are good enough to teach children, they might ask why teachers are even necessary.

Teachers expressed concern about matters of trust. They were afraid that a parent in the classroom might become a "spy," spread rumors in the community, or tell half-truths about what went on in the classroom. That would be divisive rather than supportive of the teacher. Teachers wanted to trust that parents wouldn't question their practice and wouldn't ask them to justify and explain it. Finally, teachers weren't sure they could trust parents to maintain confidentiality with regard to what they learned about individual children and what they observed.

These concerns are not unjustified. Working with parents in the classroom, inviting parents to join in the teaching, does take trust—trust in oneself as a teacher as well as trust that the parent is there to support both the teacher and the children. Yet during my years of teaching, I saw that some of that mistrust could be avoided by frank talk with parents.

I learned the importance of setting ground rules when parents came into the classroom. I could not assume that they knew what to do or knew what I would want them to do. I let parent volunteers know that I would never ask them to do work that I wouldn't do myself. I could not assume they knew about confidentiality, so I explained what was required in that regard. Though I loved when a parent or volunteer took the initiative and did what needed to be done, more often parents wanted me to give them guidance. This was not always easy for me to do, but I learned. Ground rules were: Refer questions or complaints to me; don't speak about individual children outside the classroom; please don't talk with other teachers about me or what went on in the classroom; you're here to work with all the children, not just your child.

In formal programs like the Parent Scholar program of Follow Through, parents were given "training" by that program's managers. In some school districts, all volunteers were expected to go through "training" sessions. I wouldn't call the way parents and I prepared to work together "training," but it was important to establish a common understanding. We usually talked together first about what work I believed needed to be done, and then what work that parent would be comfortable doing, including interests and talents. In addition, I had some special ways of working with children, and it was important to me that parent volunteers get to know them. I used several procedures to show parents how they could work with the children and with me. Often I showed them to all parents, volunteers or not, so that they would know how to help children at school and their own children at home. If parents decided to work in the classroom, I would be pleased, but that was not the primary reason for my carrying out this orientation.

My Newsletter

The newsletter was my first vehicle to let families know the ways in which I worked with the children, to give them examples of the things parents did when they worked in the room, and to describe ways in which they could help their children at home.

Parents' Meetings

Parents' meetings were another occasion where they learned about what they could do in the classroom and how they could do it. I took advantage of the Back to School Night for parents at the beginning of the year to describe the classroom. However, I didn't think that was enough because these evenings were always rushed. At our school there were two 45-minute meetings with two different groups of parents. We expected delays because parents had trouble finding classrooms. Parents walked in and out because they had more than two children in the school. Some parents wanted to have individual conferences with the teacher. Sometimes the principal gave us material to cover with the parents that night, which further decreased my time to explain my classroom to them. And sometimes I found those nights good for only an introduction to what I was doing with the children—a rundown of the schedule with brief descriptions of each activity—and for parents to ask questions about issues that concerned them.

At those required meetings, I always invited parents to think about helping in the classroom. There was never enough time to give them the practice they might need to help effectively. As a result, I began to hold additional get-togethers for parents both during the school day and at night in parents' homes. These gatherings gave us more time to explore what the children and I were doing. I tried to hold them regularly throughout the year. My thinking was that for those parents who were interested in working with the children, such meetings would help them feel more comfortable about offering their help. Here is an example of the invitation I sent home to parents:

9/21/76, Note

Dear Parents,
    At the beginning of each year I like to invite all parents to a meeting to discuss your goals and mine for our children. I also like to let you know some of the things we will be doing in the classroom in case you'd like to help the children and me.

There are usually two meetings: one during the day and one at night for people who work outside the home.

The day meeting will take place at 8:45–10:00 (just come inside with your child) and we will serve breakfast.

The night meeting will be at 8:00 and we will serve dessert.

If you would be willing to let us use your house for the evening meeting, please check below.

Please send the bottom of this letter back.

I hope we can get together next week. I'll let you know the exact date by Friday.

Please try to come. We'd love to meet you!

Sincerely,

L Strieb

At the meetings, I not only gave parents some sense of how a school day went and what and how I taught, but as an introduction, I also taught them some of the games I'd want them to play with the children and modeled some of the ways in which I taught the children.

10/2/81, Journal

At the parents' meeting I talked once again about the curriculum, through telling about the schedule. Then I taught several math games (Guess My Number, Guess My Rule, Vector Tic-Tac-Toe.) Adults and children played together. It was a nice feeling. Belinda's mother felt it was a good meeting, since it gave the parents insights into how I teach.

During several years of team teaching, my teammate and I prepared for parents' meetings together.[5] We held two workshops during which parents participated in an after-school example of our Project Time. We modeled some of the ways in which we taught children. We set out many of the materials used at Project Time. We gave them written directions for how to use materials such as the binocular stereoscopic microscope; classroom creatures; and construction materials like blocks, math games, marble track, and Lego. We listed questions they could ask the children. We knew that if the parents learned to play the games and were given questions they might ask the children, it would make their entry into helping easier for them and for us. At those workshops, I especially enjoyed watching parents sitting on the floor in the classroom trying to create structures as complex as those their children had made with the wooden marble track blocks.

Shadowing Me

A third way I tried to help prepare parents for helping the children was to have them shadow me as I worked with the children during the school day. I modeled as I helped children with writing, reading, playing math games, and cooking. For example, I invited parents who volunteered to help children with writing to observe writing workshops. They sat in on my conferences with individual children. I had particular ways of speaking with the children, of helping them to spell words, of helping them toward independence, and I wanted to be sure the parents understood what I did and why. For writing conferences I usually sat in a chair with a child seated to my left. I asked the volunteer to sit to the left and slightly behind the child so that she could see and hear everything that was going on. I did this for one or two visits or until both the parent and I felt ready for her to take over. Then I monitored the parent–child conferences until we both felt that the parent could hold conferences on her own.

Posters on the Wall

I listed questions parents could ask the children when working with them (for example, on writing) or suggestions they might give to the children for stories.

DIFFICULT TIMES

Working with parents in the classroom takes some flexibility, the ability to observe what's happening and to change course if it seems necessary. It takes an openness or willingness to engage in a back-and-forth, ongoing conversation with parents in which the teacher sometimes admits (at least to herself) to not knowing everything and is open to the ideas, observations, and suggestions of others. When that happens, when both parents and teacher are pleased with the situation, the children will benefit from the richness that is the usual result.

But even though I enthusiastically welcomed parents into the classroom, occasionally tensions arose between my expectations and parents' efforts, making it necessary to constantly work on them. There were times when I resolved these tensions in favor of the parents' view and times when my perspective prevailed. The goal was, of course, to attain a shared vision of what classroom experiences should prevail.

Inviting parents into the classroom means that a teacher sometimes relaxes control and keeps quiet even if things are not always as she wishes they would be. Knowing when to intervene and when to wait can be tricky. There were times when I found it difficult having parents in the classroom, though those times were actually quite rare. In any given year, it helped to remind myself of past times that were difficult and then use those examples to aid me when preparing to work with a new group of parents.

Unreliable Parents: The Case of the Gingerbread Sleighs

It was hard for me when parents didn't follow through (came late, didn't complete what they started, left early).

One of the winter traditions of my teaching from the 1970s until I retired in 2000 was to cook, construct, and decorate a gingerbread cookie house with the children. I did not involve parents in this cooking project. Each day of the first week in December, we worked on that house. Each step of its creation led to several math, social studies, reading, or literature lessons, and over the years I'd developed and shared a "gingerbread house curriculum" with parents and other teachers. When the house was complete, I covered it with plastic wrap and displayed it in a prominent place in the classroom. During December report card conferences, the children were always excited to show the house to their parents and to respond to their questions about its construction.

On the day before winter break, we always invited the principal to our classroom to demolish the house. Parents visited the room that afternoon just to observe this ritual. After the principal had everyone laughing with his dramatic antics and broke the house into many small pieces with a baseball bat, parents filled plastic bags with pieces of the house for each child. As the children left the room for vacation, I handed each one of them a large piece of the house that had been important to building community. It was a beloved activity.

At the beginning of the 1991–1992 school year, in response to my invitation to parents to work with the children, Daniel's mother, Kassie, offered to help make an entire gingerbread village, adding that she was a professional cake decorator. I believed that her contribution would add a rich layer to our tradition and to the educational benefits that always come from cooking. Unfortunately, I didn't think through the details of the activity and this offer to help.

When the time for building the village finally came, I was not sure I wanted it to happen, partly because it would take a lot of time and partly because I selfishly didn't want my gingerbread house to be overshadowed. But I had agreed to the project and promised to pay for all the ingredients. About a week before we were to begin, Kassie approached me again, this time to say she'd reconsidered and felt that we should make gingerbread sleighs instead of a village. She said she had made them the previous year in her son's class. She said she would make the five pattern pieces out of paper and would come to the classroom to help each child cut the patterns and the gingerbread sleigh parts.

To save time, I made the dough for the sleighs at home (the same dough as the dough for the gingerbread house), but as soon as another parent had helped the children trace the cookie pieces from the paper patterns, I realized that it would take much more time than I'd allotted for each child to do that task—and that I'd have to mix at least three more batches of dough to complete the sleighs.

After five days of working on this, I wrote in my journal.

12/11/81, Journal

These gingerbread sleighs are driving me crazy! This project will never again be done in *my* class. There are way too many pieces for thirty-three children to put together. I was trying to be supportive to a parent but I just wasn't thinking.

The worst part was that Kassie came in to help only one afternoon. She cut sleighs with only six children, had to leave early, and never returned. After that, Maddie (the classroom assistant), Bobbie (the Parent Scholar), and I did the work Kassie had promised to do. Though I wanted to stop making the sleighs, once we had started and the promise had been made, I had to be sure there would be one sleigh for each child.

What were the problems with this project? The ingredients became costly. The adults had to do the work for the children. It took too much time in general and too much time away from other teaching.

12/16/81, Journal

Sometimes a parent's help is a mixed blessing. I'll have to pay closer attention to the projects I agree to let parents start in the room. I must give more thought to those suggested by parents, and must be strong enough to do things on my own terms. . . . Next year I think I'll stick to my own traditions.

In years that followed, I didn't stop inviting parents to initiate projects with the children. I just made sure that I understood exactly what the parent wanted to do, exactly what the educational benefits might be, exactly what materials would be needed, and exactly how much time it would take. I also tried to be sure that the parent had demonstrated herself to be reliable, someone who could be counted on to complete a project. I'd wanted to welcome Kassie, to support her taking the initiative. I do not blame Kassie. I could have changed my usual plans for the gingerbread house, but didn't want to. I continued making gingerbread houses in December until my final year of teaching.

A Change in Routine

I sometimes found it difficult to have parents in the classroom when it meant a break from the routine or a change in (my) plans. I believed that consistency of routine was essential for calm children and calm classrooms. One afternoon Mr. Norman, Mark's father, arrived in the office at 2:15, wanting to come up to the classroom. He'd brought his 3-year-old son with him. I told the secretary that I wouldn't be able to speak with him until after I'd dismissed the children at 2:45. Mr. Norman still insisted on coming up and waiting outside the classroom.

After I'd accompanied the children to the door downstairs, we sat down for a talk. He said he would be coming to the classroom at the end of every day to pick Mark up. I told Mr. Norman that parents were really expected to meet their children outside in the schoolyard, but he insisted that he would pick Mark up in the classroom.

He told me he was very concerned about Mark's behavior and would like a behavior report every day. Some parents liked written behavior reports, which I often had trouble remembering to complete. I told him I hoped he would accept a verbal report. The end of the day was the most difficult time for me. Everything seemed a rush and, in the rush, I often had trouble completing these written reports. I agreed to let him come to the room 15 minutes before dismissal time if, in return, he would help the children prepare for dismissal. I told him that at that time I would give him a verbal report on Mark. I didn't tell him how concerned I was that bringing Mark's toddler brother with him at this difficult time of day might be too much of a distraction for the children and for him.

Though I managed to give Mr. Norman verbal reports on Mark's behavior, as I'd expected, his younger son required a good deal of his time, the children in the class were distracted from getting ready to go home by the small child's antics, and Mr. Norman rarely helped them prepare to leave. I would not have minded the toddler's visit had it come at a calmer time during the day.

There were times when parents dropped in to visit. It was important to distinguish between visits to talk with me about their child (not acceptable when children were in the classroom and I was teaching) and visits to help the children and me. Sometimes parents wanted to help but hadn't arranged to do so ahead of time. Sometimes they wanted to bring something to show the children and had forgotten to let me know. Usually when I received a call from the office announcing a parent's presence, I told the secretary to send the parent up, unless the purpose of the visit was to have a personal discussion about a child. In that case I'd set up an appointment to meet during my planning time or before or after school.

If I thought such a drop-in visit would be good for the parent, his child, and the class, I'd adjust to it. I didn't like to refuse a visit even if it meant stopping in the midst of what we were doing. Never wanting to miss a "teachable moment," I'd allow it. Spontaneous visits often happened when a parent came in with a younger sibling, as Tonya's mom did one day, and we interrupted what I'd planned so that we could observe the baby. Though I don't think parents took undue advantage of my flexibility and willingness to interrupt what we were doing, it was never easy to make the transition from what we were doing to what the parents needed.

When We Disagreed

It was hard for me if a parent did things in ways contrary to how I thought they should be done. I was responsible for the well-being of the children and for their learning. I have to admit that I, like most teachers, had certain procedures for working with children at certain tasks. I knew there might be other ways, but as the classroom teacher, I had to be comfortable that what the adults did with the children was at least consistent with my way.

Doing things her own way: Mrs. Case. Occasionally, but rarely, a parent would try to take charge in a way that was unacceptable to me. When that happened, I usually felt that I'd failed at letting her know the limits of her help. I once wrote in my journal, "What should I do when a parent's help contradicts what I want the children to do?"

Mrs. Case had been helping me since the first day of school. I had a set routine for helping children to spell words when they wrote. Before going to an adult for help, I wanted them to try to say the sounds of the letters as they tried to spell, and to write these down. I told them that if they weren't sure of a spelling, after they wrote their try they could circle the word. That way, the adult who had a conference with them would know they had tried their hardest. Mrs. Case could not get used to this system. Furthermore, she was upset with the developmental spelling.

One day as the children were writing, Mrs. Case turned out the lights (which I sometimes did to get the children's attention, but which parents never did), walked to the front of the room, pointed to the alphabet with a pointer, and directed all the children to say the words that named some pictures. She then told them to find letters by saying the alphabet as she pointed to the letters until they came to the one they needed, in this case *t*. That's not a bad way to help beginners to match letter names with letter sounds, though it's tedious. But then she said, "For example, if you want to spell the word *this*, you know it starts with a *t*, so you look until you find it and write it down." Well, that wasn't such a good example. Children know that *top* starts with *t*, but unless they've been taught that *this* starts with *t*, they wouldn't know that. *This* doesn't start with the same sound as *top*.

When she became frustrated with developmental spellings, she began to spell words for the children, allowing them to write as she spelled. This was contrary to my way of encouraging them toward independence by "sounding out." The result was that many children gave up trying and continually asked adults to spell for them.

She was also disturbed by what she called the messiness of the handwriting of these beginning writers, so she began to draw lines in their unlined drawing–writing books, which I didn't do until the children's fingers were stronger and they could write within or on the lines. After she did that, many children refused to write without drawing lines first. For example, Mrs. Case's own child, who had begun to write independently, stopped trying to write new words altogether and would only copy sentences that she first dictated to an adult on lines that she took a great deal of time to draw with a ruler.

I spoke with Mrs. Case. I explained to her my reasons for teaching as I did. I also told her how important it was to ask me before she tried something new. It was an uncomfortable discussion, but after it she worked at paying more attention to my directions to the children about writing and spelling. Little by little, with my insistence that her own daughter was able to and should try to spell independently with various supports (word wall, picture dictionary, personal word list), her child went back to writing sentences on her own.

Causing noise: Mrs. Tredwell. It was school policy to allow parents of children in early grades to celebrate their children's birthdays in school if the teacher agreed. I always gave permission to do that. The following incident happened at a birthday party during my first week in a new school. I didn't know that elaborate parties were part of that school's culture or I might have handled things differently.

9/15/90, Journal

Aaron's mom brought a birthday party for Aaron today. It was WILD! . . . I don't mind a cupcake or some cookies or a piece of cake or fruit for each child, but this was much more. Mrs. Tredwell arrived when the children were at science class, during my planning time. I had to talk to another parent on the telephone about a problem with her son, so I had to leave the room. I left thinking Mrs. Tredwell would know that she should prepare the classroom by setting up the party while I was out, but she'd done none of that. When I returned, the spelling papers and homework books were still on the desks and none of the party things were distributed. I asked her to do that while I went to pick up the children.

When I returned with the class and sent them to their seats, I noticed that ten places were missing plates, hats, and cups. Chaos ensued. That was the first exciting thing that happened. Mrs. Tredwell *loves* kids, but, because she's not worked with younger ones, she doesn't know how to keep things calm. She talked loudly and constantly; she had kids getting up and down; she moved all around the room as she talked, but didn't help me to stop kids from getting up and walking around. It seemed to me that as I got one child seated, another would pop up. She gave them whistles as a take-home party favor. WHISTLES! IN SCHOOL! In an open-space classroom connected to another class with no wall in between! It was really noisy and horrible. Yet no one got hurt, the children were good-natured and courteous to one another. I just stood there, embarrassed, worrying about the class next door, momentarily unable to get them quiet.

After the children went home, while Mrs. Tredwell and I were straightening up the classroom and talking about the party, I joked with her a little about how inappropriate her choice of party favors was because they added noise to an already noisy setting. We laughed as she apologized. I'm sure she'll never do something like that again.

Unhappiness with My Own Teaching

It was hard when I was unhappy with my own behavior or my own teaching, and the parents were witnesses to those times. Those times made me uncomfortable, and they were many. It was always easy to write about the bad times. They stood out. I often wrote in my journal, "I was embarrassed that the room was so messy—messier than I can remember a room of mine being for a long time."

The following story illustrates a time when I was unhappy with my teaching and a parent witnessed my tension about it. Abdul Khalifa was a student from Malaysia who began attending our school in January, while his father was a graduate student. Though Abdul spoke some English, he was not fluent. His mother, aware of American customs and those of our school from having volunteered weekly in the classroom for a month, arrived one February day with a birthday cake and other refreshments for a party. I noted in my journal: "I was embarrassed at what she witnessed."

Her son took a book from Jimmy, and Jimmy got angry and started to yell. Dontay entered the argument. Abdul elbowed one of them, and Dontay wouldn't stop yelling at him about it, even when I reminded him that he'd punched Abdul in the eye the day before. With some humor I wrote, "It was loud and awful, but a rich language experience for Abdul."

In addition to the fight, as I looked around the room, I noticed that there were papers everywhere, on every surface, and they seemed to have no order to them. And, finally, to make matters worse, before the party I gave out calculators for a lesson for the first time, forgetting to set some ground rules (which I usually do when I introduce a new material) and forgetting to count them. When I first collected them, six were missing. In the end, I had to say, "No party until we find those calculators" (words I hate saying). Two calculators were never returned. But yes, there was a party.

I noted in my journal that it took forever to prepare for the party and Mrs. Khalifa was watching. Yet again, I'd failed to prepare ahead of time and she'd forgotten to bring either matches or a knife, so the children had to wait until I'd asked another teacher for both. Understandably, the children became quite restless while they waited. Finally the party happened and it was lovely. Before we had a chance to sing, Abdul blew out the candles. The children were stunned. His mom explained that in their country that's what they do.

Many of the children had spent all of Project Time drawing birthday greetings to Abdul on the board and making him cards and messages. Flora and someone else saved food from their lunches and gave it to him as a little present. I found it very thoughtful, touching, and supportive. It was their idea and they carried it out beautifully.

In spite of the lovely party, I told Mrs. Khalifa that if, after all the mess, noise, and fighting, she wanted to speak to the principal about removing her son from my class, I would certainly understand. She replied, "I want you to teach him. I want him in this class." I felt good about that because, in addition to the noise and the fighting, she must have noticed the other positive things that happened.

When a Parent Seemed Unhappy

A Parent Scholar once said she was surprised that the children in my class seemed far behind those in her daughter's class. For example, by the middle of October, when she told me this, her daughter's class had already been taught how to write the whole alphabet. (It seems very strange to be writing this now because children are now supposed to be able to do that in kindergarten.) And her daughter's class had not only one sheet of dittoed, written homework but also several sheets of math problems, including fractions. I said calmly (though I was uncomfortable), "Well, not all teachers teach in the same way. I start kind of slowly. But my students usually end up doing as well as the others." Interestingly, I noted in my journal at the same time that this Parent Scholar really paid attention to the children when she worked with them and then told me her observations. I found her descriptions to be both accurate and helpful. So for me, her criticism was tempered by her helpfulness.

In spite of the time and effort it took to prepare parents to work alongside me, in spite of my embarrassment about my own teaching, in spite of the fact that some parents were unable to participate, throughout my teaching life, the richness parents brought to the children and me when they worked alongside me overcame those difficulties.

WHEN PARENTS DON'T ENTER THE CLASSROOM

When I started teaching full time in 1970, I quickly realized that I couldn't expect all parents to join me in the classroom. Many parents were unable to spend time in their children's classrooms. They worked full time and many couldn't take time off, even for report card conference, because they'd lose precious pay. Some parents didn't want to spend time in their children's classrooms. They worried that their children would be too "clingy" or would behave in a way that would embarrass both parent and child.[6] There were other reasons parents didn't help in the classroom. Some parents were too busy with small children and the many tasks in their homes; others felt that they had no contribution to make; others had had terrible school experiences as children and didn't want to have anything to do with schools; still others believed that there was no need for parents in the classroom—that it's the teacher's job to teach, not theirs.

I know that some children felt sad when they saw others' parents helping but not their own. However, I decided early in my teaching that the benefits gained from the presence of parents in the room, benefits to many of the very children whose parents couldn't come in, made it worth doing. I always spoke to the class about the reasons some parents were unable to work in the room and the children appeared, without exception, to be accepting. I was determined to not only "keep the door open" for parents but also to actively invite them in.

❧ 6 ❧

Bringing Home into School:
Parent Work in the Classroom

I owe a great debt to the many parents who worked in my classrooms. The ways in which parents can contribute to children and teachers are many and varied, and for as many parents who want to work in classrooms, and teachers who invite them in, there are that many possibilities. (For a list of everything parents did, see Appendix H.) No 2 years are the same when it comes to either children or parents. Some parents are more vivid in my journals and in my memory. The stories that follow are examples of the contributions parents made to the children and me. They describe parents who did a variety of tasks, anything that needed to be done; parents who sent things to school with their children; and parents who brought their knowledge, their babies, and their interests to school to enhance the curriculum. They stand for many others for whose stories there is not enough space.

DOING WHAT NEEDED TO BE DONE

The first group of parents worked in my classroom in a variety of ways over time. Bobbie stands out because she came every day and stayed all day. Most parents who helped came one or two mornings a week.

Every Day, All Day: Bobbie

Early on, I needed and encouraged parents to work in the classroom with me, even when I had a part-time classroom assistant. Bobbie was unusual because she wanted to be there every day. Bobbie's niece Maria was in my class; her own son had special needs and attended another school. Bobbie began working at the school as a Parent Scholar (see Chapter 5). She started in January 1980 in the classroom of a colleague with whom I shared a four-room pod. After she completed her 10 weeks as a Parent Scholar, she continued to volunteer for the rest of the term for all four of us. During that time, she managed to complete all the filing of my students' work and helped me with my school records. She also cooked with the children. We teachers were so grateful for Bobbie's help that in June we celebrated her birthday with her sister Thalia's help. On the day of the party, Bobbie's sister and son joined us. We combined the four classes and, though it was crowded, we had a wonderful time consuming cake, Jell-O, and punch as well as singing songs. Some of the children made speeches and gave Bobbie cards they had made.

Bobbie knew she wanted to do another stint as a Parent Scholar, but because Parent Scholars could not work consecutive terms, she had to wait until the next winter's round to do it. The following December, she requested to work with me as a Parent Scholar. Because I didn't have many children eligible for Title I services, I wasn't sure it would happen. One day in December, we were talking, and I told her that she might not be able to work with me. She said, "That's okay. I'll come right back here every day when I'm finished with my class. This is an education for me. I've learned so much. People notice how much my son has changed since I've been working here at Kelly." I said, "That's what this program is all about. I wasn't a Parent Scholar, but when my kids were little and in the Westside Parent Cooperative Nursery, I found I was learning so much that I used to stay every day and help after I dropped my son off, just like you do."

During the time Bobbie worked with me, she spent most of the time with the children. (For a complete list of Bobbie's contributions, see Appendix I.) At Writing Time, once Bobbie had shadowed me for a few days, she held conferences with the children. She also helped them prepare their published books for the class library, hearing what they wrote, helping them glue their drawings into their books, stapling pages together. On one occasion she helped the children collate and staple pages for a whole-class book to be sent home with the final report cards of the year.

At Reading Time, again after observing me, Bobbie listened to individual children or small groups of children read, helped children who were designated to receive Title I services in a variety of ways, helped children find books they needed for their studies (for example, finding a book in which a child could identify an insect she'd brought to school). She helped the children keep books in order on the shelves, and she repaired torn books. She also color-coded books with adhesive tape according to topic and reading difficulty. During the 1981–1982 school year, to meet the interests many children had in setting up a "real" lending library, Bobbie helped them do exactly that. Within a few weeks after she started, card pockets were pasted into the books, each book had its own card to be signed upon removal from the room, and the library had official date stamps and a storage box for signed book cards. Children took turns working at their circulation desk. This was truly the children's own library; they participated in every step of its creation, with Bobbie's support. Here is an entry from a newsletter to parents.

5/5/82, Newsletter

A large number of children have made a lending library where there were already thousands of books on shelves in the alcove. They cleaned it and organized it, asking me to please move my junk. Now Bobbie is helping them to put pockets and cards in the books. Soon, children will be on duty and the books will circulate. It's been interesting to see the children start this activity them-selves. They needed adult help, however, to organize the circula-tion of the books, and Bobbie's given that.

At Project Time Bobbie and I did many of the same things with the children, supporting them in their choices by providing materials, help-ing them when they needed help with their projects, such as sewing, weaving, and art activities. We played math games and cooked with small groups. The children often held and cared for the animals and insects we kept in the class. Though she never liked touching them, Bobbie did enjoy observing them in their various cages and discussing them with the chil-dren. If she felt too much time had passed since I'd last fed them, she re-minded me that it was time. In addition to keeping the paints and clay in good, clean, neat working order and supervising cleanup of the art area, Bobbie joined the children in working with clay. And she suffered with them when her work was destroyed. She had made a clay pitcher and somehow it had broken. At a class meeting during which I devoted time to a discussion of caring for the clay objects that had been set on the shelf to dry, I asked Bobbie to talk about her broken pitcher with the children. She held the pitcher up and the children understood. I reminded them that this drying clay is delicate and that they must not touch pieces that are on the shelves "even if they belong to you."

At Math Time Bobbie helped children to do their practice worksheets, played math games with them, and marked math papers for me. She alerted me to children who were having difficulty.

Occasionally at Story/Discussion Time, Bobbie joined the discussions. When we observed insects and natural objects, she (as did I) described along with the children. When we discussed African American history and the civil rights movement, she contributed a great deal of personal experience. At other times, when I read to the children, she filed and organized papers. She glued homework sheets into the books until the children were able to do it themselves. She checked homework, always coming to me when she had a question.

In addition to working with the children both individually and in groups, Bobbie helped me to keep the classroom running smoothly. She helped with displays and bulletin boards, did marking, sorting, filing of papers—all jobs that can overwhelm a teacher with 34 children in her class. This journal entry illustrates one way in which Bobbie helped me.

5/19/82, Journal

> In past years, at just about this time of the year, I start putting things away in the closet. My goal is always to be ready so that on the last day of school for teachers, I'm not still packing when everyone else is long gone. I'm always very torn about putting materials away or leaving them out for kids to use. For the first time, I've asked someone to help me to put the closet in order and to put things away. Bobbie has agreed to help me. Desk, closet, paint box lids, check content of boxes. In other years I've not wanted to ask someone to do (a) what I feel I should be able to do myself, and (b) what I need to do myself because otherwise I won't know where things are. I've gotten over my embarrassment and I know that Bobbie understands my "system."

By working with children, she gave them extra attention and extra time with another adult. Having an additional person in the room can be thought of as a way of reducing class size, though of course the teacher is fully responsible. When Bobbie worked with individual children on reading, math, special projects, cooking, and other activities, the children were given more time to work with an adult. It allowed me more time to work with children who needed the most help from me.

One of the most important things Bobbie did was to help supervise the rest of the children while I worked with an individual child or with a small group. She understood what needed doing in order to keep all the activities going smoothly. Sometimes we discussed matters, but sometimes she was just aware of what had to be done, without my having to tell her. This was important because it meant I didn't have to be interrupted with questions. The atmosphere was often more peaceful when a parent was helping than when I was alone with the children. Bobbie's observations of the children were not only helpful; they also gave me lots to think about. She saw and heard much of what I missed. Bobbie had a wonderful, quiet way of maintaining calm, as compared to my loud, sometimes brusque or impatient, ways. She not only helped keep the children calm; she also had a way of calming me.

In mid-June of the year Bobbie was helping me pack up the classroom, I noticed that I was becoming increasingly tense each day as the end of the year approached. I wasn't sure that my anger and tension were any different from any other year, but it felt worse.

6/18/82, Journal

Today Bobbie said to me, "Look, are you upset about something?"
    "No more than usual at this time of year," I responded. "I'm worried that I won't be able to get all the stuff put away and that I should be teaching the kids more."
    "Well, these are my last two weeks in the classroom. I won't be here next year and I want them to be two pleasant weeks. So will you please calm down. We'll get everything done. There's plenty of time."

The next day I wrote in my journal, "It *was* a better day, and I like to think it was because I was heeding Bobbie's words [and afraid of losing her and her help]."

Giving Feedback: Gayle

What stands out for me about Gayle, another parent, is the quiet way in which she slipped into the classroom on the days during which she came to help. She'd look around and get right to work, either with the children, if we were writing or reading, or on checking homework, or filing papers, or repairing library books. Gayle worked with me for the 5 years during which I taught all three of her children. She was one of those people with a quiet manner, which contrasted with my much louder demeanor, and I think it was sometimes a relief to the children to be able to work with her. Sometimes when she was in the room, she'd let me know about her own child's reaction to a homework assignment I'd given. I really appreciated Gayle's observations and "feedback" about what was going on in the room because they were often positive. I have several examples in my journal of Gayle pointing out to me how well the children were working together at Project Time, how caring they seemed to be for one another, or how purposefully they were working on reading and writing.

PARTICIPATING BY BRINGING AND SENDING

I always looked for ways to bring aspects of children's home lives into the classroom. Over the years, I invited parents and children to bring things from the world around them into the classroom. In the newsletters, I often alerted parents to what might be of interest to and appropriate for the children. I invited parents to bring or send specific items when I needed them. At other times they thought of things on their own after they read in the newsletter about what we were studying, or after I'd written thanks in the newsletter for things other parents had sent/brought in. Examples of such things were: an apple grabber, slides of the *Apollo* mission, various maps, many different books (European and Japanese fairy tales, insect books, fiction or nonfiction books with an African American focus, books about animals large and small), science experiments, a human skull, information, and food from their various cultures. I believed that any item parents brought or sent would enhance classroom experiences.

The word *bringing* had so much meaning in my years of teaching, the things that parents brought were so central to my work with children, that I wanted to do a reflection on (that is, list the meanings of) the words *bring* and *bringing* rather than merely looking up definitions in the dictionary.[1] A group of us did such a reflection; portions of Cecelia Traugh's summary follow.[2]

> Bringing implies that you are carrying something, bearing something, though bearing seems weightier than carrying, and in the process, moving it from one place to another. When you bring something, it doesn't come by itself. You accompany it and it reflects on you, is part of you. You have an investment in what you bring. You can bring objects, but you also bring with you your thoughts, your language, your culture and history, and your body.
>
> The word "bring" is almost always used with a preposition, which means it is an action or motion word: bring to, bring with, bring toward, bring forth, bring up, bring down. The word changes meanings according to the prepositions with which it appears. Bringing forth implies creating, giving birth, opening up possibilities. Bringing up implies coming from the source, deep inside, something not always pleasant and sometimes difficult. Bringing to or toward implies that there will be a receiver. Bringing down implies calling a halt to something, stopping something completely as if the foundation has been destroyed.
>
> Some bringing involves sharing with others. And, according to the circumstances, the community can be helped and enriched or inhibited and destroyed.
>
> When you are invited to or requested to bring something, the person who extended the invitation has the obligation to acknowledge, recognize and thank you for the thing you brought.

The stories in this section illustrate aspects of the reflection on bringing. The parents certainly were present not only when they brought things but also when they sent things to school with their children. They brought not only objects but also brought their bodies, their families, their thoughts, their languages, their cultures, their histories, their interests. They had a deep investment in what they brought. They brought things to share with others, taking responsibility for making good contributions to the children, and in bringing the things they did, they enhanced the group and enriched the community.

11/15/96, Newsletter

Many parents have sent things for us to use or helped their children to bring things from home: Alicia Gregoriou's dad sent us a huge roll of brown paper which we are using to trace around our bodies and which we will also use for murals; the Gregoriou family also gave us their Chinese hamsters for the school year; Janice's mom sent 1996 pocket calendars for each child; Jack brought a book about learning to tie your shoes and a box with laces so that children who don't know how, could learn; Ned brought in his Body Game; Theo brought a praying mantis; Melinda brought a garden spider; Julio's mom lent me some books to help me select CDs; Timothy has brought in many books about animals, especially dinosaurs, which he shares with the children; Ron brought in a wonderful tape of *Chicka Chicka Boom Boom* and some stickers for everyone; Theodore brought a book about a caterpillar/ butterfly; and we've had many birthday cupcakes.

Children Bringing Things, with or without Permission

I invited parents to bring things to school and I also encouraged children to do so with their parents' permission. When I invited parents to send things and children to bring things to school, I was not at all interested in traditional "show and tell" items. In traditional "show and tell" as I know it, each child has a scheduled time to bring something to school, to stand in front of the class, to talk about it, and finally to respond to questions about it. When my own children were small, I never liked "show and tell," at least the way it was carried out in their elementary school classrooms. The major reason was that children tended to bring toys to school, and, as the year went on, the toys tended to get fancier and fancier, especially after Christmas; the fuss made over them by the other children made me uncomfortable. I felt that the activity often (though not always) created competition for material things, something that I did not value at all. Through the newsletter, I invited, recognized, and thanked certain contributions. I did have some standards, and I was usually able to communicate the sorts of things that I would find acceptable for children to bring. Looking back through the newsletters, I noticed that I especially encouraged objects that were related to and enhanced the curriculum, that brought the natural world indoors, that fostered common experiences, and that did not distract from the community or aid in destroying it.

Just as my newsletters to parents were invitations to work in the classroom, they also served the purpose of inviting parents to bring or send objects from home. For example, when we were doing some thematic work on size and scale, I wrote the following entry in my newsletter, and parents responded with many objects.

1/23/81, Newsletter

Do you have any interesting but not too valuable small things (miniatures) at home? Our display table is becoming filled with teeny-tiny dishes, chairs, mice, animals, books. We are also interested in books about mice and other small creatures (elves, toads) and in tiny books.

It all started with the mice. The children love mice and I feel it is because they love small things. Last summer I started to collect books about mice, and our new librarian added about 30 books from our school library.

After we look at small things for a while, I'd like to help the children think about size and scale. "How many mice would be as tall as you?" is an example of the kind of question I'd like to raise with the children. Perhaps we'll talk about giants later. If you have any suggestions, please tell me. My plans are not completely formed yet.

Each year I encouraged the group to search for natural objects when they were anywhere outside. Over the years, children managed to find fascinating things, often with the help of their parents. For example, after a vacation in West Virginia, Jacob brought three large animal bones to school: a skull, a jawbone, and a vertebra. We described them, and the children tried to figure out which bones on their bodies corresponded to Jacob's animal bones.

At the end of June 1983, when I knew I would be keeping my first-grade class through second grade, I displayed objects that children had shared and objects from my own collection on a large table. They included bones and tracks preserved in mud; shells and things from the sea; rocks and fossils; seeds and things from trees, including feathers and nests; and flowers and plants.

6/6/83, Journal

I then put the following message, written in large print, on the table with the display: "When you are out of school during your summer vacation, please keep your eyes open for natural treasures. Many people found these treasures from nature and shared them with you and me."

This table is a wonderful review of the year and of all the natural things the children and I brought in, things we've looked at and talked about.

It worked. The following September I noticed that they had responded to my invitation of the previous June by bringing to school many found natural objects.

10/7/83, Newsletter

Our display table is filling up with natural objects. I've found some: the monarch butterfly chrysalis, the milkweed pods, the earthworms, slugs and grubs. Jalil brought the praying mantis (who enjoys the hamburger and water we feed her) and Danika brought us a 2 inch yellow and black garden spider which has spun a web between two twigs in its aquarium/cage. If you see a spider like that, don't be afraid and DON'T KILL IT. It's big, but it's harmless.

Jason's apple grabber. Occasionally, what a child brought not only enhanced the curriculum but also allowed another child to make an important contribution to the class's knowledge and experience.

10/14/97, Journal

Jason brought in an apple picker and, though the children couldn't guess what it was, they did say that it reminded them of a hand or a bear's claw. I told them that someone invented it. The inventor saw that people needed something to help them grab apples that were high on a tree, and something that would hold more than one apple, so this is it. I told them about how, when I was little and I helped in my grandmother's grocery store, it was a big deal for me to be allowed to use the grabber to reach and carry down cans placed high up on the shelves.

Then I asked Teddy (a child who has spina bifida, is paralyzed from his chest down, and is confined to a wheelchair all day) to show the class how his grabber works. It was wonderful that Teddy could teach the children, which he rarely has a chance to do. The children noticed how much that tool looks like a thumb and a finger pinching things to pick them up. I love these discussions of technology and for some reason they often come around cooking and especially apples (apple peeler, apple corer, Foley food mill for applesauce—tools and machines that make human work easier.) The children were fascinated with the grabber and I allowed lots of time for Teddy to supervise their practice using it.

Samir's lizard. I was sometimes delighted at first, but then dismayed, when parents gave permission to their children to bring animals into the class-room. Unfortunately, there were instances when things didn't work as parents and I had hoped. At those times, I wondered if they'd sent the animals to school because they were too much to handle at home. I was always willing to give animals a try, but if they wouldn't eat or if other things turned out to be wrong, I sent them home or back to the outdoors where they had been found. For example, I was never very good at rais-ing tadpoles and had trouble coaxing box turtles to eat. I usually kept those creatures for a few days, long enough for us to observe them, and then returned them to their natural habitat.

Samir attended Kelly School though he lived outside its boundaries. He'd been transferred from another school, where he wouldn't follow the rules. I was told that if he didn't behave at Kelly, he'd have to leave there, too. He wasn't an easy child to have in class; he often hurt other children and made them feel unsafe, but I didn't want to use my power to have him removed. I noticed that he was fascinated with books, and I some-times observed him copying words from books with topics (like dinosaurs) that interested him, or from other children's word lists. When he brought something to school, I liked to follow up on it immediately. Early in the year, he'd found lots of earthworms on his way to school, and they ar-rived enclosed in a potato chip bag. I suggested that he first observe them, and then make a book about them. He dictated the words to me and called his book *This Book Is About Worms*. He was delighted to discover that he was the author of that book, something he hadn't realized until I pointed to his name.

Samir often talked about his pet lizard. I encouraged him to get permis-sion from his parents to bring it to school to show to the class. In January his parents gave him permission to bring a lizard from home to school, but the results were not completely desirable.

1/6/87, Journal

Samir brought in his lizard, finally. He's been telling me for months that he was going to bring it, but I didn't expect it on this quite cold day. We passed the lizard around the circle in the jar and each child described it. . . .

I then asked the children if they had any questions about the lizard. They did. Is it a girl or a boy? What does it eat? Can it walk far? Do they like dirt? How does it grow? Where was it born? Where was it living? How are they born? Where is its mom and dad? Where do you find it? Where does it live? Why does it have little fingers? Why does it have a long tail?

Unfortunately, the lizard died. First, Samir had insisted that he should keep it in about an inch of water in a jar. Second, it was terribly cold this morning which made that inch of water really cold for a lizard. I knew it wasn't a good idea, but he wouldn't listen to me. Third, I wasn't watching as Samir and about three other children worked with the lizard and blocks. I felt really bad that the lizard died, but when Samir wants to do something that doesn't hurt other children, you want to let him do it. I know it's not a good thing to say, but he does have another one.

Jimmy's turtle. One day, after his mother and I had spoken about it, Jimmy brought his large water turtle to school. I wasn't sure I knew how to handle it, but I was willing to try. Six days later, I was writing complaints in my journal.

11/30/90, Journal

The turtle STINKS! I was dreading coming in this morning because I knew I'd have to clean the aquarium, but this was even worse than I thought it would be. Harold was gagging from the smell, and the children ran for my clothespins (usually used to hang paintings on the wire across the room) and put them on their noses. I guess I have to clean the aquarium at least once a week. Just what I need. I had to put my gloves on to keep the turtle from biting me, and I was so angry at the turtle that I left it out of the water for most of the day. I can't do that again. I don't know if I can keep it because it's lots of work. Wally tells me they fed it raw meat at home, so I might try that. But that will stink, too.

The next day I wrote in my journal,

The turtle bit me today. The nurse made me go to the doctor to get a tetanus shot.

The turtle was not only too much work but also turned out to be unclean and dangerous. The smell was horrible. I had to give the turtle back to Jimmy's family, and the children and parents understood. There was no choice.

Problem objects. There were other times when children pleaded with their parents for permission to bring certain items to school. Parents, not realizing the effect of the children's bringing these items, not realizing that the children had been asked not to bring such things, allowed them to do it. Each year—in fact, each season—brought its fad toy that children brought to school. Yo-yos, spinning tops, calculators, beepers, water pistols, trading cards of various kinds, judo or karate sticks—all created problems through the years, disappearing for a while and then returning to favor. These distracted the owners and others from concentrating in class and caused fights at recess. Just trying to hide the object from me took intense effort. In addition, sometimes children who didn't own the toy or the exact, preferred version or quantity of the toy became envious and just took it. Though I was never happy using the words *steal* or *stole*, those were the words the children used, and that is how they understood it when things that belonged to them were taken by someone else without permission.

During the course of any year, the popular item took over recess time without teachers' knowledge, and fights would break out over the object. Finally, the item would be so distracting and so prone to being stolen or causing other kinds of chaos—not only in my class but throughout the school—that the principal would have to make a blanket rule against bringing it to school and would send a letter home to parents that included that rule. At the beginning of the year, I usually listed in the newsletter to parents certain things I knew from past experience that children should not bring. But I could never anticipate everything. In the September 1988 Newsletter, after listing all the supplies the children would need for school, I wrote the following notice in large, bold letters.

PLEASE—
NO TOYS OR STOPWATCHES

NO CANDY
NO GUM
NO MONEY (except when requested for trips)
NOTHING VALUABLE IN SCHOOL

At other times, the problem with the item kind of crept up on me and I had to ask the child to stop bringing it after I'd already allowed it in the room. At least once a year, a girl would bring a purse containing lipstick or perfume or both to school. There would be a frenzy of attention around the bearer. At lunchtime (if I forgot to take it from the child and hold it until the end of the day) the girls would come in from recess smelling of perfume and looking like clowns, lipstick smeared on their faces. Those who brought the purses always insisted that their mothers had given them permission to bring them to school.

Tami, a first-grade girl, occasionally brought objects that were acceptable to me—a hamster, for example. Early in the school year, Tami brought a purse and money (coins and bills) to school. She was distracted by all the objects in the purse. She played with the purse, dropped the money, began to trade the contents of her purse with April—all at times when I was expecting them to be paying attention to whatever activity was in progress. I finally moved Tami's seat away from April's and told her that she must stop bringing things to school. She stopped for a while, but in the spring, she again began to carry a purse.

4/18/90, Journal

First, Tami smelled up the room with the perfume she had in her purse, then she kept playing with it instead of listening to the math lesson. . . . I got furious. . . . Why can't the kids keep these purses on their hooks? Or, better yet, why can't they keep them home, as I asked them to do?

Not only did I disapprove because such items distracted Tami and others from paying attention, or because they caused more children to bring in such things, but I also didn't value children focusing on their appearance through fancy clothing and makeup, didn't feel it to be appropriate for little children to want to imitate adults in these ways—at least not in school. "You're so beautiful, you don't need lipstick to make you look pretty," I would say. I often saw the humor in these occurrences but, nevertheless, had to reject the items.

Pokémon cards were all the rage in the fall of 1999. At first I allowed the children to bring them to school because they talked so much about them and because they often wrote stories about the characters. I liked the fact that the children were using something they were interested in as inspiration for exciting stories—for a while. A child made a poster with a list of the names of all the characters to make it easier for the children to spell them correctly. But . . .

10/5/99, Journal

I've had it with the Pokemon cards and it's just the first week the children have had them in school. Today Adele and a bunch of boys were playing with the cards, and Adele ended up in tears. She'd traded something that made her really unhappy. I'm not sure if she understood that once you make the trade, the trade is finished and you're not supposed to get your cards back. But I could see big problems looming with these cards. So I've banned them from school. Adele probably asked "Can I hold that Pokemon card?" For some children "hold" means "borrow." For other children, "hold" means "keep." That misunderstanding often causes arguments.

10/6/99, Note

Ms. Strieb
    Tommy explained to me about the Pokémon cards you took from him. I spoke with him and told him there is a time and a place for them and in the classroom is not one of them. He will not bring them to class again. He can only use them at recess or lunch.
    Thank you,
    Tracey Manno

It became easier to enforce the ban on Pokémon cards after the principal sent the following note home to all the parents. This is an example of the principal's action when some fad began to disrupt the entire school.

11/4/99, Note from principal

NOTICE TO PARENTS

STARTING MONDAY, NOVEMBER 1ST, STUDENTS MAY NO LONGER BRING POKEMON CARDS TO SCHOOL. WHEN CARDS ARE STOLEN IT CREATES CONFLICT BETWEEN STUDENTS AND DISTRACTS FROM EDUCATION. PLEASE DISCUSS THIS WITH YOUR CHILD. THANK YOU FOR YOUR COOPERATION.

Parents Bringing Things: Cindy's Natural Science Objects

Cindy Roberts had children in my class for 4 years. Douglas was with me from 1978–1980 and Jane from 1980–1982. As I looked over the list of things Cindy brought to the classroom, I'm struck by how she immediately caught on to the things I believed were important for children, how she understood what was appropriate to bring and how it would enrich the community. Cindy paid attention to my newsletters, especially my invitations and my descriptions of curriculum and the children's interests. The study of various aspects of science was important to my teaching. Cindy's contributions enhanced our studies in a variety of ways. Observing and describing natural phenomena (creatures, bones, shells, plants—leaves, seeds, trees, flowers) were central to the science program.

She responded to the invitation to bring specimens and brought, at different times during the fall, a praying mantis, a garter snake, a salamander, a chameleon, and a black and yellow garden spider. She came to the classroom when she was pregnant with her twins so that we could observe and describe mother and babies before and later after they were born. For at least a year, she visited regularly with them (see "Parents Bringing Their Babies," below). When we studied bones and bodies, she added to the richness of our display of skulls from various animals—such as cat, dog, cow, horse, bird, and mouse—by bringing us a human skull. Though the skull was painted green, it was in much better condition than the skull that was attached to the full-size human skeleton I owned and used in the classroom.

During the 1980–1981 school year, she responded to my plan to investigate changes in the classroom over the course of the entire year. At regular intervals throughout the year, I asked the children, "What has changed in our room?" Sometimes they noted changes that had to do with things like the display table or the bulletin boards or the room arrangement. At other times they noted changes that had happened to them and their learning. They described our pumpkin in its various forms from pumpkin to jack-o'-lantern to a rotten, smelly, moldy object that had changed considerably during the months it had been part of the classroom. Many of the changes we described were changes over longer periods of time—weeks and months.

3/11/81, Journal

Cindy Roberts responded to my/our interest in things changing by bringing us an experiment or demonstration in which something changed dramatically and quickly—the Coal Flower/Crystal Garden. Before she showed us how to make a crystal garden with coal, ammonia, bluing, and water, we sat in a circle and I asked the children, "What has changed in the room? What was it like before?" I wrote the children's responses: "The mice weren't pregnant and now they are . . . the walls have pictures of the kids' bodies and they didn't . . . the bulletin boards have changed . . . the clock used to work and now it's broken . . . the table used to have leaves and seeds, then it had holiday things and the gingerbread house and now it has tiny things . . . Ali's building is built but before it fell down" After the discussion, I felt the children were ready to observe the more rapid changes of the crystal garden.

This was not an "experiment" that I would have chosen to demonstrate to the children. Though the children had many experiences with science, I didn't often do formal science demonstrations or experiments. But because Cindy thought it would be interesting to the children, because she thought it fit into my interest in having the children observe and describe changes over time, she thought it would be a good thing to do. Later in the day, we gathered in front of the crystal garden to talk.

3/11/81, Journal

Cindy began to talk with the children about what scientists do. I know that children have strong ideas from movies and television about what scientists do. I felt that some of the things she was saying were a little beyond their understanding. I wanted to help a little. So together, we reminded the children of the things they said had changed. Then I pointed to the bowl with the coal flower experiment on it, and I asked the children if they remembered what it looked like before, when Ms. Roberts first set up the experiment. "It was coal. . . . It was liquid. . . . It smelled awful." Then we talked about how it had changed.

I said, "When Mrs. Roberts says she's doing an experiment with you, she means you're all watching or observing it to see the changes. I want you to look at this bowl whenever you think of it. It's different now from what it was in the morning. And when you leave school it will have changed some more. Keep watching." And I thanked Cindy for helping us to make a crystal garden.

The following year Cindy asked if I'd like her to again make a crystal garden with the children. She knew that over the course of my 2 years with a group of children, I liked to repeat things (read some books more than once, study the same live creatures, etc.), mostly because each time you repeat an activity, the children are not the same as the first time or even second time—they bring new experiences to what might be the same activities.

2/5/82, Journal

Cindy Roberts brought the crystal garden experiment again. This year she changed it a little. She decided to try to grow the crystals on twigs, which would be supported between bricks. While she was setting up the bricks and twigs, a child asked, "Are the bricks and twigs supposed to grow?" I asked the class. "No, there's no ground, They're not planted and the twigs are dead. . . . Yes, bricks are alive. . . . Sometimes you can see big rocks with little twigs growing between them . . . Bricks can be soil. . . . Bricks are not for seeds. They don't have soil. . . . The twigs might grow. Bricks are pressed together like the ground." I then asked, "If anything grows, what will it look like? The children surmised it might look like a tree, a leaf, a Christmas tree, a flower.

Cindy's greatest contribution by far was to our studies of plants and origins. Our school neighborhood (the neighborhood in which I also lived) was within the boundaries of the city of Philadelphia, but it was unusual in its mix of housing and in the many old trees and front, back, and side yards. The Roberts family lived in a single-family, semidetached house with a large side yard. In a way, Cindy brought her whole garden, a major part of her own life, into our classroom.

She knew that I liked children to understand where foods came from and what they were like before they were processed. She knew that we would bake bread and cook other foods "from scratch," would cook apple-sauce and vegetable soup, would make butter from heavy cream, peanut butter by grinding peanuts, and, probably, ice cream in a hand-churning machine. When her oldest son was in my class, she and the children made fresh spaghetti sauce from tomatoes, carrots, onions, garlic, sweet peppers, and herbs from her garden. She supervised the washing of the vegetables, their grinding in a hand grinder, and the cooking of the sauce on my hotplate. I'd wished we'd had time to make pasta "from scratch."

When Cindy's daughter Jane was in kindergarten, her class planted vegetables in their home garden. In September of Jane's first grade with me, Cindy reminded the children of the things they'd planted in the garden. She'd carried a sunflower, grown from a seed they'd planted, in a bag. She didn't want the children to see it. We played Twenty Questions, and the children guessed what was in the bag. She left the sunflower with us so that the children could observe it, and over the course of the next few days, they estimated how many seeds there were, took them out of the sunflower, grouped them into sets of 10, and then counted them.

In March we walked to the Roberts's home to plant seeds in the garden in a special section set aside for our class. Many of the children were more interested in running around and in using the play equipment than in preparing the soil and planting seeds, but we managed to get everyone to turn the soil with large shovels and to plant something. We planted peas, comparing those that had been soaked in water ahead of time with those that hadn't. We planted radish, beet, and lettuce seeds. By the time we got to onions, we'd lost most of the class, and those who remained had trouble planting them root down, top up.

We talked about a great many things that day: whether lettuce seeds, which are tiny, are really seeds; why the earthworms we saw everywhere in the soil are important; how it feels to put your hands into dirt. Cindy answered questions clearly and had a bucket of water ready for those children who hated the feeling of soil on their hands to wash them.

We walked to the garden three more times that spring. On the first visit we pulled weeds, thinned and transplanted sunflower seedlings, planted pumpkin seeds, and ate peas right off the vine. The second time we again pulled weeds and ate peas (this time only one per person). The third visit was in June, a few days before school ended. It was our spring harvest celebration. After a quiet lunch under the pear tree, the children played on the equipment in the yard. Half an hour later, we picked the radishes, lettuce, onions, and garlic, and some of the children washed them and made them into a salad. Then we sat in a circle on the grass, quietly eating the salad made of vegetables we had planted and cared for.

School didn't begin on time the following autumn (second grade) because of a teachers' strike, though Cindy helped me when I met the children in front of the school and we walked to my house to read for a few hours. After the strike, in November, Cindy came to school to talk with the children about the garden. She asked them to remember what we'd planted in the spring (which wasn't easy for 6- and 7-year-old children). There had been no autumn harvest because the squirrels had devastated the garden. She described, in detail, how they had climbed the sunflower stalks and eaten the seeds.

In the spring we again planted a garden. We knew that the third-grade teachers would continue this project when Cindy's daughter went to their classes. The Roberts's decided to use a rototiller to loosen the soil. We saw the garden before it was tilled. And because Cindy knew that one of my interests was instilling in children some understanding of aspects of technology (especially machines that do work formerly done by humans), we observed Mr. Roberts using the machine.

We served our spring salad as part of a birthday celebration for Bobbie. Cindy reminded the children that when we ate lettuce, we were eating leaves; when we ate peas, we were eating seeds; and when we ate radishes, we were eating roots (though not many of them ate radishes).

I was always as relaxed with Cindy as I was with Bobbie. I knew I could trust her to care for the children's safety. I knew I could trust her to be on time and to keep her appointments with me and the children. She was sensitive to the children's needs, as are most parents. For example, on our visit to the garden, sensitive to the fact that the children might be thirsty, she provided them with cups and a beverage. She was sensitive to the fact that some children might come to school empty-handed on the day of the Halloween parade, so she brought extra costumes. Cindy, like many of the parents who brought things into the classroom, taught me as much as she taught the children.

Parents Bringing Their Babies

I became aware of the educational potential of children observing babies when our oldest son went to nursery school and I was the nursing mother of Max, our month-old baby. On the days I had to fulfill my obligation by working at the nursery, I had to bring both Max and Saul, my 3-year-old, with me. When Max was hungry, I quietly nursed him without leaving the classroom, sometimes with children observing me. The teacher and I knew that many of the children had seen babies drink only from bottles, and we felt that it would be all right if they happened to observe the natural function of breasts in passing. The presence of younger brothers and sisters always made such occasions as natural as they would be at home, and the situation always sparked wonderful discussions about what the children had observed, with Peggy masterfully leading them.

Once again imitating Peggy, I invited parents to work in the classroom alongside me when I taught, even if it meant they had to bring younger children with them. Sometimes it didn't work out because the babies and younger children needed their parents' undivided attention, and then the parents quietly left. But for the most part, everyone benefited from these visits.

10/13/92, Newsletter

Do you have a baby? Are you pregnant? We're not trying to get personal. We are looking for a parent who would be willing to and interested in bringing a young baby to our class about once every six weeks. We will study science, social studies and health as we observe the baby and parent. We will observe and describe the baby and predict how the baby has changed. We'll write our predictions and then observe to see if they were correct. Visits will provide science, reading and health lessons. We will also observe and learn about how parents care for babies, especially how they keep babies safe. So, if YOU have a baby we'd LOVE you to bring her or him in. Just let me know ahead of time. Please send a note in your child's homework book.

For 20 years we had regular visits from at least one baby between the ages of 1 and 18 months for us to observe and describe. When Cindy Roberts was pregnant with twins, the children got to observe her before they were born. Another year, a father brought his two children, one 2 years old and the other 2 months old, and we observed them together during four visits. Another year, two mothers offered to bring their children, and we observed both of them.

During the late 1970s, Germantown Friends School, under the leadership of Sally Scattergood, had developed a program called Educating Children for Parenting (ECP), and although, when I started, I hadn't read their materials, I knew from newspaper articles and television programs that parents and members of the community were invited to bring babies into Germantown Friends classrooms. I decided to devise my own program.[3]

Karen. On Karen's first visit in February, the children and I sat in a circle along with the baby and her mother, Shannon Buckley. I asked the children to watch her quietly for a moment and then, if anyone had anything to say, if anyone observed something about the baby that they wanted to describe, he or she could. Fred wanted to ask questions, and I promised him there would be time for that after lunch. The children described what Karen was wearing, her size, how small everything about her was (her ears, eyes, nose, fingers), the movement her hands and feet were making, her face as she started to cry.

Robbie, Karen's brother, needed very badly to be next to her, and he kept touching her face or leaning in front of her, making it difficult for the children to see her. He also began to call her names like "Fart Face" and "Red Heinie." He giggled all the while, and his mother was quite embarrassed. I suggested to his mother that she seat him on her lap until Karen began to get restless. That calmed Robbie.

When we got back from lunch, we again sat in a circle, and the children were invited to ask questions.

2/6/81, Journal

How was she born? How does it get out? . . . How does the baby
grow? . . . What is your belly button? . . . What is pee? How does it
get yellow? . . . What is poop? . . . How come men don't have
babies? It's not fair. . . . My question—How can you usually tell if a
baby is a boy or a girl?

Three months later, in May, the children noticed how much Karen had
changed and described some of the changes. Then I said, "Mrs. Buckley told
me that Karen can clap her hands. Maybe if you do it, she'll do it, too." So
32 children, sitting in a circle, clapped their hands, while Karen sat, quiet
and still, in the middle. I couldn't see, but Mrs. Buckley said she was laughing. Then I made a motion for the children to stop clapping, saying, "Let's
watch what Karen does." Instead of clapping, Karen shook her arms, waved
her hands, and made a sound. She did it about three times. I signaled for
the children to clap again and then to stop. Once again, Karen moved her
arms furiously. By the third time, the children realized that she was telling
them exactly what she wanted them to do. They loved the game and continued for quite a while. Karen never clapped for us that day.

A month later, Shannon again brought Karen to visit. Karen was
surprisingly pleasant, considering the amount of jostling she got as the
children carried her around the room at Project Time. Then we sat in a
circle and tried the clapping game again. This time, when the children
clapped, Karen looked up, startled, and smiled. When they stopped, she
began to clap. Then she stopped, looked up, and made a sound. That sound
made the children clap. She clapped again, stopped, and made the same
sound. I thought this game would never end.

Karen's last visit was when her brother was in second grade and she
was about to turn 2:

1/19/82, Journal

Karen, Robbie's sister visited the class today. She was drawn to the
mice and guinea pigs and wanted to play with them. When she
couldn't have them she made a fuss. I asked the children, "How
does Karen get what she wants?"

We talked about her, though I have no written record of that
conversation.

I grew more experienced in having parents visit with their babies, largely
because of my association with ECP, which developed guides for teachers.

Again and again as the babies visited, the same issues were raised. The children usually asked about the baby's age, about how and what the baby ate, about whether or not the baby used a toilet, about whether or not the baby could sit up or walk, depending on its age. I usually asked the children: "How can we make the visit safe and comfortable for the mother and baby? What do you remember about the baby from our last visit?"

Predictions were important: "What do you think the baby will do today? What will the adult do for the baby?" While the baby visited, we observed and talked about whether or not our predictions matched our observations. I asked some of these questions, and the children asked some of them: Has the baby changed? In what way? What did the adult do to take care of the baby while they were visiting? How does a baby let its parents know what it wants (and other issues related to communicating)? How can you get a baby to stop crying? What happens if we sing (as we used to clap) for the baby? What's the same (or different) about this baby and that baby, this baby and her older sibling or an adult, this baby and other living things in our classroom (snake, guinea pig)?

As years went by, I gave the children half-copybooks in which to write their predictions and questions before the visit and their observations following the visit. Our discussions of what the children observed often became reading homework that they and their parents enjoyed.

Why I invited mothers with babies. There are many reasons for bringing babies into classroom for us to study. They are endlessly fascinating and fun. Everyone knows babies. Everyone has them around—if not at home, then in the family or in the neighborhood. Being with babies is an experience we've all had in common regardless of culture, race, ethnicity, gender, class, or level of education. They remind us of ourselves. We were all babies once and can usually tell stories about that—both those we may remember and those we were told by adults. As living things, babies easily provide the basis for studying science, math, health, social studies, and "critical thinking" concepts. And like many other subjects of study (leaves, rocks, apples, flowers, twigs, seeds, insects), babies are always available. I always looked for ways of bringing the home into the school through experiences that all children had in common, experiences that we could talk about that weren't dependent on objects we had at home or things we did with our parents or books we read at home. Over the years, I kept a mental list of such experiences and used them often as topics of whole-class discussion, as topics for whole-class books, and as suggestions for children as topics for independent writing. Babies met all of those criteria.

Inviting babies into the classroom enhanced parent–teacher relationships as well. Babies needed a parent to come with them when they visited, which brought parents into the classroom. Parents taught the children about parenting; and though certain practices might differ from person to person, from home to home or ethnicity to ethnicity, what is common is that babies must be cared for and that parents are able to talk about how they offer that care.

What happened in the classroom with regard to discussions and observing and caring may have provided good models for parents to emulate—for the parents of the babies who were brought to school and for the parents who heard about the visits from their children and read about them in the newsletters and homework.

The visits from babies often led to other activities. Among other things, for example, we drew pictures, read books about babies around the world, and published class books about ourselves as babies using stories parents had told us. I end this section with three examples of spontaneous writing by children about their siblings, written in different years.

MY SISTER KAREN

By Robbie

My sister does funny things. She walks and crawls up the stairs. Sometimes she falls down. She gets hurt but she lives. She gets better. I like my sister. She is fun. My sister does funny things. She crawls, and she sticks her butt up. Now that is funny. Now that is funny for her.

MY BROTHER

By Barry Boyle

My Baby Brother
My baby brother is nice.
He wears the same clothes as me.
He wears the same sneakers as me.
My brother and I wrestle.
He sleeps a lot.
He always wants my mom.
He wants my big brother.
He always wants a bottle. He always wants a baby doll.
I let him hold my car. He always wants a dog.
He bites me.
My cousin hits him all the time.
He is about to turn two.

MY BABY SISTER

By Assif

When I walk in the door my sister hits me. I pick her up then she kisses me. Then she hits me again.

I say, "Stop."

She went after my book bag. I took it and she said, "Un, un." I put it back down and she took it.

Then I went upstairs to play my game. When I got finished I played in the bed with my sister.

I got out. She cried and I took her out. I gave her to my mom and she went to sleep.

She woke up again and when she wakes up, she puts her hand up and she lies down.

She walked in the kitchen to play with the ABC. I put her in her walker. Then she ran from me and I ran after her. She screamed and then I screamed back. She ran away again.

She shook her hand and I shook my hand. She ran again.

I took her upstairs with me and when it was time to go to school my mom brought her in my room. I gave her my bubble bath and she threw it.

I put her on my bed and I put on my coat and book bag and I took her in my mom's room.

I went outside to wait for my aunt. I got on the school bus and then I went to school. The end.

Parents Bringing Their Knowledge: Sharing Work and Interests

9/97, Newsletter

I will be inviting parents to come to school to talk about their work or something they're interested in. In the past, we've had many excellent presentations and demonstrations. I'll be sending you a note. I hope many of you will be willing to do this. We'd like to start with one person per family. It's important that we also have parents who are homemakers speak about their work. So—be thinking about this.

In my continuing search for experiences that many of the children and families had in common, I realized that "work" in its broadest sense might be another possibility. I knew that it was possible that some of the parents might be unemployed, so I considered work broadly. I told parents that being a homemaker was indeed work and that I wanted to include homemakers in this invitation. It was parents themselves who showed me that in some cases, things that interested them—an avocation, an interest, a hobby, or a way in which they earned money that was not their actual livelihood—might be more important for them to talk about than what they did at their paid "jobs." Schools often invite people to visit classrooms to talk about work and call it Career Preparation or Vocational Guidance or Career Day. Often those visitors have no relationship to the children in the classrooms. One thing that made these visits to my class so successful was that the children had a stake in visits by their own parents. Because the visitors were known to the children, the visits had immediacy. Finally, I didn't tell the parents how to present their information. The thoughtfulness of the parents, their success in making their work understandable to the children, impressed me. The props they brought to help reach that goal surprised me more than once.

A cornucopia of information. Most of the parents who visited in 1998 taught us about their paid work. We were taught by a skilled carpenter, who demonstrated the uses of various carpentry tools; a social worker who places children into foster care; an emergency room nurse, who showed the children how to use a stethoscope; a high school math teacher, who posed problems to be solved on calculators; a pathologist, who brought a human heart and slides of sections of two lungs, one of a smoker and one of a nonsmoker; an internist, who led children through a process called "differential diagnosis" of a fictional woman with heart disease; an ophthalmologist's assistant, who showed the children various tests she gives in the office and brought disposable dark glasses for each child; a secretary at Philadelphia Community College, who showed the children a newsletter she worked on and who brought PCC pencils and erasers for each child; a Fairmount Park Department team leader who supervised groups working on park maintenance, who brought hip-length work boots, overalls, gloves, and a hat for the children to try on and who talked about his early experiences working in the park as a high school student in the Job Corps; a member of the Philadelphia City Council, who invited us to council chambers and spoke about his work while we were there; the owner of a local Indian restaurant, who invited us to the restaurant and talked about his work as he gave us a tour of his kitchen and then sat us at set tables for some Indian snacks; a homemaker, who talked about all the tools she uses at home and all the work she does; a filmmaker of health films, who made a special video for us that demonstrated morphing, using his own children's faces; and three architects—one who talked about terminology and then took us to a nearby church he was in charge of restoring after a fire had destroyed its nave, and two female architects, partners in a small firm, who, because the film *The Hunchback of Notre Dame* was about to arrive in local theaters, talked about medieval architecture and had the children demonstrate various buttresses using their own bodies. In all cases, the parents talked with great feeling and, of course, knowledge, about their work lives. (See Appendix J, for more detail.)

Three parents talked very little about their paid work but instead spent most of their time talking about work they really loved to do—work without which they said they would have been unhappy and unfulfilled people. There was a carpenter whose beloved work was painting signs. Using the pencils, rulers, brushes, and paints he had brought, he painted a sign for a birthday party at a bar, while describing to the children how he decides what to paint and how math plays a role in that work. An assistant to the president of a large local university in charge of community affairs brought and played drums and a synthesizer because his loved work is composing and playing jazz with a small local band. He showed us how he sometimes practices by playing along with taped music. And he showed us an advertisement in a local paper for a performance his band was planning.

Mr. Johnson. One of the most successful and meaningful visits from parents came from Mr. Johnson, an African American father, whose paid work was driving a truck. But he'd also had training to be a hair stylist and barber. That was what he loved to do and that is what he chose to talk about with the children.

The children watched as Mr. Johnson laid a white cloth on the four desks he had pushed together. He carefully put his tools on the cloth: scissors; brush; comb; shears (a clipper with a still blade and one with a moving blade); a brush to clean the clippers; guiders, which keep the clippers from getting too close; outliners, which give hair a shape and can be used for drawing; an apron "so you won't itch"; disinfectant spray "to prevent you from catching germs from the last person"; witch hazel to brush off the hair; and a Sanex napkin "in case we have a customer who has bad hygiene or had a sore on their neck; we change this every time we give a haircut."

As a lead-in to a discussion about good hygiene, Mr. Johnson placed the tools on the table and explained their uses in a relaxed, conversational way. He asked the children what "good hygiene" means, and after he established that it means good health and cleanliness, he talked about all the ways in which a barber keeps his workplace clean. He asked the children, "Would you go to a barber who sleeps with a pig?"—which made the children laugh a lot. He sprayed disinfectant on the clippers to make them clean.

During the next part of his presentation, Mr. Johnson talked about different types of hair. He pointed to various children in the classroom and described their hair. Neville's was wavy, his son David's was curly, and Carol's was straight. Neville and David were African American, and Carol was White. The children were delighted to be pointed out for the attributes of their hair. He drew some diagrams on the board of hair follicles and their differences and how those differences affect the consistency of the hair. He also asked the children, "Where does hair *not* grow on your body?" They responded with some answers: the palms of hands, lips, soles of feet, to name a few.

One of the children asked if it's necessary for people to shave their eyebrows. Mr. Johnson told them that people do that because they think it will make them look good. He asked them, "Why do we have eyebrows, especially if you're going to shave them off?" I told them about the possible practical purposes of eyebrows (to keep the sweat from dripping down into your eyes, for example), and then said, "People all over the world fix their hair, wear makeup and jewelry, put marks on their bodies, wear clothes. But what they think is beautiful might be different from what you and I think is beautiful. Some people think it's beautiful to shave their eyebrows, others don't. Some people think it's beautiful to put marks on their faces or tattoos on their bodies, while others don't. Some people think it's beautiful to braid their hair; others think it's beautiful to color their hair a different color. Usually where you live lets you know what people think is beautiful, and when you go to a new place, sometimes the people seem really strange because they're different from you."

When Mr. Johnson finally placed a chair on top of the four desks, it began to dawn on the children that something important was going to happen. Neville asked, "Is he going to cut someone's hair? Whose hair is he going to cut?" Mr. Johnson beckoned to his son, David, and placed him on the chair so that the children could watch as he cut David's hair. I was surprised and delighted by this wonderful idea. Hair—which so often separates us, which has so much emotion around it, which had been a source of learning about race early in my teaching life—was the basis of an important common experience for all of us.

Mr. Johnson first brushed his son's hair. "I do this to loosen his hair and break it apart. I can't give him a good haircut if it's 'peasey'—in tight separate curls."

And then, in a relaxed way, he began to cut his son's hair. He used one guider on his shears, then another, until David's hair was cut very close to his skull. At the end of the haircut, he used the outliners to cut zigzag lines on David's hair. "The fun part to doing this is when they smile when they're done and when they look in the mirror and think they're all pretty." All the while he was cutting his son's hair, he answered the children's questions, pausing when the task required his complete concentration. "Do you have to study to become a barber?" "You study for 1,230 hours, take a test given by the state board, and then you get a diploma." "If you want to shave your beard, would you use those things?" "I might use special scissors for shaping, but if this were a real barber shop, I might do more things. I might massage his head," which he then did to his son's head and cheeks.

This visit from Mr. Johnson was important for a variety of reasons. Mr. Johnson took a subject that is rarely mentioned in public, though very important (hair and its differences, its racial significance and meanings), and made it possible for us to talk about that subject. We talked about it as if the differences were the most natural things in the world (which they are). Hair salons and barber shops are for the most part racially segregated institutions in our culture. They are secret and hidden places. Everyone has hair. Mr. Johnson showed us what we all have in common.

The way Mr. Johnson planned for this experience was impeccable: the way he laid out the tools, the way he talked about everyone's hair texture, and the final surprise—the actual haircut and styling.

The parents who talked about their work and their interests all thought carefully about what would interest the children and what the children could understand about their work. They learned that what they did could be valued by children and their school. For that moment they knew what it might be like to be a teacher (though without all the responsibility). What did they bring to the children and me? I return to the reflection that started this chapter: The parents brought things to share with others (souvenirs, such as pencils, magnets, and dark glasses). They wanted to please the children and me. They took seriously their responsibility by bringing things that they thought would make a contribution to the group. The group was enhanced by what the parents brought. What they brought would not be part of a child's conventional school experience. Parents connected the children with the world outside the school. If some of these presentations had to be categorized, if it were necessary to attach a curricular label to them, they could be considered science or social studies, in a deep sense.

Most important, parents shared their knowledge. As much as a teacher might know, she can't know everything. As much as he tries to see, he can't see everything. As many good ideas as she has, she can't think of everything. Parents provided valuable and important perspectives in the classroom. Simply put, the children and I learned from parents.

❧ 7 ❧

Learning from a Life in Teaching

ONE OF my goals throughout teaching was to include as many parents as possible in the life of the classroom to support children and to help me with adult-intensive projects. Based on my reading of longitudinal studies, I believed that I could make a contribution with this book by looking closely at my relationships with parents over many years. I knew that such studies are valuable because of both their particularity (their great detail, particular to the teacher doing the study) and their universality (experiences teachers have in common).[1] I have described my own experiences as a parent and the ways I addressed parental involvement. I communicated with parents about my ways of teaching and about their children. I invited parents to let me know their concerns, wishes, and thoughts, and I let them know that I considered and often acted on their suggestions. I invited them to work alongside me in the classroom or to work from home (for example, by typing children's stories or making materials for math lessons and games) if they were unable to join us in the classroom. I also invited parents to teach what they knew.

At a school and district level, much progress has been made in listening to and hearing parents' voices, but I was most interested in the level of the classroom and the relationship between the parents and the children's teachers. In the years since I was a young parent, the relationship between parents and schools has changed considerably. Many more parents speak out about their concerns, both to schools and to school districts. Official policy now requires schools to include parental involvement in their plans in a variety of ways, such as parent participation in school-based management committees, school-led workshops to educate parents, or, less frequently, parent presence in the classroom. In many cities parents often have the right to choose from among neighborhood schools, magnet schools, publicly funded (sometimes for-profit) charter schools, religious or private schools; to form independent schools; to remove their children from school altogether and teach them at home. Though there are parents who continue to choose to send their children to neighborhood schools or who don't realize that they have a choice, more and more parents are expressing their wishes and concerns, and making them heard by choosing schools other than neighborhood ones.

AUTHORITY AND TRUST

In the Introduction, I said the following: "Children, most precious to parents, are in the care and under the supervision of a teacher for only 5 hours a day—a time when parents are not present. Questions of authority arise in the relationship between teacher and parent. Who's really in charge? What are the realms of authority of each? What are the areas of overlap? What are the areas of conflict?"

A teacher has authority outside the home, in the classroom, but it is a temporary authority with regard to children and parents. It exists for only a portion of 5 days a week and usually comes to an end after 1 or 2 years. Her authority extends to the home with homework and various communications. The teacher has more or less authority in the classroom according to the school and district in which she teaches. She is required to implement official policies over which neither she nor the parents have much control, whether they believe that those policies are sound or unsound. No matter what policies school districts adopt regarding parent involvement in schools and classrooms, no matter what principals urge teachers to do, within the classroom it is usually the teacher who chooses to what extent parents will influence her own thinking about her practice and whether or not to include parents. It is the teacher who creates an atmosphere of welcome or exclusion, comfort or discomfort within the classroom.[2]

A parent's realm of authority is the home. Parents can choose whether or not to acknowledge school requirements there. They are not required to be involved in their children's education in any way except to send them to school or to prove that they are being adequately educated at home. Parental authority extends into the school according to the wishes of the teacher or school administration. For my own mother, grandmother, and great-grandmother, there was no questioning of teacher or school authority. They just sent their children to school, expected them to behave and to fend for themselves socially, believed that the teacher would teach, and didn't involve themselves in any other way. They accepted what happened. They were neither invited into nor had direct involvement in the school, and they seemed perfectly satisfied. In contrast, my husband's mother, who, like my mother, was of the first generation born in the United States, was a former school secretary and was married to a physician. She fought with administrators all the way to the superintendent of schools so that her children could attend a demonstration school, purported to be better than the neighborhood school. During the 1940s, that was quite rare. Her job experience and middle-class status—as well as her personality—gave her the courage to do this.

Though parents are ultimately responsible for and in charge of the child, parents usually want their children to know that the teacher, too, has authority. When I taught their children, it was important to many parents to pave the way for my authority. They often asked my permission or cleared things with me before acting because they didn't want to detract from my authority in the eyes of their children. This desire to respect the teacher's authority was true whether it was for the Keyser School Community Mothers' Group (although it may not have been so apparent in that case) or for the parents whose children I taught.

Successful parent–teacher relationships necessitate negotiations based on trust. No matter where parents decide to send their children to school, trust is central to the relationship between home and school. Conventions, roles, and expectations enter into a consideration of trust. Trust involves a mutual understanding of and acceptance of these conventions, roles, and expectations. Teachers and parents expect certain kinds of roles and behavior from one another. If the two parties agree on their roles, it's easy to establish trust.[3] If a teacher believes that a parent's role is to sit and work with her child on homework for 3 hours after school, but the parent doesn't do that, the teacher might feel that the trust has been violated. If parents believe that they should be allowed to express their opinions about curriculum or pedagogy and to work in the classroom, but the teacher does not, parents might feel that trust has been violated. If a parent has permission from a teacher to visit or work in a classroom and then writes a public letter naming and complaining about that teacher (as I did in 1968), trust has been violated. If a teacher asks about home life—for example, how a parent disciplines a child at home—and a parent believes that it's "none of the teacher's business," the parent might feel that trust has been violated. It might be hard for a parent to trust a teacher if the parent wants school to look exactly like the school she attended, while the teacher is teaching in a different way. In other words, if there's disagreement, if it's perceived that one or the other of the parties is trying to make the boundaries between roles fuzzier or to draw boundaries in new places, then there might be a loss of trust. In the late 1960s, when we Keyser Mothers were examining these roles, when we said, "Parents and teachers are equal," it was not possible for the teachers to trust us because in their eyes we were not equal.

And though I wanted parents in the classroom and I wanted to know their ideas and wishes, in the end, if I didn't agree with something a parent suggested or requested, I had the last word on what went on in my classroom and how I taught. This is a tension embedded in the relationship, and it makes me wonder if indeed "parents and teachers are equal." The best example I can think of would be if there is a conflict between parents' and teacher's views about what classroom structures and methods will enable children to be successful in school. I believed it was important for children to learn more than just what people call "the basics." When my own children went to elementary school, my husband and I did not want them in traditional classrooms, where they would have to sit still, be quiet, work only in workbooks and on commercial worksheets. We did not believe that bringing home these papers was proof of learning. We were fortunate that the public elementary school they attended had both excellent traditional and progressive educators and that parents were given a choice—not of teachers but of classroom structures. As a teacher, I wanted children to be given choices of activities so they could pursue their interests; I wanted them to be able to learn while sewing, painting, drawing, working with natural objects, building with blocks and Lego. I believed that talking and solving problems verbally led to more peaceful, less violent interactions. I believed that all of these activities fostered the learning of "the basics."

If, however, there had been parents who told me of their disapproval of what I was doing, who believed that children should sit down and be silent all the time, should work only in workbooks and on commercial worksheets, and saw those behaviors as proof of learning, then I might have had to do the following:

1. Respect their views, and not judge them.
2. Keep them informed, and let them know why I taught the way I did.
3. Invite them into the classroom (I found this most effective in parents' gaining an understanding of and acceptance of my practice).
4. Try to find a way to work with them and their children.
5. Help them to find a better placement for their child.

This meant that the school itself had to have a procedure in place for resolving such conflicts. In three of the four schools in which I taught, there was such a procedure. As it turned out, at those schools, children whose parents were either dissatisfied with their child's progress or had difficulty with their child's teacher were more often transferred *into* my classroom in the middle of the school year. None were transferred out.

WHAT I LEARNED OR MIGHT HAVE DONE DIFFERENTLY

I learned a great deal from going through my data—my journal, my narrative records, notes from meetings of the Philadelphia Teachers' Learning

Cooperative, my newsletters to parents, notes from parents to me, and notes from me to parents. Though I began to write this book while I was still teaching, I've completed it long after I'd retired. While I was teaching, I tried to use my records to influence my teaching practice. That's no longer possible because I'm not in a classroom. As I looked back, I created a list of things I might have done differently or not at all with regard to parents, and things I didn't do but would do if I were teaching now:

- Although there was a year in which, as part of a study of houses around the world, we visited the home of every child in the class, I would have tried to visit and interview each family at home by myself, as some teachers did, at the beginning of the school year. That would have indicated to parents that I respected where they lived and that I was interested in knowing their children in a fuller context.
- I would have kept my notes to parents about behavior to a minimum, especially to parents of children who were continually difficult for me to handle. Many notes I did write were either ineffective or sometimes caused abusive punishments.
- I would have asked parents more questions about their child at report card conferences. For example, in addition to showing parents examples of the work their child did in school and discussing it with them, I would have asked them to bring to conferences something their child did at home—a drawing, a photograph, a story—in order to, again, show my interest. I would also have asked more about the child at home, with guiding questions, such as, "How do you discipline your child at home? I know that you spend all day Sunday in church. Does your child sit for a long time? How do you get him to do that? What do you do if she becomes restless or distracted?" The answers to these questions might have given me additional insight into the child as a learner.
- I would have tried even more than I did to include children's home life in the school curriculum and homework. Many assignments did involve looking at the home: mapping one's room, discussing topics with parents, involving siblings.
- I would have tried harder to give more homework assignments that didn't require help from parents. This would have meant checking ahead of time to be sure that children would be able to do the homework. This is important because of the parents who might not have been able to help their children at home.
- I would have created a written guide or handbook for parents and other volunteers who helped in the classroom. One of the volun-

teers with whom I worked for many years said that she'd never seen written directions about working in classrooms and that such a document would have been very helpful.

- I would have reviewed my journal entries and other records more often, to learn if patterns were emerging or questions were arising that would help me to strengthen my relationships with parents.
- I would have thought more about why and how to engage fathers and grandfathers in classroom life. In rereading my journals, I noticed that most of the parents who participated in my classroom and who wrote notes to me were women. I know there are many possible reasons for the preponderance of women: Many children came from single-parent families headed by women.[4] People often assume that the role of caregiver to young children belongs to women. Perhaps my choices of activities and school hours made it harder for fathers or grandfathers to participate. The major exception was when parents came into the classroom to describe their work and interests to the children. Men and women did that equally.

PRINCIPALS, ADMINISTRATORS, AND A WELCOMING ATMOSPHERE

This book enters a policy discussion about parents from a perspective outside the usual one of researcher or administrator or policymaker: the perspective from inside the classroom. I have a few suggestions for administrators that could foster parent involvement in schools. These grow both from my practice and from my thinking for so many years about this issue.

What principals say and do when they meet with parents can lead to a feeling of openness and to families' feeling that they are truly invited to participate. If principals don't want parents present in their schools, they can establish school policies whose effect is to create barriers to parent participation. If they do want parental involvement, the most important thing principals can do is to develop a philosophy that leads to openness and then to work with the staff to show parents they are an important part of what goes on in schools.[5] There are then practical things that can be done: giving parents a place to hang coats and store purses, giving them a storage place for other supplies, allowing them to use the adult lavatory, setting aside a room where they can meet and relax, and perhaps helping them to set up a babysitting arrangement for their children, providing a coffee machine and perhaps even a small refrigerator, recognizing parents who volunteer. In some schools, for example, volunteers and the teachers in whose classes they work are honored with a luncheon to recognize their contributions. These show that a school is serious about including parents.

Principals can recognize teachers who have relationships with parents—teachers who invite parents to participate in their children's education not only in official ways (PTAs, chaperoning trips, supervising fund raisers) but also directly, with children, in classrooms. This can be done in a staff newsletter or at faculty meetings. They can encourage sessions in which teachers share with one another ideas about parent participation. (See Appendix H for a list of what parents have done.)

Principals should provide books and other materials that describe successful parent–teacher relationships and experiences.

Many schools have signs at their front doors that say, "All visitors must first report to the office." Once inside, visitors meet the security staff, which directs them to sign in. In secondary schools there are also weapons checks. Visitors then proceed to the school office, where they must sign in again. Visitors who are regularly scheduled volunteers are required to obtain criminal background checks and be fingerprinted before beginning work. Considering all of this, it is now more difficult to enjoy the spontaneous parental involvement that I often experienced.

The rules and procedures are extremely important and are necessary for the safety of both teachers and children. However, it is important that security cautions not get in the way of sincere welcomes. Once a whole school or a teacher decides that parents will be invited into classrooms on a regular basis, measures should be taken to show parents that the invitation is sincere. In spite of the barriers, parents can be made to feel welcome if they are alerted ahead of time to both district and local school requirements, encouraged to go through the checks early in the year, and assured that once all the barriers have been crossed they will be able to enter with only a stop at the office to sign in.

The security staff must be trained to be cordial when directing visitors to the school office. Next, those who work in the office play a central role in making parents feel welcome. They again ask parents to sign in and occasionally must call the classroom to see if the teacher will allow that visit. Usually women, these office workers must act both as "portals" and, occasionally, as "barriers." They have to be welcoming and friendly, even when a parent seems angry or behaves in a belligerent manner. It's a fine line to walk and takes some skill to walk effectively. Their interaction with parents can leave a crucial impression of the school. It was my practice to talk with the office staff at the beginning of the school year and let them know my personal policy on parents visiting the classroom: As long as visitors stopped in the office before coming to the room and told the staff where they were going, as long as the parent did not seem to be angry or agitated, and as long as the office worker called me to alert me to the visit, all parents would be welcome to come to the room.

It is important for principals, teachers, and parents to fully understand district rules regarding one-time visits to classrooms, which are different from regularly scheduled volunteering. When parents want to speak with teachers about matters of concern, procedures should be in place so that teaching is not disrupted and safety is maintained. Having to make an appointment to discuss a concern with a teacher should not be considered a barrier to contact. It is both common courtesy and a safeguard.

Finally, many school districts have become so wary of children's allergies and the spreading of germs through foods that they no longer allow cooking in classrooms or even food contributions from parents. Some of my most wonderful experiences with parents happened when they cooked with children or sent foods from home. No one ever got sick from that cooking. This policy should be reexamined.

TEACHERS AND PARENTS

My experience with the Philadelphia Teachers' Learning Cooperative has shown me the immense value of participating in an inquiry or study group. I recommend that teachers consider forming such groups. Certain topics repeat over the course of many years, and parent–teacher relationships can be explored in a variety of ways. Topics can range from looking specifically at one teacher's relationship with one parent to a more general discussion, such as how each member of the group works with parents.

Parents could consider forming their own groups and addressing issues similar to those in the Keyser School Community Mothers' Group's position paper: the parents' role, the teachers' role, and discipline. Then, both parents and teachers might come together to discuss similarities and differences in their outlooks on these topics.

Both groups could also meet regularly to do Descriptive Reviews of Student Work or even Descriptive Reviews of the Child, either at inquiry group meetings or even at regular meetings at schools (in a parent–teacher study group). Describing student work is a nonthreatening way for parents to be introduced to the variety of student responses to school assignments and a way for parents and teachers to learn about the individual student described and about many students over time. These descriptive processes proceed with each person speaking in turn and with the chairperson making sure there are no interruptions. Participants' words and perspectives are considered to be equal in importance, regardless of role or position in the world. We have found over the years that this discipline of listening to others creates a space where adults can truly hear one another.

SOME FURTHER CONCERNS

I am left with some concerns about parent involvement. A child's school success has become a more important measure of parent success than ever before. Many people believe that if a child doesn't go to college, that child and his parents have failed. Emphasis on success in school has made parents (and children) anxious and competitive. Most parents who worry have children who will do quite well in school. Yet I certainly understand the worries of parents whose children belong to groups that have been under-served in schools and have often had more difficulties. Does an emphasis on parent involvement foster inequities? Will programs that have begun to provide training in childrearing to groups of expectant parents make a difference, especially given that once the children are old enough to at-tend elementary school, their experiences may be limited to drill and prac-tice for standardized tests? I worry that programs that teach parents how to parent may be based on assumptions that might be considered insult-ing or racist. I worry that they might imply that there is only one "right" way to parent.

My other concern fits side by side with a child's school success as a measure of parent success. Once schools decide that parents should be involved and that parents need to be taught how to parent, with school success in mind, what happens to those who don't or won't or can't? What happens to the children in large families whose parents must work day and night to provide food and shelter or are simply overwhelmed? Should these parents be judged as inadequate? Should their children have to suf-fer because their parents can't do what is now expected of them? Obvi-ously these parents must be considered rather than dismissed.[6]

FINAL THOUGHTS

In summary, involving parents in a variety of ways was important to me for several reasons. My personal experience with the Keyser School Com-munity Mothers' Group shaped my attitudes. It was humiliating and hurt-ful when we tried to show our willingness to help but our position paper and our knowledge and strengths displayed in the paper were rejected. A little bit of planning by the principal would have gone a long way toward avoiding the negative ways in which the teachers reacted to our ideas and words. If ways of addressing parent involvement had been developed in the school beforehand, our ideas and support might have been welcomed. Teachers might have understood the anger underlying some of our words and worked to change the situation. Our experiences stayed with me and made me more attentive to parents when my role changed and I became a teacher. Those experiences helped me to prepare, in advance of teaching, for including parents. They remain with me now as my own adult children attempt to contribute to their children's classrooms and sometimes meet with barriers constructed by administrators and teachers.

Parent involvement was also important to me because I saw opportunities to educate parents in an informal way. I believed that educating parents was part of my work as a teacher. I did this by modeling and supporting and by offering experiences, rather than by "lecturing." Inviting parents into the classroom, sending a newsletter home, speaking with parents, discussing examples of their children's work at conferences, demonstrating various methods—all made a difference in the ways parents thought about and worked with their children at home.

Making my practice public by inviting parents into the classroom so that they could see what was going on and letting them know why I taught the way I did made a difference in our relationships. Opening the classroom doors to parents helped them to understand and accept my role and strategies as a teacher, and I was much more accepting of their ideas as parents.

Finally, parent involvement was important to me because of the many contributions parents made. They were additional adults in the classroom. They listened to children, read to them, and helped them with academic work. They allowed us to do intensive hands-on activities like cooking and crafts, which would have been much more difficult otherwise. They taught the children and me about themselves and things they knew. They enriched our studies with their knowledge, experiences, and resources. Though I taught for many years and taught many of the same things year after year, it was the children and their parents who made each year different and special. Forty years ago, those of us in the Keyser School Community Mothers' Group insisted that we be included in our children's education, in the schools, alongside the teachers. After examining my practice, I see that our ideas extended to my own teaching.

Data Sources

Source of Data	Estimated Number of Pages	Types of Information
Journals	10,000 (handwritten, some on computer)	Daily notes written on my teaching, on children's work, and on specific incidents regarding children and their parents
		Records of and reflections on curriculum, major events, my teaching
Classroom newsletter	250 (handwritten, some on computer)	Monthly communications sent home to parents to thank them, to inform them about the classroom, and to teach
Daily and narrative records on children; report card comments	14,000 pages (since 1990 on computer)	Daily jottings, one for each child
		Every 2 to 3 weeks— Narrative summaries that reflect on daily records
		Three times/year—Report card comments
Homework samples	About 20 years' worth, in loose-leaf binders	Include homework and explanatory notes to parents
Letters and notes I sent home	50 (most on computer)	Communications sent home to parents to inform and teach; some personal, some to whole class; different format from newsletters
Letters and notes *from* parents	80 (now on computer)	Pre-1996, incomplete
		1996–2000, complete; express parent concerns and interests

| My correspondence and position papers from before teaching | 25 (now on computer) | 1967–1972—My ideas about schools and education, questioning administrative practices, taking action, raising issues of justice and equality that I wrote as a parent and community activist |

Timeline

Year	Personal	Philadelphia	National
1961	Graduated from college; undergraduate major in history of art and history	Largely segregated system	The Peace Corps
1961–1962	Graduate work in history of art; visited kindergartens	Picketing outside of Woolworth's Great Cities School Improvement Program, Ford Foundation	Civil rights activities; the Peace Corps
1962–1963	Year-long substitute teacher in kindergarten; oldest child born December 1963	Picketing construction sites to employ African American workers	Civil rights activities
1964–1970	Certification and master's program in elementary education; gave birth to two more children; per-diem substitute teacher 1965–1970	Northern Student Movement	Civil rights activity; Martin Luther King Jr. assassinated; Ford Foundation Model Cities Program
September 1967–1972	Parent participant in Westside Parent Cooperative Nursery; Keyser School Community Mothers' Group; letters to superintendent, etc; read and distributed articles about open classrooms	Open-classroom movement; distributed articles on open classrooms	National science reforms; classroom reforms; federal government War on Poverty
September 1970–June 2000	Taught kindergarten, first grade, and	John B. Kelly School opens and includes	Head Start and Follow Through,

	second grade in Philadelphia public schools	English infant schools model of the Follow Through program; teachers' centers opened in Philadelphia	federally funded programs for pre-school and grades K–3, part of Title I, ESEA
September 1978		Philadelphia Teachers' Learning Cooperative founded	Teachers' centers lose funding
2000–present	Retired	No Child Left Behind	No Child Left Behind

First Letter to Mr. Gideon, Principal of Fitler–Keyser Schools, February 1, 1968

Mr. Edwin Gideon
Principal
Keyser School
Coulter St. at Morris
Philadelphia, Pa., 19144

Dear Mr. Gideon:

Last year I heard you, along with other principals in the Germantown-Mt. Airy area speak at Vernon House [the meeting space of the Germantown Community Council] to the community about the results of the Iowa Achievement Tests. You said that you were not surprised that the children in Keyser school had done so badly. At that time I asked you if children who do badly in tests, or, more important, who fail to learn what they are supposed to learn in schools are also those children of whom little is expected in school. In other words—does not achievement match expectation? I cannot remember your answer, but I do remember that I was not satisfied with it.

On Friday, January 26, Mrs. Zatella Jenkins and I visited the Keyser School kindergarten. On Monday, January 29, we visited the three kindergartens at the Fitler School. You are the principal of both schools, and while at Fitler, last year's meeting came to my mind. Several other things came to me in light of the question I asked one year ago:

1. The Keyser School is dilapidated and you are obviously anxiously awaiting the construction of the new Kelly School to replace both Fitler and Keyser. Nevertheless, Fitler recently added a new, beautiful kindergarten with wonderful physical facilities. It has two other lovely rooms which also have wonderful materials. Why could Keyser have not received some of these materials? After all, *both* schools are being replaced and the materials could be moved as quickly from Keyser as Fitler. The poor teacher in Keyser seemed, at a glance, to have very little to work with. It must be quite demoralizing to her to compare herself with her equals at Fitler.

2. An SRA math course was being given to the kindergarten children at Fitler. Reading readiness was also being taught there. At Keyser, all we saw on the walls was an incomplete alphabet and *no numbers*. Certainly children will do poorly in achievement tests if they are not taught. Or do you have so little expectation that the children at Keyser's kindergarten will be able to learn that you did not even bother to try to have the teacher teach them? It is easy to say "Oh, those children can't learn." But it is certainly the duty of the school to show evidence of having tried.

3. *Now* I know why the Supreme Court ruled that separate but "equal" facilities are unconstitutional. Here is a perfect example of what happens in the black school and the

white school when both are under the same administration. (No wonder my friend, Mrs. Jenkins, sends her oldest daughter to the Catholic School.)

4. I know that a teacher's personality has a lot to do with the appearance of a room, and that Keyser's room is largely the result of its teacher. I don't think I saw Mrs. T. smile at the children once while I was observing. But even more important, there was no evidence that this teacher made any effort to make up for the lack of materials. She could have made numbers and an alphabet herself to put up on the walls. Perhaps the teacher has personal problems of which I am unaware and which keep her from spending time thinking of how to overcome the obstacles thrown in front of her. But you, as the principal are to be held responsible for letting such inequalities as we saw Friday and Monday get past him.

5. Is it necessary for parents to complain before their children are treated equally? I think that it is *your* duty as an educator to be sure that they all have the same opportunities to learn even if their parents have not reached the point of feeling comfortable about complaining.

Finally, I must tell you why *I* made this visit. I have a child who lives within the boundaries of Keyser and who will be eligible for kindergarten next year. He is currently attending the Westside Parent Cooperative Nursery, run by the Board of Education at the Enon Baptist Tabernacle Church. (We, too, have little in the way of physical facilities that have been given to us by the Board of Education. But our teacher, Mrs. Peggy Perlmutter, has made up for this lack by begging, borrowing and even trash picking. Our children do not mind using second hand materials.) I have wondered why so few of the parents in our section of Germantown have chosen to continue their children in the public schools after such a wonderful nursery experience. These visits made the answers almost clear. It is almost too much to fight years of neglect; they will wait until the new school is built in the wild hope that the new building plus integration will bring improvements; and finally, they are people who *have* a choice. But what about those who have no choice? I have felt that for many reasons, my child would benefit from a public education. But not at the Keyser School. Not even for one year. The combination of the teacher and the materials, and the knowledge of what the children at Fitler are getting is holding me back. I have *not* applied to private school and do not intend to. What can I do? What can *all* the parents whose children are to go to Keyser School next year do?

I await your immediate reply by mail or in person.

Sincerely,
Lynne Y. Strieb
(Mrs. Bertram L. Strieb)

Cover Letter to the School Board and Administrators for the Previous Letter

February 1, 1968

Enclosed you will find a copy of a letter which I sent to Mr. Edwin Gideon, Principal of the Fitler-Keyser School. It is self-explanatory. I would like to add three comments:

1. It is imperative that you visit the Keyser School, Fitler School and the Westside Parent Cooperative Nursery as soon as possible.

2. The kindergarten at Keyser School, as far as I can see, should be closed tomorrow. At least, next year's five-year-olds must not have to be kept behind. The new Kelly School

will be completed in September of 1969, but they will have suffered for having been born one year too early.

3. I see three alternatives and I am sure you can think of more:

   a. Send all Keyser kindergarten children to Fitler. This would cause great overcrowding at Fitler

   b. Get a new teacher and new supplies at Keyser, even for one year.

   c. Start a new kindergarten made up of children who went to the Westside Nursery and the kindergartners from Keyser. It could be housed in church space or space elsewhere in the community. It would be wonderful if it could in some way be related to the cooperative nursery school experience, complete with parents active as teacher aides, and to the concept of the "Infant Schools" of England which were described by Joseph Featherstone in the *New Republic* magazine. Of course, all arithmetic and reading readiness programs given at Fitler, and all materials at that school would be available to the children and presented to them when they are ready, on an individual basis. Parents could be used effectively for such individual work.

It is quite clear which plan I would favor. Whichever one is used, things *must not* go on as they are now, not even for just one more year.

Sincerely,
Lynne Y. Strieb
(Mrs. Bertram L. Strieb)

Second Letter to Mr. Gideon, Principal of Fitler–Keyser Schools, February 28, 1968

Mr. Edwin Gideon, Principal
Keyser-Fitler School
Coulter & Morris Sts.
Philadelphia, Pa.

Dear Mr. Gideon:

At this time I would like to acknowledge some of the things that have happened as a result of my letter to you of February 1st. It is quite heartening to see such quick results.

1. The meeting which you set up with Mrs. Hawkins—the Kindergarten Supervisor of District 6, yourself, my husband and me was very interesting. It was at that time you told us of the immediate changes taking place. In addition, we discussed the idea of parent cooperation in the school, the SRA arithmetic program, the Westside Parent Nursery, and your eagerness to communicate with the parents at Keyser School. By the time you receive this letter a meeting with some of the parents will have taken place.
2. Mrs. Hawkins told of materials which were to be ordered for Keyser's kindergarten. She had an appointment that afternoon with Mr. Leonard to order the supplies. I do not know whether or not they have arrived, but I am sure you are keeping after them.
3. Mrs. Hawkins had spent the entire week at Keyser helping Mrs. R. She told us of some of the teacher's ideas which she felt were very good.
4. Dr. Staples (the associate superintendent in charge of curriculum) visited the kindergarten and wrote to me telling me that curriculum changes were being recommended.
5. Parents' Visiting Day was held on February 15 at Keyser. I visited the kindergarten at that time. The room looked bright and cheerful; materials which may or may not have been available before were more readily accessible. Readiness materials had been made by the teacher, and a number corner had been put in a prominent place in the room. Slippery surfaces on walls which originally could not hold papers were covered with materials to which they could adhere. Paintings were beautifully displayed on a clothesline.
6. The most exciting thing that I saw happen on Visiting Day was that you asked parents to sign up to help in the kindergarten if they have time. You had an excellent list of ways in which they could help, and almost every parent signed up. One father took a rocking chair home to paint. Your open acknowledgment to them that this idea is new to you and the teacher, but that you are interested in trying it out was wonderful. I sincerely hope that it works, and you must know that there are additional people in the community who are anxious to give time in the school.

I have some additional comments:

1. I feel that all parents need to be told what to do by the teacher. They also need her encouragement that they are doing a good job. I still feel that some visits to cooperative nurseries would be helpful to a school starting out on such a program.
2. Hopefully the SRA program will be *available* to all the children, but not compulsory. Active interest in numbers can be stimulated without forcing children to do workbooks every day.
3. All the new materials in the world will make no difference if a teacher is not happy with the children or if she feels they cannot learn. Neatness in a room is not nearly so important as a room with a comfortable atmosphere. (Parents are great for cleaning up!)
4. We want our children to be happy with learning. They *are* happy in the nursery, and they are learning at an extremely rapid rate. We can see there that children will be relatively quiet, work, and listen when they are stimulated. Yesterday a child from the nursery found a piece of coal in the street and brought it to school. The teacher discussed it with the children. Today when my son arrived there were at least five books about coal and mining on the table for him and the other children to look at and discuss. When my husband came home tonight our son jumped up and down excitedly and said, "Daddy, after dinner, let's talk about coal. I learned more about coal. I built a coal mine in the sandbox today too!" Every day is like this. If a public nursery school can be like this, why not the upper grades?

Sincerely,
Lynne Y. Strieb
(Mrs. Bertram L. Strieb)

copies to: members of the board of education,
kindergarten teacher
kindergarten supervisor
associate superintendent
district superintendent

Suggestions (Notes from Meeting with Principal, Edwin Gideon), Early March 1968

1. Keyser school should have its own principal.
2. Principals should insist that police patrol neighborhood during lunch and after school. (Reports of sexual deviant in car. Man loitering in school yard last year.)
3. There should be someone on yard duty after school and during lunch for emergencies. That person should have at least access to a telephone. Mothers are willing to help. What about a matron?
4. A room in the school should be open during lunch for supervised play, reading games, etc.
5. Children should be taken on more field trips. They now have two per term, always the same ones. Parents are willing to accompany groups on trips. Not all of them need transportation. We have a list of people and places in Germantown. Public transportation could be used.
6. School should make many more books available to children. The Scholastic Book Service makes soft cover reprints of good children's books that sell for 30 and 40 cents apiece. We feel that children need more practice in reading other than reading books.
7. School should allow mothers to bring younger children when they visit.
8. School should create situations which allow children to teach each other.
9. Efforts should be made immediately to individualize the school program.
10. We have a list of community volunteers who wish to help in the school.
11. We as parents would like to find ways of supporting the teachers and making real contributions to the school. We would like to meet with them and talk with them about such things as community involvement in the schools. It is most important that parents, teachers and administrators be able to discuss such a thing together without feeling threatened.

Keyser School Community Mothers' Position Paper

Note to Teachers

We do not want the teachers at Keyser to feel that this is happening only to them. All over the city, in fact nationwide, parents are reassessing their role in the education process, without really being organized. We want to work together *with the teachers* for the good of *all* the children. The verbal communication we feel is so important for children is also important for adults. With this in mind we hope to calmly and sensibly discuss the following points.

A group of mothers from the Keyser School Community

The Parents' Role

1. Parents and teachers are equal. Only their roles differ, and even these only slightly. Every parent, regardless of education or background is deserving of respect from people in the school. As parents we credit ourselves considerably with the success we have had in teaching our children to speak which represents a far greater achievement for the child than any other in his childhood.
2. We are due the respect of having courteous treatment, which includes appointments being kept, and being given truthful, even if personally unpleasant answers to questions. That truth includes admission by the teacher that sometimes she honestly does not know how to deal with a problem. Parents can understand this without losing respect for a teacher. In short, we do not hold an honest answer to be indicative of incompetence.
3. Parents have the right to say what they expect from the schools. Their children are most precious to them.
4. Parents see their role as different from the old one of selling pretzels and aiding in Play Day. We see our interest and our help as essential to our children's success. We have the potential for making real contributions to our children's education by supporting the teacher in classroom situations, doing meaningful tasks. This might mean a change in the classroom as it now exists. Such classroom help could solve several problems:

    a. The teacher who complains that her parents have not prepared their children properly for school would be able to show them, right in the classroom, what learning is all about.
    b. The teacher who complains that her class it too large and undisciplined for individualized or small-group work would have the daily help she needs. Parental help on a daily basis would allow for greater flexibility.
    c. We believe that gradually, the parents who seemingly have not been interested in their children's education, but who have stayed away through fear of authority, would be anxious to help once a small group of parents began. Mothers who help in cooperative nurseries generally share common interest with the

teacher *because they feel welcome from the beginning and because they have been re-spected for their contributions by the teacher.* They are on her side.

5. We know that we have responsibilities and obligations which go along with this offer of parental help.
6. We have a list of people from the neighborhood with talents who are willing to work and could be fitted into the curriculum.
7. We do not want the teachers at Keyser to feel this is happening only to them. All over this city, in fact nationwide, parents are reassessing their role. We want to work together *with the teachers* for the good of *all* the children.

The Teacher's Role

1. The teacher must respect the natural intelligence and curiosity of all children. She must have faith that almost all children want to and can learn. And she must continually ask the questions: "How *do* children learn?" and start from that point.
2. The teacher should treat all children as the individuals they are. This may mean a change from the typical "egg carton" classrooms with all desks in rows and the teacher giving out information to all children at once. It may mean breaking the structure down so that the atmosphere is more fluid. It may mean more freedom for each child to choose what to read. It may mean an entire overhaul in the way children learn reading and arithmetic.
3. The teacher herself should continually question her role. Is she a guide in helping children discover for themselves (much as a parent) or is she the sole beginning and end of all information in the learning situation? All adults (parents included) should continually evaluate their attitudes toward children. We should be honest to them, (and to ourselves and each other.)
4. The teacher should respect her children and parents. This means encouraging children to bring things from their homes to discuss. It means having an interest in the community in which she works; perhaps even taking her class to visit the homes of children.
5. Teachers should not say "His parents did not prepare him for school" and give up.(Few teachers do.) If children have not had certain experiences at home, they must get them in school. If they cannot get them as schools are set up now, then the setting should change.
6. Teachers should encourage children to talk with one another and teach one another. We want a classroom structure, which encourages conversation. Children need to speak fluently before they can read or write. Furthermore, successful verbal communication is the only control of violence that men inflict on one another when breakdown of communication occurs.
7. Teachers should help children to see that it is fun to learn.
8. Schools should prepare children as if colleges did not exist. Higher education is not always the answer for all children. Many must be prepared for survival. They must be able to make it on their own, without taking orders from someone else. Initiative is to be encouraged at every opportunity.
9. We are including a list of books and articles that we have found interesting and relevant to our experiences:

    a. Joseph Featherstone, "The Primary School Revolution in Britain," *The New Republic,* August and September, 1967. Available in reprint.
    b. John Blackie. *Inside the Primary School.* London, Dept. of Education and Science, HMSO, 1967

c. Jonathan Kozol, "Teaching the Unteachable," *The New York Review of Books,* available in reprint.

d. John Holt. *How Children Fail.* Dell Publishing Corp., c1964

e. John Holt. *How Children Learn.* Recently published

f. Paul Goodman. "Mini-Schools: A Prescription for the Reading Problem" *New York Review of Books.* January 4, 1968

g. "The Negro in America", *Newsweek,* November 20, 1967. Reprint

[The reading list was followed by a list of classrooms we recommend visiting.]

Discipline

1. Our rights and our children's rights are clearly defined in Bulletins 22A, 22B, and 22C. 22B #4, p. 6 states: No corporal punishment, no isolation in cloakrooms, no repetitious writing, no public humiliations. *In loco parentis,* the Penna. School law, passed around 1911, while it does not exclude corporal punishment can, by its very loose wording, cover a much more tolerant definition of parental and child behavior.
2. Children rarely cause trouble when they are interested in what they are doing.
3. We want our children treated as teachers would have their own children treated.
4. Children do not fight all the time at home. They use fighting as a weapon to distract the teacher. It disrupts the class and gets them attention.
5. If children have to continually be put out of the room or isolated; if threats must be used continually to keep them quiet and paying attention, then perhaps the system should be re-examined rather than blaming the parents and children for their shortcomings.
6. It is wrong to expect children to sit still and pay attention for long periods of time. Adults are rarely asked to do this.
7. Sending a child to the office to be disciplined does not really get rid of the problem. It is the teacher's responsibility to individually discipline verbally (and privately). When treated with respect, children will respect the teacher and work to the utmost of their capacities.
8. Children can be very self-disciplined but are not encouraged to develop this. They are often taught that they have to be forced to learn under threat of punishment rather than that learning is fun.
9. We would like children to be given real responsibility rather than just be told to follow orders. If they just follow orders, when they are left alone they do not know what to do. We feel that although chaos might be an immediate result of any relaxation of discipline, it is a chaos which has to be encountered. It is *not permanent,* and is a creative chaos which will pass when the children become more responsible. The rewards of self-discipline and responsibility far outweigh the drawbacks of this early chaos.
10. Children should not be punished for talking. We want a classroom structure which encourages free conversation, not one which gives punishment for talking. Talking is an aid to learning. Violence is a result of a breakdown in verbal communication.

Suggestions

1. Some suggestions have been included under the other headings.
2. If working with all children doing the same thing at the same time causes a situation in which a single distraction becomes a discipline problem, then perhaps the class structure should be changed. Nursery and kindergarten children rarely have to be disciplined when they have their "free play." It is usually when attention is required by all of them

at the same time, for any extended period of time, that greater discipline problems arise. Children can appear to be listening in a large group, but many have "turned the teacher off." Why not adapt the system to give more guided freedom during the day? Active participation, moving, walking, *doing*, is one way for children to learn. The teacher, especially the experienced one, is indispensable as a guide, for she knows the curriculum requirements. Parents could help when and where the teachers need them. This would help to immediately individualize the program in the school.

3. Schools should allow situations which allow children to teach each other.
4. Children have to want to read before they actually learn how to. To want to read, they must have access to all kinds of books in large quantities. Suggestions: Scholastic soft covers, comics, newspapers, *Ebony* magazines, books children make themselves, information books, simple nature books, a full encyclopedia for each room, including the kindergarten. Children should certainly not be punished for reading ahead. IF they want to read, then they should just be encouraged to read.
5. We would like to see less fuss made over lining up and going to the bathroom. At home, children do not constantly use the toilet. In school it is a great way to bother the teacher and waste time.
6. Children should be taken on more field trips. Parents are willing to accompany groups on trips. Not all of them need transportation. We have a list of people and places in Germantown. Public transportation could be used when buses are not available.
7. A room should be open during lunch for free play, reading, games.
8. School should allow mothers to bring younger children when they visit. This would help break down barriers between home and school. If small children (and visitors) disrupt things as they are now, perhaps they should be changed.
9. Parents can be instrumental in helping teachers get needed materials. They are also willing to help in any way to get more teachers more free time for planning. This would be in the best interests of our children.

Sample Newsletter to Parents

FRIDAY, NOVEMBER 17, 1996 • THE 205 NEWS • FIRST GRADE • LYNNE STRIEB, TEACHER

HAPPY OCTOBER BIRTHDAYS TO
Tamara Brenner
Mattie Kaye

Here comes a

GREAT BIG THANK YOU to all of the parents who have helped with the children. I hope I haven't missed anyone!

These parents joined us on **trips**: Maria Gregoriou, Emma Stedman, Mr. Martin, April Gray, Mr. Boston, Mrs. Cory (Lucinda's grandmother), Liana Shenken, Doris Branson (Julio's mom), Laura Brenner, Bob Brown invited us to have lunch in the amphitheater of his law office in the Curtis Building. Not only did we have a wonderful, quiet lunch in luxurious swivel chairs, but Mr. Brown also directed us to the beautiful Tiffany glass mosaic in the building lobby.

These parents have helped **in the classroom:** Laura Brenner, Emma Stedman, (Project Time, homework) April Gray, Ashika Boston, (reading, writing, Project Time), Ms. Wynne (Ned's mom,

who accompanied singing of 204 and 205 with her guitar.) Many parents have sent things for us to use or helped their children to bring things from home: The Gregoriou family sent us a huge roll of brown paper which we use for body tracings and for murals; they also gave us their Chinese hamsters for the school year; Janice's mom sent date books for each child; Jason brought a book about learning to tie your shoes and a box with laces so that children who don't know how, could learn; Ned brought in his Body Game; Theo brought a praying mantis; Melinda brought a garden spider; Julio's mom lent me some books to help me select CDs; Timothy has brought in many books about animals, which he shares with the children; Ron brought in a wonderful tape of **Chicka Chicka Boom Boom** and some stickers for everyone; Theodore brought a book about a caterpillar/butterfly; and we've had lots of birthday cupcakes.

We've had many offers of help: Mrs. Valdez and Mr. Avila have offered to help us with Spanish; Mrs. Lyons, a medical student, has offered to teach us about our bodies; Dr. Kaye, a dentist, has offered

to teach us about our teeth; Mr. Shenken has offered to help us with our computers.

All of you have been supportive and helpful with getting notes in on time, helping your children with homework, getting your children to school on time, sending in absence notes, giving your children money for trips and supplies.

BOTH THE CHILDREN AND I THANK YOU FROM THE BOTTOM OF OUR HEARTS! AND A BIG THANK YOU TO TEACHER KATHRYN, TOO. WE ARE SO FORTUNATE!

Sandy Cummings, a University of Pennsylvania graduate student, works in our classroom one and a half days each week. She has been teaching small-group lessons in reading, and has been supervising children in writing and reading.

THE BABY

On Monday, October 28 Dr. Kaye, Mattie's mom, brought her baby Paul to visit our classroom. I've invited parents and their babies to visit the classroom every 6 to 8 weeks for the children to

181

observe. I hope Paul will be able to visit through our two years together. If you have a baby, please visit with us too. That way we can learn what's the same and what's different about individual children. I'll be writing more about these visits in the future.

★ ★ ★ ★ ★

READING - We have spent the first two months of school getting excited about books. The range of readers in the class is great. Some children are beginners, others are already able to read difficult "chapter books."

I have done reading instruction in a variety of ways. **First**, the children write daily in their writing books. As they "sound out" words, they are practicing (and often learning) phonics.

Second, in class we read the homework poems and discussions. Those are good for the beginning readers because as children memorize the words, they point and recognize the connection between what they say and the words on the page. It's GOOD to memorize. Historically, many people have learned to read by first memorizing. We have read books with predictable words in books like **When Will I Read?** and **Chicka Chicka Boom Boom**, and **Pierre**. We also read a weekly children's newspaper and I write messages to the children on the board.

Third, children spend about 20 - 30 minutes reading, either alone or with one or two others. Children often learn effortlessly by reading with other children. They have surprised themselves (and probably you) when they discovered that they could read. As you know, that discovery spurs them on to greater concentration on and excitement about books.

Fourth, for those who are beginning, I do more formal reading instruction, with more teacher direction. So far, besides their own writing and predictable books and poems, they have worked on rhyming words (word families) and flashcards, with words from graded readers.

Fifth, in addition to having the whole class read books together, I read to the children every day.

Some of this may change as the year goes on. Your comments about their reading at the back of their reading homework books have been very helpful. Soon the children will begin to keep their own reading records.

As I said at the Open House, "The best way to become a good reader is by reading." Your child should read at home for at least ten minutes each night. It doesn't have to be a whole book. You can take a few days to complete a book. Don't forget to use the bookmark your child made. Please don't spend hours on "sounding out" words or drilling endlessly. A little might help, but it could get boring and cause a child to dislike reading.

Play rhyming games ("I'm thinking of a word that rhymes with 'day' and it's something you like to do; I'm thinking of a word that rhymes with 'day', and you do it with money when you buy something"); play "I Spy" with initial or ending consonants. Try to read advertisements in the food section of the newspaper. Read labels and signs. There are many words around us!

Watch for three class-made books to come home for you and your children to read. All the children contributed to them (unless they were absent.) The books are: **What I Will Be for Halloween, I Can Read, and On Halloween Night**. Enjoy those books that have predictable words. The children are quite proud of them.

On the Tuesday before Thanksgiving, we will be having a celebration at 1:00 in the afternoon to which you are all invited. We will probably need help that morning. **THANKS AGAIN** for everything you do for us. Come visit us soon. (Please stop at the office first.)

IN THE NEXT NEWSLETTER:
Birthdays, Math, and Writing.
Please let me know what else you'd like to know. Any questions?
Send them to me. I'll respond.

Note: Portions of the original newsletter have been abridged and modified for inclusion in this book.

Parent Contributions in My Classroom, 1970–2000

Arts and Crafts
Prepare clay, paints
Create something out of clay
Supervise printing, paper-making, tie-dyeing, making picture frames for Father's Day
Help with sewing (threading needles, teaching knotting and running stitch, cutting patterns and quilt squares), with weaving
Teach about and make pysanki (Ukrainian and Yugoslavian Easter eggs)
Talk about work as an artist
Make books of all kinds
Make mailbox

Behavior
In to help all the children, son's behavior improved

Parties and Gatherings
Birthday
Halloween (costumes and makeup, cooking, cutting pumpkins, parade)
Thank-you parties for student teachers, volunteers
Thanksgiving (contribute food, supervise cutting, crack nuts, set up, serve food, teach Swahili words for our song, clean up)
Authors' breakfasts and teas (bring food, flowers, decorations; decorate; set up; help serve; clean up)

Clean and organize room and class library
Beginning of the year—help unpack
End of year—help pack up
Class library of about 7,000 books

> Beginning of the year—remove books from boxes and put them on shelves
> Label and color-code books
> Organize books on shelves
> Repair books
> Create a lending library with the children with cards and pockets
> Teach children the system for borrowing and replacing books to shelves
> End of the year—put books back into boxes, label boxes

Sort, organize, and file papers
Put names on folders, workbooks, homework books
With the help of a few children, organize my desk when it gets messy
Clean desks, sink, painting area

Cooking
Help the children cut apples and pumpkins using real knives
Cook and bake with the children: Peanut butter fudge; breads such as challah, scones, pizza,
    cornbread, pretzels; birthday cakes, cookies; gingerbread sleighs; marinara sauce and
    salad from our class garden; potato latkes; apples and honey; chapati; stone soup;
    graham cracker houses
Help me write a grant to buy cooking equipment
Lend me pots and utensils

Cover for me
When I was called out of the room in emergency
When I was late getting the children in line

Share Cultures and Backgrounds
Written and spoken words, songs, stories in Swahili, Chree, Hebrew, Russian, Serbian,
    Japanese, Spanish, Mandarin, Malay, French, German, Urdu, and American Sign
    Language
Foods of

> Ireland (scones)
> Eastern European Jewish people (potato latkes, challah, matzoh)
> Pakistan and India (chapatti, pakora, rice)
> China (spring rolls, dry fried string beans, rice)

Share Cultures and Backgrounds
Customs and celebrations of

> Ireland (songs)
> Unions (songs)
> U.S. African American (street songs and games, how to hold a picnic, a bake sale,
>   Kwanzaa)
> Ukraine (pysanki)
> U.S. Jewish (high holidays, Hanukkah, Passover)
> India (Devali, dance)
> China (chopsticks)

Curriculum
Share origins of children's names
Bring dogs for us to observe—science
Teach about dental and physical health
Bring babies for us to observe and describe

Errands to home and store for things I forgot to bring
Film and batteries
Pots and utensils
Ingredients

Give me suggestions
Linda, about theater (complaint: play about Teddy Roosevelt during Black History Month)
About handling difficult kids

About rumors after the strike
For end-of-year picnic
About tension
About things children want for classroom
To put list of helpers' names on poster
About what cooking equipment to request in a grant proposal
About how to make homework directions clearer
About dating homework
About a child's observed behavior—another eye helps
A contract for behavior for own son
About a take-home quiz
About getting children to practice spelling homework
To make a list of words all authors use

Homework
Take notes on discussions
Copy
Put into books
Mark
Talk with children about

Help with Children
Solve problem of pills brought to school
Practice handwriting
Write stories
Walk out with child afraid of Halloween stories
Walk children to bathroom
Stop fights
Calm child having a tantrum when mom left
Help complete hard homework
Line children up in schoolyard when I'm late
Notice who seems to need help and who doesn't

When I needed help to make things go smoothly
Sewing
Reading
Writing
Project time
Math
Cooking
Playing games at school
Making games at home
Setting up computer, teaching me

Make games, teach them to the children, play games

Marking
Math papers at home
Homework

Math workbook
Reading worksheets
Spelling tests

Math
Practice with measuring
Play games (dice and cube, three-men morris, checkers, chess, Othello, tic-tac-toe, 100
    board, Chutes and Ladders, number base games)
Supervise math groups
Read workbook directions
Help with math
Help with writing numbers 1–1,000

Observe
Twigs with kids through microscope
My reading lesson
Calm in room
Parent seems critical
Lesson on Frederick Douglass
Animals (mice, silkworms)

Parents teach about their work and interests
Sign painter and carpenter
Interior designer
Three doctors: pathologist, pediatrician, internist
Ophthalmologist's assistant
Legal secretary
Homemaker
Assistant to president of a university in charge of community affairs
Barber and truck driver
Lawyer
Computer experts
Union organizer
Musician
Music teacher
Peace worker from Pendle Hill
Secretary at community college
Fairmount Park team leader
Three architects
Filmmaker and videographer

Photographs
Fix children's hair and clothes on picture day
Take pictures of celebrations and everyday events

Prepare Gifts
Collect money
Supervise making

Reading/writing
Help at my home during the teachers' strike
Listen to individual children read
Listen to a small group read
Read with own child
Make books
Read to class (English, Spanish, Serbian, Mandarin)
Choose book to read to class
Write and read to visually impaired helper
Type stories
Make and show flashcards
Show me folder for list of words all authors use

Set up/fix
Bulletin boards with student work
Aquarium
Computer
Broken bookcase
Blocks (sanded)

Singing and guitar
Irish songs
Street songs and games
Union songs
Raffi
Hebrew songs
Mexican songs
French songs
Serbian songs
Russian songs

Trips
Parents prepare name tags, take children to the bathroom, keep me calm
Walks through neighborhood

Walking trips (Kelly and Lingelbach Schools)
Insect walks
Friends Free Library
Northwest Regional Library
To my house during strike
To Fernhill Park for picnics and seeds
To the class garden at the Roberts's house
To visit all the children's homes
To observe the trees
To the train and downtown to City Hall
To the supermarket

Walking Trips (Greenfield School)
Indian restaurant for tour and snacks
Taney Park for picnics, to find insects and seeds, to let the monarch butterflies go

Free Library and picnic at Rittenhouse Square
Supermarket
City Hall tower
Annenberg Theater, University of Pennsylvania
Franklin Field and the Palestra
University of Pennsylvania Museum of Anthropology and Archeology
Tour of the housekeeping areas of the Rittenhouse Hotel
30th Street Train Station
Post office at 30th Street
Academy of Natural Sciences
Franklin Institute
Pennsylvania Academy of Fine Arts
Reading Terminal Market
Westin Hotel, Liberty Place to see gingerbread houses and the school choir
Architectural tour of church at 22nd & Spruce to see repair after fire

On buses, trains, trolleys, subway
Zoo
Philadelphia Museum of Art
Italian market
City Hall tower
Chew estate
Balch Institute & Law office
Klein Gallery
African American Museum
Blockson African American Collection, Temple University Library
Wagner Free Institute of Science

Parent-organized trips
Class garden at Roberts's house
Visits to all children's homes
Franklin Field & Palestra
Tour of housekeeping areas of Rittenhouse Hotel
Main post office, 30th St.
Tour of church, 22nd & Spruce, to see repair after fire
Law office
City Council offices

Typing
Stories for class library
Class discussions

Things Bobbie Did to Help the Children and Me (*Grouped*)

Animals
Feed animals
Observe and care for animals though doesn't like them, 6/15/82

Art materials
Work with clay, model, 12/16/81
Clay ruined—lesson, 12/16/81
Put out paints and clay, 2/5/82

Attention to children
Talk with children, 2/5/82
Work with small group on problems (pills), 3/9/82
Small group—to library to find book, supervise finding a picture, 6/4/82

Cook with children
Cook peanut butter fudge, 6/24/81
Cook gingerbread sleighs—cut pieces, 12/11/81
Cook gingerbread sleighs—assemble and wrap, 12/22/81

File, sort, organize my things
File and sort, 6/11/81
Organize and clean room and closets, 3/19/82
Organize and put things away—end of year, 5/26/82
Help with school records, 6/30/82
Help me pack, 5/31/83

General help
Help with party, 12/23/81
Help with school records, 6/30/82
Use contact to get us into courtroom, 5/18/82

Mark
Mark workbooks, spelling tests, 2/5/82

Math
Make games, 1/20/82
Make math board games, teach them, 1/82
Games, 2/5/82

Review, 2/5/82
Make coin game, 3/9/82
Help with reading and arithmetic, 3/25/83

Organize with children
Organize class library (cards, stamps, pockets, kids), 5/5/82
Organize circulation of books, 5/7/82
Show interest in condition of library, 10/2/82
Collate pages of a class book for each child, 6/22/83

Organize parents
Supervise gift from parents to me, 6/11/82
Organize gift from parents, 6/18/82, 6/25/82

Other eyes/ observer
Her observations help me, hears and sees what I miss, 2/5/82
Give advice about children's behavior and parents, 4/16/82
Help train volunteers, 5/28/82
Calm me, 6/15/82
Problem—talking about me with another teacher; told me about the conversation,
     5/28/82

Reading/writing
Small reading group, 12/22/81
Reading with one child, 1/7/82
Reading, 2/5/82
Make alphabet printing set, 3/9/82
Model reading, 5/28/82
Small group—to library to find book, supervise finding a picture, 6/4/82
Help with reading and arithmetic, 3/25/83

Work on displays
Bulletin board, under my direction, 1/11/82
Bulletin board—hang new one, 6/8/82

Newsletter: Parents Tell the Children About Their Work

FRIDAY, JUNE 17, 1996 • THE 206 NEWS • SECOND GRADE • LYNNE STRIEB, TEACHER

THE AUTHORS' BREAKFAST

was a great success! There were 24 guests. The children were very excited to read their stories to all of the adults. Their reading and the stories themselves were really impressive. They'd practiced a lot to speak loudly and to read accurately. It meant a lot to them to have another audience (different from their classmates) for their writing. Publishing their books, putting them into the class library, reading them to others not only gives the children a purpose for writing beyond writing for their own enjoyment (which IS important, too.)

The food was delicious, thanks to all of you. We really appreciated all your contributions. There was plenty, and the children were so well-mannered. I'd talked to them ahead of time about taking a little and then going back for just as much as they could eat, not more. They listened well.

I want to especially thank those of you who were able to come ahead of time to help with setting up: Charles' grandfather, Bert Strieb, Teacher Kathryn, Jillian Benton, Arlene Kennedy, Mrs. White, Mr. and Mrs. Sinicki, Mrs. MacDonald, (Larry's mom.)

Since the last 206 NEWS we have had more parents come to talk about their work. Each of the presentations was so very thoughtful and clever. It's hard to hold the interest of young children, and they managed for the most part, to do it. Again, I can't do justice to the wonderful presentations and to the questions the children asked, but you can ask your children more about them.

Gloria's dad is a carpenter for his day job. But the job he loves to do is to paint signs. He told us what he was doing as he designed and painted a large sign for an imaginary party. He showed us the tools he uses - different kinds of brushes, paint, pencil. He talked about how he uses math to measure and said it's important to make the letters for signs large and bright. The sign stayed up in our room for a few days.

Lily's mom is a doctor. She talked about her work and then got the children to diagnose two illnesses. She pretended she was the patient, telling the children her symptoms. They asked questions to narrow their guesses, and then they figured out that she had a sore throat that might be a strep infection.

They then predicted the treatment. She also pretended to be an old woman who felt very tired and got out of breath when she walked up steps. The children narrowed it down to lung cancer or heart problems. One child's final question let them know that it was her heart. Your children were doing "differential diagnoses" like real doctors! They are good questioners (though I'm not ready to be treated by one of them yet.)

★ · ★ · ★ ·

Jordan's dad is a Ground Maintenance Crew Chief at Fairmount Park. He got the children to explain what those words mean. He brought a helmet, gloves, goggles, earphones, rubber hip boots, brightly colored vests and other equipment and he dressed Jordan and Zerena in this work uniform. He showed us pictures of different kinds of grass cutters, from smallest to largest. He told us that before he was a crew chief, he was cleaning fish ladders on the Schuykill River, and fell in. He had a safety harness, so he wasn't swept away by the water. He told us about all the animals that live in the park. He described the hard work he did during the recent blizzard. We thanked him for cleaning all that snow. At the end, he used his walkie-talkie to tell his co-worker that he was ready to meet him outside.

On Friday, June 11, we had a trip and a wonderful lesson given by Mandip's father, Mr. Singh, who owns a restaurant. We have been planning this trip for the whole year.

Mr. Singh gave a lot of thought to our visit. We were seated at a long set table. Mr. Singh told us a little about the restaurant and, with Mandip's help, about the Taj Mahal, which was pictured in a silk embroidered wall hanging. Suddenly food came out. There was a plate of three different Indian appetizers for each child with a sauce for dipping. You would have been very proud of your children! Before we left school we had to talk about foods that look or smell different from the ones we usually eat. I reminded them that it would be bad manners to say "Eeuw" or to make a face. As many times before, I reminded them that people all over the world eat strange to them, but other people (the people in India) think it's delicious. (And I think it's delicious.) They heard what I'd said. Most of the children tasted each appetizer and though some left food on their plates, no one said anything insulting. When one of the appetizers was spicy hot, Mr. and Mrs. Singh rescued us with icy soda.

After eating, Mr. Singh responded to the children's excellent questions about running that restaurant. We then had a tour of the kitchen and saw how the Indian bread *nan* is made in a *tandoor* (a special oven.) Before we left, we tasted it. Some said it tasted like a pancake. All agreed that it was delicious.

As I said, you would have been so proud! I was. And I appreciated Mr. Singh's thoughtful preparation for our visit. Thank you, Mr. Singh.

Thank you Mrs. Benton for joining us on our last two trips. Without you we couldn't have gone.

There's more to be proud of about the children. Recently some teachers visited the class and they pointed out things that are very important to me. They noticed how well and quietly the children were talking and working together. They remarked that no one was fighting, that the children showed interest in one another's work, and that they said wonderful, supportive things as they helped each other. These visitors said that all of this was very unusual. Creating community among children is very important to me but that it's hard to know if we've been successful. Now I know we have (for the most part).

As for summer, you already know how many of the things you can do to help your child: Set aside time to read every day; visit the Free Library and join a book club; read every sign in sight; play spelling games; write letters to friends and family; write notes to your child and encourage him or her to write back; start a journal - draw in it too.

For math: practice counting by twos, threes, fives, tens, forward and backward from 100; play cards and keep scores; play "Guess My Number," count money; make change; do things by the clock. ("We'll eat lunch at 11:30." "Let me know when it's 4:00 and we'll read a story."). Give your child word problems to solve. "How many legs would five children have? Write the number story."

Read to and talk with your children. Even if the TV is on (not too much, I hope) you can at least sit and talk about one or two of the programs. Here are some words for books or TV: "What do you think will happen next?" "How do you think it will end?" "What was your favorite part?" "Why did you like it?" ("Because it was good" is not a good answer.) "Could you think of another way it could end?" "What happened first? In the middle? At the end?"

Now is the time to give a special thank you to Teacher Kathryn for all of her hard and wonderful work in our classroom. She helped me and worked directly with your children. We've all learned so much from her.

It's been a challenging and wonderful year. I'm looking forward to seeing you next year.

Note: Portions of the original newsletter have been abridged and modified for inclusion in this book.

Notes

Introduction

1. I do not address parent-teacher conferences in detail in this book. Lawrence-Lightfoot's (2003) book *The Essential Conversation: What parents and teachers can learn about each other* is an important, comprehensive book on that subject.

2. Lawrence-Lightfoot (1978) wrote:

> Children in the family are treated as special persons, but pupils in school are necessarily treated as members of categories. From these different perspectives develop the *particularistic* expectations that parents have for their children and the *universalistic* expectations of teachers. In other words, when parents ask the teacher to "be fair" with their child or to give him "a chance," they are usually asking that the teacher give special attention to their child (i.e., consider the individual qualities, the developmental and motivational characteristics). When teachers talk about being "fair" to everyone, they mean giving equal amounts of attention, judging everyone by the same objective standards, using explicit and public criteria for making judgments. With fairness comes rationality, order, and detachment. (Lawrence-Lightfoot, p. 22)

Though in general I agree with Lawrence-Lightfoot that teachers and parents may have different perspectives, this does not mean a teacher must be detached, must treat children as categories, and must always judge everyone by the same objective standards. Children are individuals, each with distinctive strengths and vulnerabilities. I tried to keep this idea central to every aspect of my teaching—from my classroom layout, to the schedule, to finding ways to make it possible for me to observe students' individual interests and ways of learning.

3. A longer description of my observing, describing, and documenting will appear in my forthcoming essay "Drawing the Individual Forward."

4. See L. Strieb, "Visiting and Revisiting the Trees," in Cochran-Smith & Lytle, 1993; and Strieb, 1985, for detail about how I used my journal.

5. The Descriptive Review of the Child is also the subject of Himley with Carini, 2000. Prospect's processes are copyrighted, and The Prospect Center should receive full attribution when they are used.

6. The Philadelphia Teachers' Learning Cooperative has been meeting every Thursday since 1978. We started when funding for the Advisory Center, a teachers' center, was withdrawn by the School District of Philadelphia. Our group of

teachers had been discussing educational issues over dinner at the Center on Thursdays after we finished making curriculum materials or attending workshops after school. We found those discussions valuable to our practice, and we wanted to continue to meet. Because we did not want to have to worry about funding, we made the decision to have no membership fee. Starting in the early 1970s, many of the founding members had attended seminars led by Patricia Carini, Corinne Biggs, and Jessica Howard, and other staff at the Prospect School, both at the Advisory Center and at the Prospect School in North Bennington, Vermont. We decided to focus our meetings on children and classrooms, using the Descriptive Review Processes developed at the Prospect School. To learn more about this group, see Philadelphia Teachers' Learning Cooperative, 1984, and Abu El-Haj, 2003.

Chapter 1

1. As I wrote this, I came across the following quote from an essay by Elizabeth Graue (2005). I believe that it applies to all teachers, whether pre-service, beginners, or experienced.

> Individuals come into their professional education with cultural scripts that shape interaction and meaning making (Biklen, 1995; Goldstein & Lake, 2000; Hollingsworth, 1989; Kagan, 1992). These beliefs, which provide a framework for appropriation of knowledge and values in professional development, are quite stable and form the foundation for an emerging professional identity (Kagan, 1992). Images of education figure prominently in the formation of beliefs, shaped by notions of good teachers, ideas of the self as teacher, and memories of self as student (Kagan, 1992). We can better understand the genesis of home-school relations by examining the beliefs held by prospective teachers as they begin their professional program. (p.159).

2. Yiddish word meaning "village."

3. Dunbar was one of the first schools in Philadelphia named for an African American. It was located in an economically distressed neighborhood in North Philadelphia (now surrounded by Temple University and newer homes), and because at the time many Philadelphia schools had segregated staffs, its faculty was all African American. Many of the teachers were community leaders and members of prestigious churches, fraternal groups, and volunteer organizations.

4. Cutler (2000) gives a comprehensive history of the relationship between parents and schools. Though national in its reach, many of the examples are from Philadelphia and its suburbs.

5. See Countryman (2006) for a detailed history of the civil rights struggle in Philadelphia.

6. One exception to this was the Henry School, a public school in West Mount Airy, the area immediately north of Germantown, where many fairly middle-class White and Black people lived. When African Americans began to buy homes in

the Henry School neighborhood, the Jewish principal of Henry School, the rabbi from the local synagogue, and many of the White Jewish residents, vowed that there would not be a White flight from that neighborhood and its schools. They succeeded. Currently, 40 years later, Henry School is a majority African American school. A small group of White parents of young children are trying to convince their White neighbors to join them in sending their children to Henry. Most of the White families in Mount Airy, though they choose to live in that integrated neighborhood, now send their children to independent or religious schools.

7. The Westside Neighborhood Council met monthly in the community room of a local federal high-rise housing project. The Germantown Community Council, another integrated group, was made up of civic and business groups from the lower northwest section of Philadelphia. During the late 1960s, these civic groups were struggling on a variety of fronts. Among those struggles was the one for the community to have a say in the placement, curriculum, and staffing of planned new public schools. For example, Westside, with the help of the Germantown Community Council, had successfully fought for the location of the planned John B. Kelly School to be built in 1969. The original plan had called for destroying several blocks of row homes owned by African Americans, while leaving untouched a large block of open land with only one house on it, situated across the street from the private Germantown Cricket Club. The original plan would have been much more expensive to carry out, but more important, it seemed to the community that by tearing down those homes, those in power were trying to force long-time working-class African American homeowners to move away.

8. The Westside Parent Cooperative Nursery School was one of several cooperative nurseries in Philadelphia. One of the founders of the program was Ruth Bacon, mother of the actor Kevin Bacon and wife of the well-known city planner Edmund Bacon. The program ended in June of 2005.

9. The federal Follow Through program provided tuition to classroom assistants who pursued degrees.

10. The following African American parents had children in the Westside Parent Cooperative Nursery: Barbara Brown, Joan Countryman, Zatella Jenkins, Berry Coverdale. The following White parents had children in the Westside Parent Cooperative Nursery: Lynne Strieb, Anne Weir. The following African American parents had children who had also attended Westside, at Keyser School: Fay Bennett, Florine Brown, Barbara Brown. Joan Benjamin was the only White parent who had children old enough to attend Keyser. Two of the African American mothers had children who attended Germantown Friends School. Husbands/ fathers are mentioned only occasionally in this story because, though those of us who had husbands (not called "partners" in the 1960s) found them to be interested in, and supportive and proud of what we were doing. They were working days or nights and were unable to join us in this work.

11. Notes, meeting of the Keyser School Community Mothers' Group, January 29, 1968.

12. Annette Lareau (2000) takes social class to be a defining issue in parental involvement in schools. Though she says, and I agree, that this is not always the case, it is interesting to look at the Westside situation (and at other situations

where social action joins together people who are different) in this light. Lareau wrote:

> Social class—specifically education, occupational status, income, and the characteristics of work—provides parents with unequal *resources* and dispositions, differences that critically affect parental involvement in the educational experience of their children.
>
> First . . . upper-middle-class parents have the capacity to understand the diagnostic and instructional language used by teachers, or, more generally, the *competence* to help their children in school. . . . A college education provided them with the confidence that they were capable of understanding teachers. . . .
>
> Second, social status itself also provided a resource. Upper-middle-class parents approached teachers as social equals. . . . Their occupational success led most Prescott parents to believe that they were capable of being school teachers. . . . Parents' education and social status in turn influenced their belief in their proper role in schooling, especially their right to take a leadership role in education. . . . A college education provided them with the confidence that they were capable of understanding teachers. . . .
>
> Third, *income and material resources* also played a role in facilitating family-school relationships. [Lareau talks here about paid house cleaners and two cars as indications of upper-middle-class status. Nobody in the group of parents with whom I was associated had either of those; they had one car, no paid house cleaners.]
>
> Fourth, there were indications that the style, routine, and purpose of parents' *work* affected family-school relationships in important ways. [For three of we Keyser Community Mothers, our work was on hold while we were at home caring for our children: psychiatric nurse, architect, and teacher (me). Three of us were homemakers with a high school education. One of the mothers worked at night. One of the mothers was a city planner, working in educational administration. Our husbands worked in a variety of jobs: truck driver, recreation center director, college professor, elementary math teacher, political activist, security guard. One of us did not live with her husband. Four of us later became involved in education as classroom assistants and after-school program workers.]
>
> Finally, *networks*, themselves linked to social class position, provide parents with different amounts of general information about schooling. . . . These social connections mediated parents' connections to the school . . . I would maintain that higher social class provides parents with more resources to intervene in schooling and to bind families into tighter connections with social institutions than are available to working class families. (pp. 170–172)

Chapter 2

1. Begun by President Lyndon B. Johnson, Follow Through was a program created to give low-income children and families the same services that were

available to them in the federal Head Start preschool program. According to Mary Kennedy (1978), the program changed into a research and delivery program. Various providers developed models for educating elementary school children, and the models were implemented in sites all over the country. Philadelphia was home to eight different models.

2. Dr. Marcus Foster was the principal at Dunbar School from 1958 to 1964. He went on to become the first male African American secondary school principal in Philadelphia, and in 1970, he became Superintendent of Schools in Oakland, California. In 1973 he was ambushed and killed there by the Symbionese Liberation Army. John Spencer (2009) writes:

> At the dawn of that new era [of accountability], Marcus Foster helped pioneer a more pro-active leadership role for heads of schools. The hallmarks of his leadership—especially his deep-rooted faith in the capacity of all children to learn and his commitment to engage and empower all members of a school community—anticipated the findings of subsequent research on principals who foster high achievement.

3. Mrs. Battle's position was funded by the Ford Foundation's Great Cities Improvement Program, a precursor to the federally funded Follow Through program. Home and School Coordinators became a staple in all Title I Schools in Philadelphia. Mrs. Battle, Miss Chambers, and Connie are pseudonyms.

4. At Kelly School, parents were permitted to choose their child's placement in either an open classroom or traditional track.

5. During the 1970s, two meanings for *open classroom* emerged. For progressive educators, *open classroom* meant a classroom in which children were taught in less traditional ways; where children had a choice of a wide variety of books, math, and arts materials and activities from which they could learn at some time of the day; where teachers did not always teach to the entire class, but rather to individuals and small groups. For administrators and architects, *open classroom* could refer to schools built with clusters or pods of classrooms with no walls between them. These classrooms (which we open classroom teachers preferred to call *open-space classrooms*) were designed for team teaching, usually traditional teaching (teacher standing in front of the class, children seated). It was also less expensive to build schools with fewer walls. Kelly School was an open-space school, but within the school, even in the open spaces, there were traditional teachers and open classroom teachers.

6. The stories about Mrs. Collier and Tonya in Chapters 2 and 4 originally appeared in different form in Strieb, 1985.

7. This letter was sent to the superintendent of schools, who then sent me a copy.

Chapter 3

1. This chapter is not an argument with research on homework or an attempt to justify what I did. It describes what I did and my reasons for doing it in the light

of my experience in the classroom, with parents who expected homework and policy that required it.

2. Over the years in Philadelphia, I taught only four children whose parents did not speak English: three who spoke Spanish and one who spoke Cantonese. I was not able to translate the homework into those languages. The school did not have translators. I know that it's not fair if even one child can't do the homework because of language differences, and I regret that I did not try harder. If I had taught more children who spoke other languages, I would have found ways to make the homework understandable to them. For example, if I had had classes in which there were more Spanish-speaking children, I would have given homework in both English and Spanish. And if I had taught classes in which children spoke many different languages, I might have given homework that involved no reading at all (though that would have been difficult for me).

3. Linda Bean, a teacher in the Philadelphia Teachers' Learning Cooperative, described doing this work with her second graders, and I adopted the practice.

4. See, e.g., A. Kohn, 2006.

Chapter 4

1. Personal conversation, 10/98. When I describe a child's behavior that was disruptive and difficult for me, I also acknowledge that a child is more than his or her "bad" behavior. There are whole persons behind any of these brief descriptions—children who have interests and interactions that are pleasant as well as difficult.

2. These rules were part of a larger behavior program called Assertive Discipline, developed by Lee and Marlene Canter (1976/1982), which included the teacher's clearly stated expectations for good behavior, scripts and methods for rewarding good behavior, such as external rewards for getting caught being good, and a hierarchy of punishments, among other things. This way of handling classroom behavior was very popular in Philadelphia schools and many teachers practiced it with ease. I never did get these practices straight when directed to use them by my principal, probably because I didn't really approve of external rewards.

3. "Mrs.Strieb, Theo S. Donald J and Shawn is messing with me. I told them to stop. They keep doing it. Can you tell them to stop. they hit me and one time kicked. they call me name's. they do it after school. they call it beat up girl time. they do it to more people too. it gets on our very last nerve. my dad said get them. I try to. the names they call me: fatso, fat mama, fat, chubby, ugly, freak. Can you remind me to stay away from Donald and Theodore. Nayomi Bodin"

4. Though Mrs. Booker and I did this Descriptive Review of Denise 7 years before *From Another Angle* was published, "[T]he five headings . . . though they have been revised and renamed over time, are the consistent framework for every Descriptive Review of the Child presentation" and have been since the process was developed (Carini, 2000, p. 15).

5. Notes, meeting of the Philadelphia Teachers' Learning Cooperative, January 21, 1993.

Chapter 5

1. Begun under President Lyndon B. Johnson, Follow Through was a program under Title I, created to give low-income children and families the same services that were available to them in the federal Head Start pre-school program. According to Kennedy (1977, 1978), the program changed into a research and delivery program. Various providers developed models for educating elementary school children, and the models were implemented in sites all over the country. Philadelphia was home to eight different models.

2. As I understood it, the law stated that assistance supported by Title I legislation must be given to only Title I–eligible children. Title I help was to be given by classroom assistants and Parent Scholars as an addition to the ordinary work done by the classroom teacher. In reality, two things often happened. First, classroom assistants and Parent Scholars were used to increase the adult-to-student ratio, and they were often assigned by the teacher to work with non–Title I children. That allowed the teacher more time to spend with the less well achieving students. Second, after the law was enforced, many teachers assigned their Title I assistants and Parent Scholars to work with Title I–eligible children while they (the teachers) worked with the non–Title I children. Of course, both practices defeated the purpose of the funding, which was to give children eligible for Title I support in addition to the classroom teacher, not instead of it. In later years, to be certain that aid was going to exactly the children who were supposed to be served, and probably as recognition of classroom implementation realities, only schools with at least 70% of the children below the poverty level were designated Title I schools, and the assistants and Parent Scholars were allowed to work with everyone in the class.

3. I'd taught them, as I'd taught many parents how to help the children cut apples in such a way that they wouldn't cut their fingers: Sit the apple stem side up so that it doesn't roll around. Hold the knife over the stem end of the apple and put both hands on top of the knife—one hand over the blade, the other over the handle. Warn the children not to wrap their fingers around the blade. Press down on both the handle and blade, rocking the knife until one's weight pushes the knife through the apple and cuts it in half. Place the halves flat side down on the table and press the knife through again to make quarters. The delicate part is making sure the fingers are not wrapped around the knife blade. Yes, an adult must be present when children do this, but I never had a child cut a hand or a finger.

4. Occasionally volunteers who were not parents worked alongside me in the classroom. Kathryn Keeler was one of these people. Kathryn had heard me speak to the Network of Executive Women in a panel discussion; and immediately following the program she came to me and asked if I could use a volunteer. She had just retired from her executive position in a local corporation; because she had always enjoyed working with children, she was looking for more regular volunteer work. For 5 years, once and sometimes twice a week, "Teacher" Kathryn worked with the children and with me. The parents knew her from the first days

of school, when we picked up the class outside in the schoolyard. Although she was not a parent and thus was not included in the stories in this book, she did many of the tasks that are described in Chapter 6. I prepared volunteers and parents in the same way and they did similar things in the classroom. The major difference is that volunteers did not have their own children in the room. Kathryn continues to work with children and teachers in Philadelphia on a regular basis. The children and I owe a great debt to her. Perhaps one day I will write about working with her.

5. My teammate, Eve Adler, had a gift for organizing such group activities, and I followed her lead. These workshops were very popular with parents.

6. If that happened (and it didn't happen often), I talked with both parent and child together and let them know that the parent was there to help me by working not only with her child but with all the children. I also told the parent to be sure to spend a few minutes with her own child at the beginning of each visit to the classroom. I can't remember a child ever making it uncomfortable for me to have a parent in the room.

Chapter 6

1. Prospect's Reflection on a Word is described in Carini, 2000, pp. 13–14.

2. Notes from a summary of a Reflective Conversation on *bring/bringing* by Cecelia Traugh, Chair, Prospect Summer Institute on Descriptive Inquiry, 2003.

3. Over the years, I learned that the way I worked with parents and babies and the way Educating Children for Parenting (ECP) did things were quite similar. When ECP's program was brought into some Philadelphia public schools, I worked with it and encouraged other teachers in my schools to do so. More information can be found at info@ecparenting.org.

Chapter 7

1. Essays by M. Resnick, D. Jumpp, and C. Chin in *Cityscapes: Eight views from the classroom* (Peterson, Check, & Ylvisaker, 1996) were written when the authors were classroom teachers. There are few such examples of writing by teachers about parent teacher relationships. A thoughtful, outstanding book filled with suggestions from several schools is *Creating Welcoming Schools: A Practical Guide to Home-School Partnerships with Diverse Families* (Allen, 2007).

2. Another excellent book that addresses parental involvement from a whole-school perspective is *In Schools We Trust: Creating Communities of Learning in an Era of Testing and Standardization* (Meier, 2002). Before she became an administrator, Meier was a kindergarten teacher. In this book, she speaks primarily from the perspective of a school director rather than a teacher. Chapter 3 has a detailed discussion of parents, schools, and trust.

3. Bryk and Schneider (2002, pp. 20–22) call this *relational trust*. My words are remarkably similar to theirs, though I wrote them long before I read their book.

4. I taught three children whose fathers were sole parents and one whose male cousin was his guardian. One father shared joint custody with his ex-wife; he wanted a role in his son's education but lived far from the school. One of the single fathers believed that his child should take all responsibility for getting school-work done at home but didn't allow his child enough time to do it. One father took short periods of time off from work to repair classroom furniture and to talk with me about his daughter's progress in academic work and about her behavior. The guardian worked alongside me in the classroom when he was able to, but because of many health problems, often had to cancel. I've already written about Mr. Howard (Chapter 4).

5. Bryk and Schneider (2002) talk about the importance of power in relational trust.

> Individuals' discernments about intentionality are influenced by the differential power associated with relative social status in an organization. Most relations in schools are asymmetrical with respect to power. Principals hold considerable authority over teachers, and local school professionals in turn hold status over parents. . . .
>
> Although important variations exist in the power distribution across roles in an urban school community, no one person exercises absolute power. Even principals—the single most influential actors in schools—remain dependent on both parents and teachers to achieve success in their work. (p. 128)

6. Guadalupe Valdes (1995) writes eloquently and in depth about this topic in *Con Respeto: Bridging the Distances Between Culturally Diverse Families and Schools.*

References

Abu El-Haj, T. (2003). Constructing ideas about equity from the standpoint of the particular: Exploring the work of one urban teacher network. *Teachers College Record, 105*(5), 817–845.

Allen, J. (2007). *Creating welcoming schools: A practical guide to home-school partnerships with diverse families.* New York: Teachers College Press.

Booth, A., & Dunn, J. F. (1996). *Family school links: How do they affect educational outcomes?* Mahwah, NJ: Lawrence Erlbaum.

Bryk, A., & Schneider, B. (2002). *Trust in schools: A core resource for improvement.* New York: Russell Sage Foundation.

Canter, L., & Canter, M. (1976). *Assertive discipline: A take-charge approach for today's educator.* Los Angeles: Canter and Associates. (Original work published 1982)

Carini, P. F. (2001). *Starting strong: A different look at children, schools, and standards.* New York: Teachers College Press.

Carini, P. F. (2002). Format for close reading documents, texts, etc. In M. Himley (Ed.), *Prospect's descriptive processes: The child, the art of teaching, and the classroom and school* (pp. 49–51). North Bennington, VT: Prospect Center. (Original work published 1996)

Chin, C. (1996). Are you the teacher that gives parents homework? In A. Peterson, J. Check, & M. Ylvisaker (Eds.), *Cityscapes: Eight views from the classroom* (pp. 146–163). Berkeley, CA: National Writing Project.

Cochran-Smith, M., & Lytle, S. L. (1993). *Inside/outside: Teacher research and knowledge.* New York: Teachers College Press.

Countryman, M. (2006). *Up south: Civil rights and black power in Philadelphia.* Philadelphia: University of Pennsylvania Press.

Cutler, W. W., III. (2000). *Parents and schools: The 150 year struggle for control in American education.* Chicago: University of Chicago Press.

Graue, E. (2005). Theorizing and describing preservice teachers' images of families and schooling. *Teachers College Record, 7*(1), 157–185.

Himley, M. (1991). *Shared territory: Understanding children's writing as works.* New York: Oxford University Press.

Himley, M. (Ed.). (2002). *Prospect's descriptive processes: The child, the art of teaching, and the classroom and school.* North Bennington, VT: Prospect Center.

Himley, M., with Carini, P. F. (Eds.) (2000). *From another angle: Children's strengths and school standards.* New York: Teachers College Press.

Jeynes, W. (2005). A meta-analysis of the relation of parental involvement to urban elementary school student academic achievement. *Urban Education, 40*(3), 237–269.

Jumpp, D. (1996). Extending the literate community: Literacy over a lifespan. In A. Peterson, J. Check, & M. Ylvisaker (Eds.), *Cityscapes: Eight views from the classroom* (pp. 133–143). Berkeley, CA: National Writing Project.

Kennedy, M. (1977). The Follow Through program. *Curriculum Inquiry, 7*(3), 183–208.

Kennedy, M. (1978). Findings from the Follow Through planned variation study. *Educational Researcher, 7*(6), 3–11.

Kohn, A. (2006). *The homework myth: Why our kids get too much of a bad thing.* Cambridge, MA: Da Capo Press.

Lareau, A. (2000). *Home advantage: Social class and parental intervention in elementary education.* Lanham, MD: Rowman and Littlefield.

Lawrence-Lightfoot, S. (1978). *Worlds apart: Relationships between families and schools.* New York: Basic Books.

Lawrence-Lightfoot, S. (2003). *The essential conversation: What parents and teachers can learn about each other.* New York: Random House.

Lytle, S. (2008). At last: Practitioner inquiry and the practice of teaching: Some thoughts on *Better. Journal for Research in Teaching of English, 42*(3), 373–379.

Meier, D. (2002). *In schools we trust: Creating communities of learning in an era of testing and standardization.* Boston: Beacon Press.

No child left behind: A parent's guide to NCLB. (2003). Washington, DC: U.S. Department of Education, 31–35.

Peterson, A., Check, J., & Ylvisaker, M. (Eds.). (1999). *Cityscapes: Eight views from the classroom.* Berkeley, CA: National Writing Project.

Philadelphia Teachers' Learning Cooperative. (1984). On becoming teacher experts: Buying time. *Language Arts, 51*(7), 731–736.

Resnick, M. (1996). Making connections between families and schools. In A. Peterson, J. Check, & M. Ylvisaker (Eds.). *Cityscapes: Eight views from the classroom* (pp. 115–132). Berkeley, CA: National Writing Project.

Spencer, J. (2009). A "new breed" of principal: Marcus Foster and urban school reform in the United States, 1966–1969. *Journal of Educational Administration and History, 41*(3), 285–300.

Strieb, L. Y. (1985). *A (Philadelphia) teacher's journal.* Grand Forks, N.D.: University of North Dakota.

Strieb, L. Y. (1993). Visiting and revisiting the trees. In M. Cochran-Smith & S. L. Lytle (Eds.), *Inside/outside: Teacher research and knowledge* (pp. 121–130). New York: Teachers College Press.

Strieb, L. Y. (1999). Communicating with parents: One teacher's story. In J. W. Lindfors & J. S. Wells Townsend (Eds.), *Teaching language arts: Learning through dialogue* (pp. 121–130). Urbana, IL: National Council of Teachers of English.

Valdes, G. (1995). *Con respeto: Bridging the distances between culturally diverse families and schools.* New York: Teachers College Press.

Williams, R. (1961). *The Long Revolution.* London: Chatto and Windus.

Index

About the Author

LYNNE YERMANOCK STRIEB taught kindergarten, first grade, and second grade classes in Philadelphia public schools for 31 years. She also taught a reception class for 4-year-olds in an Infants School in Smethwick, West Midlands, England, as a Fulbright Exchange Teacher. After undergraduate and graduate studies in art history at the University of Pennsylvania, she received her M.Ed from Temple University. As a parent, she was active in community groups concerned with education and equity in local public schools. She is a founding member of the Philadelphia Teachers' Learning Cooperative. Though she retired from teaching in 2000, she continues to participate in PTLC's weekly meetings. She is a member of the Philadelphia Writing Project, where she is a teacher-consultant, and she attended summer institutes sponsored by the Prospect Archives and Center for Education and Research from 1973 to 2005. All three groups engage in collaborative descriptive inquiry. She is a member of the North Dakota Study Group on Evaluation and was president of the Board of Trustees of Prospect from 2004 to 2006. With these groups she continues to address such issues as equity in education and the loss of play and playfulness in classrooms, especially for young children. She is interested in practitioner research that informs classroom practice. She has published articles and essays about teaching and practitioner research. Her monograph *A (Philadelphia) Teacher's Journal* was published in 1985 by the University of North Dakota. Portions of her journal have been translated into German and Dutch.